The Constitutional Law Dictionary

THE CONSTITUTIONAL LAW DICTIONARY

VOLUME 2: GOVERNMENTAL POWERS SUPPLEMENT 1

Covering the 1987–1996 Terms
of the Supreme Court

Ralph C. Chandler
Richard A. Enslen
Peter G. Renstrom

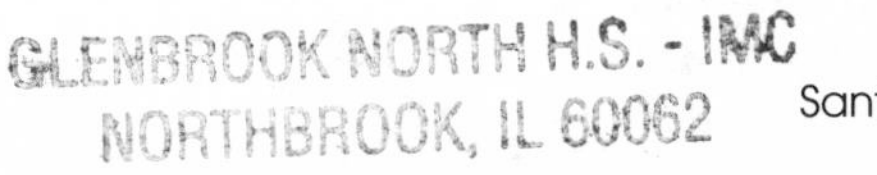

ABC-CLIO
Santa Barbara, California
Denver, Colorado
Oxford, England

Library of Congress Cataloging-in-Publication Data
Chandler, Ralph C., 1934–
The constitutional law dictionary.
Includes indexes.
Contents: v. 1. Individual rights—v. 2. Governmental powers.
1. United States—Constitutional law—Terms and phrases. 2. United States—Constitutional law—Cases.
I. Enslen, Richard A., 1931– . II. Renstrom, Peter G., 1943– . III. Title.
KF4548.5.C47 1985 342.73 84-12320
342.302

ISBN 0-87436-925-8

04 03 02 01 00 99 98 9 8 7 6 5 4 3 2 1

ABC-CLIO, Inc.
130 Cremona Drive, P.O. Box 1911
Santa Barbara, California 93116-1911

This book is printed on acid-free paper ♾.

Typesetting by Letra Libre

Manufactured in the United States of America

CONTENTS

A NOTE ON HOW TO USE THIS BOOK

Students of constitutional law are fully aware that the law is never static. Each new term of the Supreme Court brings rulings that review previous decisions in the light of current legal and social circumstances. Modifications that emerge are typically incremental. The Court may wish to simply apply an established doctrine or more clearly define a standard in a particular case as it weighs "real world" situations. Occasionally the Court sweeps aside an entire line of previous rulings and embarks on a wholly new course. A systems theorist would say constitutional law has a well-defined and dynamic feedback loop.

This dynamic creates something of a problem for writers and publishers of constitutional law books. In some respects, volumes may be out of date on some particular constitutional issues before they are even released. In this case, *The Constitutional Law Dictionary, Volume 2: Governmental Powers* was published in 1987. Significant decisions of the Court rendered later than 1986 are not included in the original volume. This supplement, the first for Volume 2, is offered to represent some of the significant decisions made in the ten years since 1987. As with the three supplements produced to accompany Volume 1, some basic guidelines apply:

1. Chapters 1, 9, and 11 of the original volume, the chapters on "Constitutionalism," "Contract Clause," and "Legal Words and Phrases," have not been revised.
2. The other eight chapters have been renumbered but closely correspond to the chapters covering the same content in the original volume. The cases on the taxing and spending powers and state economic regulation have been placed in a single supplement chapter.
3. All *See also* page-number references are keyed to the original work. It is a good idea to have the original *Dictionary* at hand when using this supplement.

4. A number of new cases have been selected to provide the definitional base for the new entries. Other new cases have been represented in the *Significance* section of the entry. In all, 138 new cases have been included in this supplement. An alphabetical list of all new cases and their respective supplement page numbers appears at the beginning of the supplement. The case names that are capitalized are cases chosen to provide the definitional foundation. Cases that are lowercase are discussed only in the *Significance* section of an entry.
5. The reader can find related information or explore the implications of a topic by using the cross-references provided at the end of each definition paragraph. The references point to related material included in the original volume.
6. If the reader is unsure about which chapter to consult for a particular case or subject, consult the comprehensive Index at the end of the supplement. It includes every case contained in the supplement, either as a definitional entry or as a referenced case in the *Significance* section. Cases that predate the supplement and are represented in an entry will appear in the Index as well.
7. For some of the most recent cases complete citations were unavailable at the time of publication. The citation from the *United States Supreme Court Reports: Lawyers Edition* is included for every case.
8. Five new justices have been appointed to the Court since Volume 1 was first published. Appendices B and C have been updated to reflect these changes, and the portions of those appendices covering the last several decades are provided in this supplement.

PREFACE

We are very grateful for the positive reception *The Constitutional Law Dictionary: Governmental Powers* has received, and we sincerely hope this supplement will make it even more useful to students of American constitutional law. As in the original Volume 2, the cases and concepts chosen for this supplement are intended to advance the understanding of American constitutional law. We acknowledge in the initial volume those who had assisted and influenced our work on this project. A special thanks needs to be extended to Joelle Renstrom, who offered her considerable writing talent to making the manuscript for this supplement presentable.

—Ralph C. Chandler
Professor of Political Science
Western Michigan University

—Richard A. Enslen
U.S. District Judge
Western District of Michigan

—Peter G. Renstrom
Professor of Political Science
Western Michigan University

ALPHABETICAL LIST OF NEW CASES

One hundred thirty-eight new cases are contained in this supplement. Capitalized cases are discussed in the definition portion of a new entry. Cases that are lowercase are discussed in the *Significance* sections of other cases.

1. *Judicial Power*

Judicial Review

***Dalton v. Specter*, 511 U.S. 462, 128 L.Ed. 2d 497, 114 S.Ct. 1719 (1994)** Senator Arlen Specter and others brought suit against John Dalton, secretary of the navy, under the Administrative Procedure Act (APA) and the Defense Base Closure and Realignment Act of 1990 in attempt to prevent implementation of President Bush's decision to close the Philadelphia Naval Shipyard. Under terms of the act, a Base Closure Commission, acting on recommendations from the Defense Department, makes an initial judgment about which bases to close. The president cannot revise or amend the commission's list but rather has 15 days to approve or reject the entire list. The president's decision is final unless Congress reverses it. A U.S. district court ruled that the act precluded federal judicial intervention. The Court of Appeals for the Third Circuit reversed the district court decision, but its ruling was summarily vacated and remanded by the Supreme Court for reconsideration. On remand, the Third Circuit adhered to its earlier ruling and held that reviewing the president's action for compliance with the Base Closure Act was permissible. A unanimous Supreme Court disagreed. The Court relied heavily on its opinion in *Franklin v. Massachusetts* (505 U.S. 788: 1992), where it had ruled that the APA could not be used to challenge the apportionment of seats in the U.S. House of Representatives. Chief Justice Rehnquist said that the prerequisite for review under the APA is "final agency action." The reports prepared by the secretary of defense and the commission "carry no direct consequences" for base closings. The only action that will directly affect the military bases is taken by the president. The reports of the secretary and the commission are not "final" and thus not subject to review. Rather, these reports serve "more like a tentative recommendation than a final and binding determination." The president's actions, in turn, are not reviewable under the APA because the president is not an "agency" for purposes of the APA. It was argued that because the president's authority regarding base closures is sufficiently limited—he may only accept or reject the commission's closure report in its entirety—the commission's action may be regarded as final. The Court was unpersuaded. This argument ignores the "core question" for determining finality: "whether the agency has completed its decision making process, and whether the result of that process is one that will directly affect the parties" and "underestimates" the president's authority under the act. Without the president's approval, "no bases are closed under the Act." That the president cannot pick and choose among bases is "immaterial." What is critical is that the president and not the commission "takes the final action that affects the military installations." The Court also rejected the argument that the president's statutory authority to close bases would be deficient if the secretary and commission violated the procedural requirements of the act in fashioning recommendations. Previous Court rulings do not support the proposition that every action by a president in excess of statutory authority is "*ipso facto* in violation of the Constitution." While some claims about presidential violation of statutory mandates are judicially reviewable, such review is "not available when the statute in question commits the decision to the discretion of the President." The president's authority to act in this instance is not contingent on the secretary's and commission's "fulfillment of all the procedural requirements imposed on them by the Act." Indeed, nothing in the Act "prevents the President from applying or disapproving the recommendations for whatever reason he sees fit." How the president "chooses to exercise the discretion Congress has granted him," the Court concluded, is "not a matter for our review." *See also* JUDICIAL REVIEW, p. 627; *UNITED STATES DEPARTMENT OF COMMERCE v. MONTANA* (503 U.S. 442: 1992), p. 65 (Supp.).

Significance The Administrative Procedure Act was passed in 1946 and serves as a process baseline for administrative agencies. The act requires that agencies generally follow processes that resemble those used in courts. The act establishes procedures for developing regulations and deciding controversies, and it defines the scope of agency discretion and the extent to which agency actions may be reviewed by courts. A recent issue arising under the APA can be seen in *Lincoln v. Vigil* (508 U.S. 182: 1993). Under authority of the Snyder Act and the Indian Health Care Improvement Act, the Indian Health Service (IHS) is annually funded by Congress on a lump-sum basis. The appropriation is to be used to provide health services for American Indians and Alaskan natives. From 1978 to 1985, the IHS provided clinical services for handicapped Indian children in the Southwest from these funds. Congress did not directly or expressly fund this particular program but was aware of its existence. In 1985, the IHS indicated it was discontinuing clinical services under the program as part of an attempt to develop a nationwide program in its place. A challenge was filed on behalf of the children eligible for services under the regional program. It was claimed that the decision to discontinue the regional program violated several provisions of federal law including the Snyder Act, the APA, and the Due Process Clause of the Fifth Amendment. A U.S. district court granted summary judgment for the challengers, ruling that the IHS decision was subject to judicial review. The district court did not rule on the merits of the program discontinuation as such but concluded that the decision to end the program was a "legislative rule" subject to the notice-and-comment rules of the APA. These requirements had not been met by the IHS in this instance. The Court of Appeals for the Tenth Circuit affirmed. The Supreme Court, however, reversed.

The Court reiterated the position taken in cases such as *Franklin v. Massachusetts* (505 U.S. 788: 1992) where the APA has been interpreted to preclude judicial review of certain categories of administrative decision that courts have traditionally regarded as "committed to agency discretion." The primary reason for this conclusion is the "impossibility of devising an adequate standard of review for such agency action." This principle was clearly applicable here. The allocation of funds from a lump-sum appropriation is the kind of decision traditionally regarded as falling within agency discretion. The very point of lump-sum appropriation, said Justice Souter, "is to give an agency the capacity to adapt to changing circumstances and to meet its statutory responsibilities in what it sees as the most effective or desirable way." A "fundamental principle" of appropriations law is that when Congress appropriates lump-sum amounts without restrictions on what can be done with these funds, a "clear inference arises that it does not intend to impose legally binding restrictions. . . ." Congress "may always circumscribe agency discretion," and an agency is not free to disregard any such statutory restrictions. Nevertheless, as long as an agency allocates funds from a lump-sum appropriation to meet permissible statutory objectives, the APA "gives the courts no leave to intrude." The Court also concluded that the IHS was not obligated to comply with the notice-and-comment rulemaking provisions of the APA. Even assuming that termination of the program is a "rule" within the meaning of the APA, it would be exempt from the notice-and-comment requirements because it affects rules of agency organization. Furthermore, an agency's "general statements of policy" are also exempt from the notice-and-comment requirements.

***Honda Motor Corp. v. Oberg,* 512 U.S. 415, 129 L.Ed. 2d 336, 114 S.Ct. 2331 (1994)** David Oberg was seriously injured while riding an "all-terrain" vehicle manufactured by Honda Motor Corp. Oberg brought suit in Oregon civil court and won a large judgment—$735,000 in compensatory damages and $5 million in punitive damages. Honda appealed, pointing out that by provision of the Oregon Constitution Oregon courts were not able to review whether such judgments were excessive. It was Honda's contention that without judicial review of the size of punitive damage awards, the award violated the Due Process Clause of the Fourteenth Amendment. Both the Oregon Court of Appeals and the Supreme Court of Oregon affirmed the trial court outcome. In a 7-2 decision, the U.S. Supreme Court reversed. The Court saw the question as focusing on what procedures are necessary to "ensure that punitive damages are not imposed in an arbitrary manner." It was the Court's judgment that awards for punitive damages "pose an acute danger of arbitrary deprivation of property" and that due process requires that some form of judicial review be available to examine whether an award is excessive. Jury instructions in such cases typically leave the jury with "wide discretion in choosing amounts." Furthermore, the presentation of evidence of a defendant's net worth "creates the potential that juries will use their verdicts to express biases against big businesses, particularly those without strong local presences." Justice Stevens called judicial review of the amount awarded "one of the few procedural safeguards which the common law provided against that danger." Oregon removed that safeguard "without providing any substitute procedure and without any indication that the danger of arbitrary awards has in any way subsided over time." *See also BMW OF NORTH AMERICA, INC. v. GORE* (517 U.S. 559: 1996), p. 206 (Supp.); JUDICIAL REVIEW, p. 627.

Significance Punitive damages are different from compensatory damages. The latter addresses actual losses stemming from a civil defendant's conduct and provides restitution for those losses. Punitive damages, on the other hand, are designed to deter future misconduct by imposing a penalty or punishment on the civil defendant. The Court has had several opportunities to consider punitive damage awards in state cases. *Oberg* focused on the procedural issue of appellate review of awards, and the Court concluded that the absence of such posttrial review was a denial of due process. Substantive due process issues have proven more difficult.

The case of *BMW of North America, Inc. v. Gore* (517 U.S. 559: 1996) provided the Court with its most recent opportunity to address the issue of excessive punitive damage awards. BMW had a policy of repairing damage occurring during shipment of their cars if the damage was "minor"—less than 3 percent of the vehicle's list price. Repairs of this order were not disclosed to prospective purchasers, and the vehicles were sold as new. Gore purchased a new BMW; the vehicle had been damaged, repaired, and repainted under the "minor damage" policy. Almost a year later, Gore became aware that his car had been repaired. He brought suit in an Alabama court, seeking both compensatory and punitive damages. A jury ruled in Gore's favor and awarded $4,000 in compensatory damages, an amount calculated to represent the value lost by the damage done to the original finish. The jury also awarded punitive damages of $4 million, a figure that was based on the reduced value of 1,000 vehicles BMW had restored and sold as new nationwide. The Alabama Supreme Court reduced the award to $2 million, largely on the ground that the jury impermissibly took out-of-state sales into account. BMW of North America appealed to the U.S. Supreme Court, which set aside the punitive damage award as "grossly excessive." It was the Court's judgment that punitive damages could be awarded based on BMW's nondisclosure policy, but it required that a "rational relationship" exist between the misconduct of the defendant and the amount of the award. The Court assessed the relationship, or "fit," between the misconduct and the damages awarded. Misconduct punished as severely as in this case must be "reprehensible." The Court concluded that this level of misconduct was not reached by BMW. In other words, the difference between the punitive damage award and the harm actually caused by the plaintiff must be reasonably related. Further, the misconduct did not endanger the purchaser in any way. Finally, the Court suggested that any punitive damage award should be substantially greater than other civil or criminal penalties for the same or similar misconduct. In this case, the Court found that the award here was a thousand times greater than the $2,000 civil penalty authorized under Alabama law.

Jurisdiction

***McNary v. Haitian Refugee Center*, 498 U.S. 479, 112 L.Ed. 2d 1005, 111 S.Ct. 888 (1991)** The Immigration Reform and Control Act created, among other things, an amnesty program for certain alien farmworkers—a "Special Agricultural Worker" (SAW) status. The Immigration and Naturalization Service (INS) administered the program and determined eligibility for SAW status by interviewing each applicant for the program. The act precludes judicial review of the INS determination except in the case of a deportation order. The Haitian Refugee Center and a number of unsuccessful SAW applicants brought suit in U.S. district court, claiming that INS reviews of the applications were conducted in an arbitrary manner that violated both the act and due process protections of the Fifth Amendment. The district court case did not review individual determinations but focused on the way in which INS administered the program in its entirety. The district court found that INS practices violated both the act and the Due Process Clause, a ruling that was affirmed by the Court of Appeals for the Eleventh Circuit. The narrow question before the Supreme Court was whether language in the act that prohibits review of individual determinations (except in the instance of deportation) also precludes "general challenge to the INS's unconstitutional practices." The Court held that it did not. The language in the statute refers to review of a "determination respecting and application for SAW status." It was the Court's judgment that reference to "a determination describes a single act rather than a group of decisions or a practice or a procedure employed in making decisions." In other words, the Court did not see this language as referring to "general collateral challenges to unconstitutional practices and policies used by the agency in processing applications." Furthermore, the "abuse of discretion" standard for judicial review contained in the Immigration and Nationality Act (INA) "would make no sense," said Rehnquist, if the Reform Act was read to require that constitutional and statutory challenges to INS procedures be "subject to its specialized review provision." Given Congress's choice of language, the Court concluded that challenges to the procedures used by INS "do not fall within the scope" of INA provisions. Rather, the review standards of the INA "appl[y] only to review of denials of individuals SAW applications." *See also* JUDICIAL REVIEW, p. 627; JURISDICTION, p. 629; *MOTOR VEHICLE MANUFACTURERS ASSOCIATION v. STATE FARM MUTUAL INSURANCE COMPANY* (463 U.S. 29: 1983), p. 97; *UNITED STATES v. CAROLENE PRODUCTS COMPANY* (304 U.S. 144: 1938), p. 93.

Significance The jurisdictional authority of courts to review decisions of administrative agencies has been limited historically. As the federal bureaucracy expanded, the general view was that administrative agencies were as well equipped as courts to address problems of policy implementation. It was believed that the substantive expertise located within administrative agencies should free many decisions from judicial scrutiny. A doctrine of deference to administrative agencies evolved suggesting that courts should only intervene in cases where constitutional violations were found or where administrative actions exceeded established legislative boundaries. More recently, this deference has diminished somewhat because of the vulnerability of some agencies to "capture" by the very interests it was designed to regulate. In addition, the scope of agency discretion involving policy implementation has grown, which has produced situations where such discretion is not always exercised appropriately.

An example of the tension between deference to agencies and the need to review the exercise of agency discretion can be seen in *Motor Vehicle Manufacturers Association v. State Farm Mutual Insurance Company*

(463 U.S. 29: 1983). The National Highway Transportation Safety Administration (NHTSA) required automobile manufacturers to provide passive restraint devices in their cars by a specific date. The requirement, however, was rescinded by the NHTSA before it took effect. State Farm and a number of other insurers challenged the NHTSA decision. The Supreme Court ruled that the decision to rescind was defective. Agency decisions may be set aside if they are arbitrary, capricious, an abuse of agency discretion, or insufficiently justified. In this case, the Court chose to apply a more demanding standard than it would have had the agency refused to fashion a rule at all. The Court said that "revocation of an extant regulation" is substantially different from failure to act. To take this narrow approach would put most agency decisions "close to the borderline of nonreviewability." The Court then considered whether the NHTSA's rescission of the passive restraint requirement was arbitrary and capricious. Review of an agency's actions must be upheld on the basis "articulated by the agency itself." In this case, the Court found the agency's justification for the rescission insufficient. Since the 1930s, the Court has tended to refrain from reviewing substantive decisions of regulatory agencies. This deference is based in large part on the view that creating such regulation is primarily a legislative rather than a judicial function. At the same time, cases such as *State Farm* suggest that the Court has at least a threshold expectation that agency actions be based on reasoned analysis, and that agencies provide sufficient support for their decisions. The explicitly stated principle from *State Farm* is that in reviewing agency decisions the Court is not to "substitute its judgment" or preference for that of the agency. Instead, the Court is to focus on the explanation offered by the agency for its actions, an explanation that must include a "rational connection" between the facts found and the choices made by the agency.

Standing

***Lujan v. Defenders of Wildlife*, 504 U.S. 555, 119 L.Ed. 2d 351, 112 S.Ct. 2130 (1992)** The Endangered Species Act of 1973 assigns responsibility for the protection of endangered species to both the secretary of the interior and the secretary of commerce. The act further requires all federal agencies to "consult with the relevant Secretary" to ensure that activities funded by an agency are not likely to "jeopardize the continued existence or habitat of any endangered species." The secretaries of interior and commerce fashioned a joint rule extending coverage of the act to activities occurring in foreign nations. The rule was subsequently changed to apply only to the United States and the high seas. The Defenders of Wildlife and other organizations filed action in federal district court, seeking to enjoin implementation of the new and narrowed rule. The district court dismissed the suit for lack of standing, but its decision was reversed by the Court of Appeals for the Eighth Circuit. On remand, the district court denied the secretary of the interior's motion for summary judgment and ordered the secretary to fashion another rule; that decision was then upheld by the Eighth Circuit. The Supreme Court reversed, however, and held that environmental groups did not have standing to challenge those regulations not extending to actions taken in foreign nations. The Constitution's "central mechanism" for separating powers depends, said Justice Scalia, on a "common understanding of what activities are appropriate to legislatures, to executives, and to courts." One of the "landmarks" defining justiciable controversies is the doctrine of standing. The "core component" of standing is an "essential and unchanging part of the case-or-controversy requirement of Article III." The "irreducible constitutional minimum" of standing contains three elements: the suffering of an "injury in fact"; a causal connection between the injury and conduct complained of; and the likelihood that the injury will be "redressed by a favorable decision." The party invoking federal jurisdiction "bears the burden of establishing these elements." When a plaintiff is the object of a challenged governmental action, there is usually "little question" that the action has caused direct injury, and standing is established. In a case such as this, however, where the asserted injury arises from the government's regulation of someone else, "causation and redressability ordinarily hinge on the response of the regulated (or regulable) third party to the government action or inaction." Thus, when the plaintiff is not the object of the government action (or inaction) under challenge, "standing is not precluded, but is ordinarily substantially more difficult to establish." In this case, the plaintiff was an organization bringing suit on behalf of two of its members. No facts were presented, however, showing how damage to the species will produce "imminent injury" to the members. That the members had visited the areas of the project prior to the commencement of the projects "proves nothing." Further, indicating an intention to return to these locations and be deprived of the opportunity to observe the endangered animals was "simply not enough." Such "some intentions," the Court concluded, "do not support a finding of the actual or imminent injury that our cases require." It is "pure speculation and fantasy" to say that anyone who observes or works with an endangered species, "anywhere in the world, is appreciably harmed by a single project affecting some portion of that species with which he has no more specific connection." Beyond this failure to show injury, it was the Court's view that the Defenders of Wildlife failed to "demonstrate redressability." When a plaintiff raises only a "generally available grievance about government" and seeks relief that no more directly and tangibly benefits him or her than it does the public at large, he or she "does not state an Article III case or controversy." *See also* ARTICLE III, p. 73; JUSTICIABILITY, p. 630; MOOTNESS, p. 634; STANDING, p. 655.

Significance The standing requirement is designed to keep the courts within bounds; it is a means of implementing the separation of power principle. Confining judicial power to bona fide controversies prevents the courts from entertaining hypothetical questions or rendering advisory opinions that, in turn, lowers the possibility that courts will encroach on the legislative function. As can be seen in *Lujan,* the standing requirement precludes the Court from reviewing certain substantive legislative decisions.

A related concept is mootness. A dispute becomes moot when courts can no longer provide a party with legal relief because the dispute has been resolved or ceases to exist any longer. Standing requirements may have been met at the outset of a court case, but subsequent circumstances may alter that status. As with the broader doctrine of standing, a moot case no longer has an active question to put to courts, thus it is no longer a bona fide controversy. A case in which mootness was a factor is *Northeastern Florida General Contractors v. Jacksonville* (508 U.S. 656: 1993). A Jacksonville, Florida, ordinance provided that at least 10 percent of the city's contract expenditures go to minority businesses. The Northeastern Florida Chapter of the Associated General Contractors of America (AGC), an organization of contractors (most of whom could not qualify as minority-owned businesses), brought an action in federal district court against the city, claiming that some members would have bid on work but for the set-aside restriction and that the ordinance violated the Equal Protection Clause. The district court ruled for the AGC, but the Court of Appeals for the Eleventh Circuit reversed, concluding that the association lacked standing to challenge the ordinance. While review on the standing issue was pending before the Supreme Court, Jacksonville modified the ordinance but retained the set-aside component for minority- and female-owned businesses. Jacksonville attempted to have the case dismissed as moot on the basis of the modifications made to the original ordinance. The Supreme Court ruled that the case was not rendered moot by the changes in the ordinance but also ruled that the Eleventh Circuit should not have dismissed the AGC's challenge for lack of standing.

The issue in *Darby v. Cisneros* (509 U.S. 137: 1993) was whether federal courts have the authority to require exhaustion of remedies before reviewing administrative actions of the Department of Housing and

Urban Development (HUD), where neither statute nor agency rule required exhaustion. Gordon Darby, a real estate developer, was prohibited from participating in any program in South Carolina administered by HUD for a period of one year. Two months later he was barred indefinitely from participating in any HUD procurement contract and any nonprocurement transaction with any federal agency. He appealed, and an administrative law judge upheld the one-year sanction but changed the indefinite sanction to one lasting 18 months. Neither Darby nor HUD sought review of this ruling. Under HUD's procedures, a hearing officer's determination is final unless a party requests review by the HUD secretary within 15 days of receipt of a hearing officer's judgment and is notified by the secretary within 30 days of a decision to review the findings of the hearing officer. Darby sought to enjoin these sanctions through an action filed in federal court. The suit was filed, however, well beyond these deadlines. Darby contended that the sanctions imposed by HUD violated provisions of the Administrative Procedure Act (APA). The HUD secretary sought dismissal of the suit on the grounds that Darby had failed to exhaust administrative remedies by not seeking review by the secretary. The district court denied the motion and granted summary judgment for Darby. The Court of Appeals for the Fourth Circuit reversed, ruling that the district court ought to have dismissed the case. The Supreme Court disagreed. The Court found the doctrine of exhaustion of administrative remedies to be "conceptually distinct" from the doctrine of finality. Use of the exhaustion doctrine requires inquiry into congressional intent, whether legislation limits the authority of courts to "impose additional exhaustion requirements as a prerequisite to judicial review." It was the Court's judgment in *Darby* that statutory language in the APA limited the availability of the exhaustion doctrine to "that which the statute or rule clearly mandates." In situations where the APA applies, the Court concluded, an appeal to "superior agency authority is a prerequisite to judicial review *only* when expressly required by statute" or in the event that an agency rule requires appeal before review and the administrative action is made inoperative pending that review. Courts "are not free to impose an exhaustion requirement as a rule of judicial administration where the agency's action has already become final under [provision of the APA]."

The voters of Arizona approved a constitutional amendment (Article XXVIII) in 1988 that made English the "official" language of the state. Article XXVIII also provides that all government business conducted by the state and its political subdivisions must be done in English. The constitutionality of the amendment was challenged by a bilingual state employee, Maria-Kelly Yniguez, who used Spanish when conducting business with non–English-speaking residents of Arizona. A federal district court ruled Article XXVIII unconstitutional on the ground that it barred constitutionally protected speech. The governor of Arizona chose to not appeal the ruling. Arizonans for Official English, a citizens group that had led the effort to place the question on the ballot in 1988, was permitted by the U.S. Court of Appeals for the Ninth Circuit to intervene in order to carry the case to appeal. The court of appeals sitting *en banc* ruled that Article XXVIII was constitutional. Before considering any First Amendment claim in *Arizonans for Official English v. Yniguez* (137 L.Ed. 2d 170: 1997), the Supreme Court resolved questions involving both standing and mootness. Since Arizonans for Official English had not been a party to the original challenge, there was a question about whether it had standing to appeal the lower court decision. In addition, it was asserted that Yniguez's claim was moot because she had left her state job and was no longer a state employee and because she was never directly threatened by enforcement of the English-only requirement. The mootness consideration proved decisive, for the Court concluded that because Yniguez had left her job before any appellate court ruling the federal courts lacked jurisdiction to examine the free speech issue. While the Court did not fully review the standing issue, Justice Ginsburg indicated that there were "grave doubts" that a private group such as Arizonans for Official English had standing to initiate an appeal since the organization was not authorized by state law to represent the state's interests, nor had any of its members suffered "concrete injury."

The Court focused on three particular errors of the lower courts in this case. First, the district court had failed to allow the state supreme court to first interpret the language of the amendment despite a request from the state attorney general to that effect. Federal courts ought not, said Justice Ginsburg, hear constitutional challenges prematurely, particularly when a federal court is "asked to invalidate a State's law." A federal court risks "friction-generating error when it endeavors to construe a novel state act not yet reviewed by the State's highest court." Second, the district court also erred when it did not consider the Arizona attorney general's opinion that state employees such as Yniguez retained the capability to use other languages to "facilitate delivery of governmental services" to non–English-speaking persons. Third, the Ninth Circuit ruled on this case despite the likelihood of it being moot. The Ninth Circuit had proceeded based on its judgment that Yniguez had an ongoing claim for damages. It "should have been clear" to the Ninth Circuit that a claim for damages, "extracted late in the day from Yniguez's general prayer for relief and asserted solely to avoid otherwise certain mootness, bore close inspection." Such inspection might have suggested to the Ninth Circuit that Yniguez's "plea for nominal damages could not genuinely revive the case." This First Amendment issue will likely return to the Supreme Court, as a separate suit on the "official English" question is pending before the Arizona Supreme Court.

One of the most interesting recent decisions on the standing question is *Raines v. Byrd* (138 L.Ed. 2d 849: 1997). In 1996, Congress passed the Line Item Veto Act, which authorized the president to "cancel" certain items in spending bills that he otherwise approves. The act was challenged immediately after its effective date by a number of members of Congress, including Senator Robert Byrd of West Virginia. They argued that their constitutional role in the legislative process had been diminished, which, in turn, disturbed the power relationship of the legislative and executive branches. A lower federal court ruled on the merits of the challenge and struck down the act as an unconstitutional transfer of legislative power to the president. The Supreme Court reversed this decision because it concluded that the members of Congress did not have standing to challenge the act. The Court ruled that the plaintiffs did not suffer either a direct or "concrete" injury to a "protected interest." Their injury was "institutional" rather than personal and therefore "too abstract" to satisfy standing requirements. Chief Justice Rehnquist said Senator Byrd's claim of a right to challenge the act was based on a "loss of political power, not the loss of any private right, which would make the injury more concrete." The challengers were not "singled out for specially unfavorable treatment" nor did they claim that they had been deprived of "something to which they personally are entitled—such as their seats as Members of Congress after their constituents had elected them." As a result of concluding that the challengers lacked standing, the Court did not address the constitutionality of the line-item veto itself. The Court made it clear, however, that a constitutional challenge might be pursued by a party who is injured by the use of the line-item veto, such as a person who lost benefits because of a "canceled" program. Justices Stevens and Breyer dissented. They concluded that presidential line-item veto power diminishes legislators' capacity to approve what ultimately becomes law.

Federal *Habeas Corpus*

***Felker v. Turpin*, U.S., 135 L.Ed. 2d 827, 116 S.Ct. 2333 (1996)** Upheld new restrictions on federal *habeas corpus* review of state criminal convictions. Congress enacted the Anti-Terrorism and Effective Death Penalty Act in April 1996. Many members of Congress were concerned that current rules governing federal *habeas* review lead to protracted appellate proceedings in which guilty prisoners, particularly those on death row, can effectively and indefinitely delay implementation of sentences. The law limited the authority of federal courts to consider *habeas corpus* petitions and was designed to restrict the access of state prisoners to federal courts. Section 106 of the act provided that any second or successive *habeas* petition had to meet very difficult standards and could not be filed without prior approval. Failure to obtain such approval cannot be appealed. Provisions of the act were challenged by Ellis Felker, a Georgia prisoner convicted of a 1981 rape and murder. Felker unsuccessfully filed a *habeas corpus* petition in 1993 and sought to file again shortly after the act was signed by President Clinton. A second *habeas* petition may be considered, however, only after a federal appeals court grants permission to file the petition. Felker failed to obtain the necessary permission. The Supreme Court reviewed the new law only a few weeks after its enactment and unanimously upheld the challenged portions of the act.

The Court considered two issues in *Felker*—whether *habeas corpus* has been unconstitutionally "suspended" by the act and whether the Court had impermissibly denied appellate review by the "gatekeeping" function assigned to the courts of appeal. The Court ruled that the act did not "suspend" the writ in violation of Article I, Section 9 of the Constitution. The Court, said Chief Justice Rehnquist, has "long recognized" that the power to award the writ by any federal court "must be given by written law." Similarly, Rehnquist said that "judgments about the proper scope of the writ are normally for Congress to make." The restrictions added by the act on second *habeas* petitions are "well within the compass of this . . . process, and we hold that they do not amount to a 'suspension' incompatible with Article I, section 9." The Court further concluded that the new provisions did impose "new conditions on our authority to grant [*habeas*] relief," but because the "gatekeeping" system applies only to second petitions filed with district courts, the Supreme Court retained its jurisdiction to "entertain original *habeas* petitions." Although statutory language did not directly apply to the Court's original jurisdiction, Rehnquist thought the restrictions, though not binding as such, would "certainly inform our consideration" of original *habeas* petitions. *See also: COLEMAN v. THOMPSON* (501 U.S. 722: 1991), p. 140 (Supp.); *HABEAS CORPUS,* p. 616.

Significance The writ of *habeas corpus* was a procedure in English law designed to prevent the arbitrary detention of prisoners. The primary purpose was to bring detained persons before judicial officials prior to the initiation of criminal trials to determine if their detention was lawful. Most *habeas corpus* petitions currently are filed after, rather than before, trials. The *habeas* process largely became a second avenue of appeal, a collateral process for reviewing criminal convictions. Access to federal courts through the *habeas corpus* petition by persons convicted of crimes in state courts has been substantially limited by recent rulings of the Rehnquist Court. In *Coleman v. Thompson* (501 U.S. 722: 1991), for example, the Court ruled that a prospective petitioner would have to exhaust all possible remedies at the state level before attempting to access federal courts. Indeed, failure to satisfy state processes would constitute procedural default, a "deliberate bypass." Justice O'Connor said for the Court the case was "about federalism" and the respect federal courts owe state court processes. It was the Court's view that the more permissive access policy needed to be replaced because it was "based on a conception of federal-state relations that undervalued the importance of state procedural rules."

The issue in *McCleskey v. Zant* (499 U.S. 467: 1991) was whether a petitioner's failure to include all claims in a first *habeas* petition precluded his raising a withheld claim in a second. The key to resolving this issue was whether the petitioner's second petition constituted an "abuse" of the writ. The Court concluded that it did. Justice Kennedy said for the Court that doctrines such as "abuse of the writ" are based on concerns about the "significant cost" of federal *habeas* review. The writ "strikes at" the finality of state decisions, which suggests an ongoing disrespect that "disparages the entire [state] criminal system." Relatively easy access to federal *habeas* review may also give prospective petitioners "incentives to withhold claims for manipulative purposes." Under the new standard fashioned in *McCleskey*, petitions following the first one will be dismissed unless the petitioner can demonstrate cause for not asserting the claim earlier. This requires a showing of "some external impediment" preventing the raising of a claim. A petitioner is also required to demonstrate that he or she suffered "actual prejudice" resulting from the claims raised in a second petition.

Under *habeas* standards that applied prior to 1992, a state prisoner was entitled to *habeas* review of evidence not adequately developed in state criminal trials as long as the evidence was not deliberately withheld. In *Keeney v. Tamayo-Reyes* (504 U.S. 1: 1992), the Court ruled that review of underdeveloped evidence could occur only if "cause and prejudice" could be shown. That is, a prisoner must show cause for the failure to develop the evidence at trial and demonstrate "actual prejudice resulting from that failure." This new standard, said Justice White, "will appropriately accommodate concerns of finality, comity, judicial economy, and channeling the resolution of claims into the most appropriate forum."

The challenge brought in the *Felker* case raised somewhat different constitutional questions. The ruling did not center on federalism as such but rather focused on the suspension and jurisdictional aspects of *habeas corpus*. The Court concluded that the act did not suspend the writ but merely codified policy governing second (or more) petitions. The majority of the Court was certainly not troubled by the direction of this policy because it incorporated the substance of the Court's own rulings on this matter. The Court was also satisfied with the statutory language preventing its review denials of permission to file *habeas* petitions. Since the act did not disturb the Court's authority to consider original *habeas* petitions, a power conferred by Congress in the Judiciary Act of 1789, the Court concluded that it retained a sufficient role in the current debate about federal *habeas* review. *Felker* did not examine the statutory standards that must be met before permission is granted to file a second or successive petition. Issues relating to these standards are likely to be before the Court in the near future.

Judicial Immunity

***Mireles v. Waco*, 502 U.S. 9, 116 L.Ed. 2d 9, 112 S.Ct. 286 (1991)** A county public defender brought a "Section 1983" federal civil rights action against a California Superior Court judge and two police officers. Howard Waco sought damages by claiming that the judge had ordered the two officers to forcibly escort him to the judge's courtroom when he was not present at the time the morning calendar was called. The judge moved to dismiss the complaint against him for failure to state a claim upon which relief could be granted. The district court dismissed the action against the judge on grounds of "complete judicial immunity." The Court of Appeals for the Ninth Circuit reversed, concluding that Judge Mireles was not immune in this case because his actions "were not taken in his judicial capacity." The Supreme Court summarily reversed. The Court held that judicial immunity is "not overcome by allegations of bad faith or malice"; immunity applies even when the judge is accused of acting "maliciously or corruptly." Instead, immunity is overcome in only two sets of circumstances: when an action is taken that is outside the judge's judicial capacity and when an action is taken in the "complete absence of all jurisdiction." The Supreme Court disagreed with the Ninth Circuit that the actions here were not taken in a "judicial capacity." Whether an act is judicial relates to the "nature of the act itself," whether it is a function "normally performed by a judge, and to the expectations of the parties." A judge's direction to court officers to bring a person who is in the courthouse to the judge's court is a function "normally performed" by a judge. The public defender who was called to the courtroom by reason of a pending case was "dealing with Judge Mireles in the judge's official capacity." The judge's order to bring Waco to his courtroom with excessive force is not a normally performed function, but if "only the particular act in question were to be scrutinized, then any mistake of a judge in excess of his authority would become a nonjudicial act." If judicial immunity "means anything," it means that a judge will not be deprived of immunity because the action he or she took was "in error . . . or was in excess of his authority." The relevant inquiry is the "nature and function" of the act, not the "act itself." The Court also rejected the contention that the judge's order became executive rather than judicial because it had been carried out by police officers. Immunity analysis, said the Court, is informed by the "nature of the function performed, not the identity of the actor who performed it." A judge's direction to an executive officer to bring counsel before the court is "no more executive in character than a judge's issuance of a warrant for an executive officer to search a home." Justice Stevens dissented, concluding that a judge's alleged order to "commit a battery on the public defender was not an action taken in a judicial capacity." *See also* JUDICIAL IMMUNITY, p. 626; *STUMP v. SPARKMAN* (435 U.S. 349: 1978), p. 87.

Significance Judicial immunity insulates judges from civil actions for conduct done in the performance of their judicial function. This immunity is intended to protect judges from fearing civil lawsuits brought by litigants who do not prevail in matters heard by the judge. Immunity is designed to protect the public interest by having judges who can act with independence. The scope of the immunity doctrine was addressed in *Stump v. Sparkman* (435 U.S. 349: 1978). The Court held that Stump, a general jurisdiction trial judge in Indiana, was immune from damages for authorizing the sterilization of a minor in an ex parte proceeding where the minor was neither given notice nor represented by counsel. The central issue in this case was whether Stump has jurisdiction over the matter before him. The Court held that the scope of jurisdiction must be "broadly construed" with regard to the judicial immunity issue. Immunity exists even if the action taken by the judge is "in error, done maliciously, or was in excess of his authority." As long as the judge has not acted in the "clear absence" of jurisdiction, a judge must be immune from liability for any judicial acts," and no flaw in performance makes a judgment "any less a judicial act." Disagreement with a judge's action is not sufficient to deprive a judge of immunity. Notwithstanding some "unfairness" that may sometimes result, judicial immunity is critical to the administration of justice because it allows a judicial officer to act "without apprehension of personal consequences." That an issue before a judge is particularly controversial is "all the more reason" that a judge must be able to act without fear of suit. The *Mireles* ruling clearly reaffirms the view expressed almost 13 years earlier in *Stump v. Sparkman.*

Impeachment

***Nixon v. United States,* 506 U.S. 224, 122 L.Ed. 2d 1, 113 S.Ct. 732 (1993)**
Walter L. Nixon, a federal district court judge, was convicted of making false statements to a federal grand jury. Nixon chose not to resign his judgeship on conviction, and impeachment proceedings were initiated in the U.S. House of Representatives stemming from his criminal misconduct. Three articles of impeachment were ultimately adopted, two charging him with giving false information, the other for "bringing disrepute on the Federal Judiciary." When the articles were presented to the Senate, it chose to use one of its impeachment rules, Rule XI. It authorizes the presiding officer of the Senate to appoint a committee of senators to gather evidence for the trial and then report findings to the full Senate. Following the submission of final briefs to the full Senate by Judge Nixon and the House impeachment managers, the Senate voted to convict Nixon, and he was removed from office. Nixon brought an action in the U.S. District Court for the District of Columbia, seeking to overturn his conviction on the grounds that the Senate rule by which the evidence-gathering committee had been selected violated the impeachment provisions found in Article I. The district court dismissed on the ground that the claim was nonjusticiable; a ruling affirmed by the Court of Appeals for the District of Columbia Circuit affirmed. The Supreme Court unanimously affirmed as well.

Article I directs that the Senate shall have the "sole power to try all impeachments." Nixon contended that the word "try" imposes an implicit requirement that Senate impeachment proceedings must "be in the nature of a judicial trial." The Court concluded that the term has "considerably broader meanings" than Nixon proposed. As a result, the term was seen as lacking sufficient precision to "afford any judicially manageable standard of review of the Senate's actions." The Court found this view "fortified" by the three "very specific" constitutional requirements that are placed on the Senate when it tries impeachment: the members must be under oath, a two-thirds vote is required to convict, and the chief justice presides when the president is tried. These requirements set "quite precise" requirements, and their nature suggests that the framers "did not intend to impose additional limitations of the form of the Senate proceedings by the use of the word 'try' in the first sentence." The Court then turned to the more general issue of whether the judiciary, particularly the Supreme Court, ought to play any role in impeachments. The Court concluded that any such role for the judiciary was inappropriate for two reasons. First, impeachments are likely to produce two sets of proceedings—the impeachment trial itself and a separate criminal trial. The framers, said Chief Justice Rehnquist, "deliberately separated the two forums to avoid raising the specter of bias and to insure independent judgment." Second, the Court noted that impeachment was the "*only* check" on the judiciary by the legislative branch. Judicial involvement in impeachment proceedings, even if only for purposes of judicial review, is "counterintuitive because it would eviscerate the important constitutional check placed on the Judiciary by the Framers." Thus, in addition to language in Article I that "textually commits" impeachment to the legislative branch, the Court was also persuaded that the "lack of finality and the difficulty in fashioning relief counsel against justiciability." *See also* ARTICLE I, p. 183; ARTICLE II, p. 139; IMPEACHMENT, p. 618; JUDICIAL REVIEW, p. 627.

Significance The impeachment language found in Articles I and II defines the way federal officials may be removed from office. The accusation or article of impeachment must come from the House of Representatives. An article of impeachment or charge may be adopted by the House by majority vote. Once the House adopts such article(s), a trial is conducted in the Senate. Conviction by the Senate requires a two-thirds vote on at least one of the impeachment charges. The *Nixon* ruling underscores the breadth of discretion residing in Congress. Impeachment is not a process that Congress initiates frequently. Nonetheless, it is quite clear that the process is political rather than legal in character. The grounds on which impeachment articles are based may be defined by the House. There is no requirement that the charges involve criminal conduct. President Andrew Johnson came within a single vote of conviction by the Senate in 1867, and President Richard M. Nixon resigned the presidency in 1974 rather than submit to impeachment proceedings that had begun in the House. The first removal of a federal judge occurred in 1804, but only six other federal judges have been impeached since. More than fifty judges, however, have resigned when impeachment proceedings were begun. The Court's ruling in the case of Judge Nixon clearly shows that the processes used by the Congress with regard to impeachment are largely unreviewable by the courts. The Senate first utilized the Rule XI approach in the 1986 impeachment of a federal district court judge, Harry E. Claiborne. In 1989, the Senate convicted both Judge Nixon and Judge Alcee L. Hastings using the Rule XI committee. The Court's ruling in the *Nixon* applies to all three removals.

Remedial Power: School Desegregation

***Freeman v. Pitts*, 503 U.S. 467, 118 L.Ed. 2d 108, 112 S.Ct. 1430 (1992)** A unanimous Court ruled that lower federal courts may incrementally relinquish remedial control over desegregation orders as particular school district operations are found to be unitary in character. The DeKalb County, Georgia, schools had been under a desegregation order since the late 1960s. The school district filed for dismissal of the order in 1986, and a federal district court determined that the district had made sufficient good-faith effort to comply. More specifically, the lower court found that a dual or segregated system of student assignment no longer existed and ended the remedial order as it applied to student assignment practices. The U.S. Court of Appeals for the Eleventh Circuit, however, reversed, ruling that the lower court must retain supervisory control over the district until it achieved desegregation across the full range of activities covered by the order. The Supreme Court upheld the district court's partial termination of supervision. A federal district court "need not retain active control over every aspect of school administration" until a district has shown "unitary status in all facets of its system," said Justice Kennedy. In addition to their remediating of any violations, lower federal courts must also "restore state and local authorities to the control of a school system that is operating in compliance with the Constitution." Returning schools to local control at the "earliest practicable date is essential to restore their true accountability." Kennedy acknowledged that the potential for discrimination remains in our society and that a state and its subdivisions must "ensure that such forces do not shape or control the politics of its schools systems."

Justice Kennedy pointed to several factors that lower courts must examine when considering partial withdrawal from supervision of a school district. They include: (1) whether there has been "full and satisfactory compliance with the decree in those aspects of the system where supervision is to be withdrawn"; (2) when retention of control is still needed to "achieve compliance with the decree in other facets of the school system"; and (3) whether the local district has shown to the public and those among the "once disfavored race" its good-faith commitment to the "whole of the court's decree and to those provisions of the law and the Constitution that were the predicate for judicial intervention in the first place." Kennedy then turned to the lower court judgment to return control over several school operations to the DeKalb County school system. The most important of the good-faith criteria here was student assignment. The district court found that measures taken by the DeKalb schools had indeed achieved desegregation, at least for a period. The lower court held that the subsequent resegregation was the result of population shifts unrelated to any misconduct by the school district. The Supreme Court agreed, stating that a finding of racial imbalance in attendance zones was not itself a showing of school district noncompliance with the court order. "Racial balance," said Kennedy, "is not to be achieved for its own sake, it is to be pursued only in response to a constitutional violation." Once a de jure violation has been remedied, a district is "under no duty to remedy imbalance that is caused by demographical factors." Resegregation produced by private choices rather than state action "does not have constitutional implications." To the contrary, it is "beyond the authority and . . . practical ability" of federal courts to try to "counteract these kinds of continuous and massive demographic shifts." To pursue such an end would require "ongoing and never-ending supervision by courts of school districts simply because they were once *de jure*-segregated." Finally, Kennedy said that although vestiges of past discrimination are a "stubborn fact of history" that we cannot escape, neither should federal courts "overstate" history's consequences in fixing legal responsibilities. The vestiges of segregation under review by federal courts may be "subtle and intangible but nonetheless they must be so real that they have a causal link to the *de jure* violations being remedied." As de jure violations become "more remote in time," and as demographic changes occur, the likelihood that a student assignment imbalance is a vestige of a previous de jure violation is lessened. Furthermore, the causal link between any current imbalance and prior violations is "even more attenuated if the school district has demonstrated its good faith." *See also* EQUITY JURISDICTION, p. 600.

Significance The Rehnquist Court has faced issues of scope and duration of remedial orders aimed at relieving unconstitutional racial discrimination in public schools on several recent occasions. A year prior to *Freeman v. Pitts,* the Court considered the terms under which a school district might be released from a busing order even though the district's schools may have become resegregated. Litigation in *Board of Education of Oklahoma City Public Schools v. Dowell* (498 U.S. 237: 1991) dated back to the early 1960s, when a federal district court found that Oklahoma City was operating a "dual" or intentionally segregated school system. Desegregation efforts were commenced, but the district court found those efforts inadequate in 1972, and an order including student busing was issued. After the busing order had been in effect for five years, the school district sought to close the case. The district court concluded that the objective of achieving a "unitary" district had been accomplished and issued an order, unchallenged by the original plaintiffs, terminating the case. The demographics of the district then changed, and the district devised a new student assignment plan that had the effect of busing some African-American students farther from their own homes to outlying areas. The district adopted a plan in 1984 designed, at least in part, to alleviate the burden on the students who were bused. While some busing continued under the plan, it was contended that the plan had the effect of resegregating the district. Nonetheless, the district court concluded that the prior decree should be vacated on the grounds that the underlying residential segregation was the result of "private decision making and economics, and that it was too attenuated to be a vestige of former school segregation." The Court of Appeals for the Tenth Circuit reversed, saying that an original decree must remain in effect until a school district can demonstrate that a "grievous wrong evoked by new and unforeseen conditions . . . that impose[s] extreme and unexpectedly oppressive hardships." Applying this standard, the court of appeals ruled that conditions in the school district had not changed enough to justify modification of the initial decree.

The Supreme Court reversed, ruling that the Tenth Circuit applied the wrong standard. Through Chief Justice Rehnquist, the Court said decrees such as those in the *Oklahoma City* case are not intended to "operate in perpetuity." Displacement of local authority by injunctive decree can only occur when local officials are party to unlawful discrimination. Relinquishing federal authority by dissolving a desegregation decree should occur "after the local authorities have operated in compliance with it for a reasonable period of time." Dissolving an order under those circumstances properly recognizes the value of local control of school systems and reflects the proposition that a federal court's regulatory control of local systems "not extend beyond the time required to remedy the effects of past intentional discrimination." While courts should not accept at face value a district's profession that it would no longer discriminate in the future, compliance with previous court orders is a factor that is "obviously relevant." In addition to determining whether a district had made good-faith compliance with a prior desegregation decree, a court must also determine whether the "vestiges of past discrimination have been eliminated" as far as "practicable."

Similarly, the Kansas City, Missouri, school district had operated under federal court order since the late 1970s. A federal district court had found that the school district had failed to desegregate its schools as mandated by *Brown v. Board of Education (Brown I)* (347 U.S. 483: 1954) and *Brown v. Board of Education (Brown II)*(349 U.S. 294: 1955). The district court framed remedies around the conclusions that segregation had (1) adversely affected student performance in the district and (2) prompted white students to leave district schools. The court ordered the district to undertake a variety of programs designed to address these problems. The actions ordered by the court were extensive and required the expenditure of significant resources. The school district sought appellate review of the remedial orders on several occasions, one of which reached the Supreme Court in 1990. The district court had ordered a property tax levy in the district to enable financing of some of the desegregation costs. The Supreme Court ruled in *Missouri v. Jenkins (Jenkins I)* (495 U.S. 33: 1990) that the order exceeded the remedial authority of the court. The 1995 case, *Missouri v. Jenkins (Jenkins II)* (515 U.S. 695), asked the Supreme Court to find that the vestiges of unlawful segregation had been effectively addressed and that a partially unitary status had been achieved. Such a finding would lead to ending the lower court's oversight of the district's operations. The school district also pursued an alternative objective if the district court's oversight was not terminated. It contended that the district court had improperly relied on achievement test scores when it ruled that partial unitary status as to educational quality had not been attained. The school district argued that the court had again exceeded its remedial authority by ordering the expenditure of resources to improve student achievement as measured by standardized testing and by ordering pay increases for district teachers and support staff. In a 5-4 decision, the Supreme Court did not end the lower court's supervision of the district but did vacate the court's remedial order.

Chief Justice Rehnquist characterized the Kansas City desegregation plan as the "most ambitious and expensive remedial program in the history of school desegregation." The district court had sought to create a school district that was "equal or superior to" surrounding districts. Rehnquist suggested that examination of the district court's remedial orders that pursued "desegregative attractiveness" and "suburban comparability" were "instructive" for the resolution of the issues of the present case. Drawing extensively from *Freeman,* Rehnquist indicated that "vestiges of segregation" must both be "real" and have a "causal link to the *de jure* violation being remedied." The Court concluded that the record in this case did not support reliance on "white flight" as a justification for expansion of its remedial authority in its pursuit of desegregative attractiveness. It was the Court's view that desegregative attractiveness has been used too broadly as a "hook on which to hang numerous policy choices about improving the quality of education in general" in the district. Pursuit of desegregative attractiveness results in "so many imponderables" and is "so far removed" from the task of eliminating the racial identifiability of the schools that it cannot be properly used to support the remedial order. The Court also rejected the conclusion that the district was not "anywhere close to its maximum potential" based on standardized achievement test results. This was "not the appropriate test," said Rehnquist, to be used when deciding whether a previously segregated district has achieved partial unitary status. Rather, the basic task of courts is to determine whether the reduction in achievement by minority students "attributable to prior *de jure* segregation has been remedied to the extent practicable." The Court offered the three-part test from *Freeman* as the only basis allowable for remedial orders. Such orders must recognize that the state's role, with respect to quality educational programs, has been limited "to the funding, not the implementation, of these programs." A district court should also "sharply limit, if not dispense with" its reliance on achievement test scores. The Court noted that too many "external factors" beyond the control of the school district affect minority achievement. To the extent that these external factors are not the result of segregation, they "do not figure in the remedial calculus." The district court's "insistence on academic goals unrelated to the effects of legal segregation unwarrantably postpones the day when the [district] will be able to operate on its own." Rehnquist suggested that the lower court's "end purpose" is to remedy the violation as fully as practicable, but it must also "restore state and local authorities to the control" of the system.

Justice Thomas offered a lengthy and outspoken concurring opinion in *Jenkins II.* "It never ceases to amaze me," he said, that the courts are "so willing to assume that anything that is predominantly black must be inferior." Instead of remedying the injury done by segregation, the district court has tried to convert the school district into a "magnet district" that would "reverse the white flight caused by desegregation." Thomas pointed to two threads in our jurisprudence that have produced this "unfortunate" situation and prompted the district court to "experiment" with the education of the district's minority students. First, the Court has read case law to support the notion that minority students "suffer an unspecified psychological harm from segregation that retards their mental and educational development." The Court's approach relies on questionable social science but also rests on an "assumption of black inferiority." Second, federal courts have been permitted to exercise "virtually unlimited equitable powers to remedy this alleged constitutional violation." The exercise of this authority has "trampled upon principles of federalism and the separation of powers" and has allowed courts to "pursue other agendas unrelated to the narrow purpose of precisely remedying a constitutional harm." The "mere fact that a school is black," Thomas continued, does not mean that it is the "product of a constitutional violation." A "racial imbalance" does not itself establish a constitutional violation. The existence of one-race schools is not necessarily an "indication that the State is practicing segregation." Federal courts must not, he concluded, "confuse the consequences of *de jure* segregation with the results of larger social forces or of private decisions." The dissenters, Justices Souter, Stevens, Ginsburg, and Breyer, were critical of the scope of the Court's review in this case, a review that returned the Court to the broad issues underlying this case from its inception. They also supported the specific remedies ordered by the district court, including the attempt to attract white students into the district's schools. In other words, they did not feel the district court had overstepped its remedial authority.

The Court will continue to struggle with the issue of federal remedial authority in the school desegregation context. The effect of the *Freeman, Oklahoma City,* and *Jenkins II* rulings is that lower federal courts will not be permitted to issue remedial orders as broadly scoped as those 20 years ago. Furthermore, the foundation of any appellate review of remedial orders will be the criteria set out in *Freeman*—degree of compliance with previous orders, whether a good-faith effort had been made generally to achieve a unitary system, and whether any causal link remains between a de jure violation and any portion of district activity remaining under federal court supervision.

Abstention

***Pennzoil Co. v. Texaco, Inc.*, 481 U.S. 1, 95 L.Ed. 2d 1, 107 S.Ct. 1519 (1987)** This case arose out of a 1984 dispute between the Pennzoil Company and Texaco. Pennzoil wished to purchase a substantial number of shares of Getty Oil and had negotiated an agreement to that end. Texaco, however, purchased those same shares of Getty Oil stock at a higher price. Pennzoil filed suit in a Texas court, seeking damages from Texaco on the grounds that Texaco had induced Getty Oil to break its agreement with Pennzoil. A Texas jury awarded Pennzoil in excess of $10 billion in actual and punitive damages from Texaco for its tampering with the Pennzoil–Getty Oil purchase agreement. Texaco responded in two ways: It appealed the award itself in the Texas courts but also filed suit in a federal district court in its home state of New York, challenging a Texas law that required Texaco to post the entire $10+ billion as bond throughout the period of the appeal. The federal court stopped Pennzoil from collecting the judgment while the case was under appeal and required that Texaco post a bond of only $1 billion. The district court's ruling was affirmed by the Court of Appeals for the Second Circuit. The Supreme Court, however, ruled that the district court must abstain from enjoining enforcement of the state court judgment. Justice Powell said that a court ought not intervene in a case when the party seeking such intervention "has an adequate remedy at law." More importantly, the principle of comity should discourage intervention. Comity is a notion that reflects a "proper respect for state functions, a recognition of the fact that the entire country is made up of a Union of separate state governments." In addition, the abstention doctrine allows courts to avoid "unwarranted determination of federal constitutional questions." The Court noted this concern as having "special significance" in this case. Because Texaco did not present to the Texas courts the constitutional claims present in this case, it is "impossible to be certain that the governing Texas statutes and procedural rules actually raise these claims." It is possible, Powell suggested, that the Texas courts would have "resolved this case on state statutory or constitutional grounds, without reaching the federal constitutional questions" raised by Texaco. This case involves challenges to the processes by which the state compels compliance with court judgments. Not only would federal injunctions in such cases "interfere with the execution of state judgments, but they would do so on grounds that challenge the very process by which those judgments were obtained." When, like Texaco, a litigant has "made no effort" to present federal claims in related state court proceedings, a federal court "should assume that state procedures will afford an adequate remedy, in the absence of unambiguous authority to the contrary." Accordingly, it was the Court's judgment that the lower courts should have deferred on principles of comity to the pending state proceeding. *See also* ABSTENTION, p. 575; FEDERALISM, p. 27; *YOUNGER v. HARRIS* (401 U.S. 37: 1971), p. 271.

Significance The Court based its ruling in *Pennzoil Co. v. Texaco, Inc.* on the abstention doctrine at least in part. This doctrine is designed to minimize conflict between federal and state courts. The doctrine instructs federal courts that they should not intervene in a state matter until all appropriate state courts have addressed the matter. *Pennzoil* builds on the Court's ruling in *Younger v. Harris* (401 U.S. 37: 1971). *Younger* involved a state prosecution of a political radical for violation of a state law that banned membership in an organization that advocated the use of criminal means to achieve political objectives. A similar criminal statute had been struck down previously, and Harris argued that the statute on which his prosecution was based was similarly unconstitutional. He was eventually able to enjoin the prosecution by order of a federal court. The Supreme Court, however, reversed, concluding that considerations of federalism must generally preclude federal court interruption of a state prosecution. *Younger* was a broadened application of the abstention doctrine, and it made access to federal courts more difficult for many state litigants, as seen in *Pennzoil.*

2. *Executive Power*

Foreign Affairs

***Reno v. Flores*, 507 U.S. 292, 123 L.Ed. 2d 1, 113 S.Ct. 1439 (1992)** The Immigration and Nationality Act (INA) authorizes that alien juveniles may be arrested and detained if there is suspicion they are deportable. Under terms of the law, these detained juveniles may be released only to their parents, close relatives, or legal guardians except under "unusual and compelling" circumstances. The INA procedure allows the juvenile to request a hearing on deportability and detention before an immigration judge. Jenny Flores and other alien juveniles brought suit in U.S. district court arguing that they were entitled to release into the custody of "responsible adults" other than those enumerated in the statute. The district court agreed and ruled the regulatory process unconstitutional on due process grounds. The U.S. Court of Appeals for the Ninth Circuit, sitting *en banc,* affirmed. The Supreme Court, however, reversed in a 7-2 decision.

The problem prompting Congress to give the U.S. attorney general broad discretion in these cases was characterized by the Court as a "serious one." The INS arrests "thousands of alien juveniles" each year, and as many as "70% of them [are] unaccompanied." Nonetheless, the Court noted the presence of two factors affecting the nature of its review in this case. First, the challenge was "facial" in character. That is, there was no particular case to which the regulations had been applied. Rather, the challenge was exclusively directed toward the language of the regulation itself. Second, the conditions that existed at the time the suit was commenced had changed. New and extensive requirements have been set out that "substantially settled claims" regarding detention conditions, and the INS was presumably in compliance with these requirements. These two factors influenced the Court's response to the three-pronged challenge to the INS regulations. The challengers first asserted that a child who has no available parent or close relative has a right to placement with a private custodian rather than a government-operated child-care institution. The Court concluded that there was no constitutional right to placement with a private custodian. Such a "novel" claim, said Justice Scalia, cannot be considered as "so rooted in the traditions and conscience of our people as to be ranked as fundamental." Further, the Court found the regulation "rationally connected" to the government's interest in promoting the welfare of detained juveniles and neither punitive nor excessive in relation to that objective. The challengers also asserted a violation of procedural due process because the INS is not required to make individual determinations as to whether a detained juvenile's best interests are served by remaining in INS custody or by release to a "responsible adult." The Court saw this contention as the substantive due process argument "recast in procedural due process terms." Finally, the Court held that the regulation did not exceed the scope of the attorney general's "discretion to continue custody over arrested aliens." Those approved as guardians reflect "the traditional view that parents and close relatives are competent custodians, and otherwise defers to the States' proficiency in the field of child custody." *See also* ARTICLE II, p. 139; *UNITED STATES v. CURTISS-WRIGHT EXPORT CORP.* (299 U.S. 304: 1936), p. 144.

Significance As a general rule, the Supreme Court has deferred to executive authority in matters having to do with international relations. Although executive power cannot exceed those limitations found in the Constitution, the Court has been inclined to recognize executive power in the field of foreign affairs that is more extensive than the enumerated powers read literally. Such deference is seen in the *Flores* ruling. The INS arrests "thousands" of alien juveniles each year, and a large proportion of them are unaccompanied. Under these circumstances, the Court deferred to the "broad discretion" given to the attorney general to determine "whether and on what terms" an alien arrested on suspicion of being deportable should be released pending the deportation hearing. Another good example is the Court's ruling in *United States v. Curtiss-Wright Export Corp.* (299 U.S. 403: 1936). A more recent and more extreme example can be seen in *United States v. Alvarez-Machain* (504 U.S. 655: 1992), in which the Court ruled that agents of the United States may ignore the terms of extradition agreements and forcibly bring a criminal suspect from a foreign country to the United States to stand trial. Alvarez-Machain, a Mexican citizen and physician, was sought by the United States for his alleged involvement in the kidnapping and murder of a Drug Enforcement Administration (DEA) agent. Under the terms of a 1980 agreement with Mexico, the United States could have requested extradition. Because Alvarez-Machain was a Mexican citizen, Mexico could then have chosen either to extradite him or to undertake its own prosecution. No extradition request was made, however. Instead, Alvarez-Machain was seized in Mexico by Mexican bounty hunters, taken to El Paso, Texas, and delivered to DEA authorities. Alvarez-Machain contended that having an extradition agreement would make no sense "if either nation were free to resort to forcible kidnapping to gain the presence of an individual for prosecution in a manner not contemplated by the treaty." Chief Justice Rehnquist spoke for a six-justice majority, saying, "We do not read the treaty in such a fashion." Rather, Rehnquist said the treaty "does not purport to specify the only ways in which one country may gain custody of a national of the other country for the purposes of prosecution." Viewing the terms of the treaty literally, Rehnquist said the agreement "says nothing about the obligations of the United States and Mexico to refrain from forcible abductions . . ." and should not be read as though such limitations are contained implicitly. Justice Stevens, in a dissent joined by Justices Blackmun and O'Connor, argued that failure to specifically prohibit forcible abductions should not be interpreted to create an "optional method of obtaining jurisdiction over alleged offenders. . . ." Indeed, Stevens concluded, it is "shocking that a party to an extradition treaty might believe that it has secretly reserved the right to make seizures of citizens in the other party's territory."

The Supreme Court upheld the U.S. policy of intercepting vessels attempting to illegally transport Haitians to the United States in *Sale v. Haitian Centers Council, Inc.* (509 U.S. 155: 1993). Interception typically occurs before the vessels reach U.S. territorial waters. The Haitian passengers are summarily returned to Haiti without determination of whether they might qualify as refugees. The policy was challenged on the grounds that it violated the 1980 amendments to the Immigration and Nationality Act and Article 33 of the United Nations Protocol Relating to the Status of Refugees. With only Justice Blackmun dissenting, the Supreme Court ruled that neither the act nor the U.N. Protocol were violated. The Court concluded that aliens residing illegally in the United States may be deported following a formal hearing. Aliens arriving at the border are subject to removal following a less formal exclusion hearing. In either situation, the alien may seek asylum as a political refugee. Provisions of the act afford hearings only to aliens who reside in the United States or have arrived at the border. For a number of years, the interdiction policy challenged in this case prevented Haitians, among others, from getting to "our shores and invoking those protections . . . ." Under terms of the law when enacted in 1952, the attorney general was given authority to stop deportation proceedings for any alien "within the United States" who would be deported to a country where the alien would be persecuted "on account of race, religion, or political opinion." The act was amended in 1980, and the phrase "within the United States" was removed. The word "return" was added making the phrase "deport or return." It was the Court's judgment that the addition of the word "return" was intended to clarify Congress's intent to prevent summary return of two kinds of aliens: those who had been admitted to the United States and were subject to deportation and "excludable aliens" who were in the country or at the border but had never been admitted. It was the Court's view that removal of the phrase "within the United States" was simply an effort to protect the latter category in the same way "deportable aliens" are protected. The 1980 amendment "erased the long-maintained distinction between deportable and excludable aliens . . . but it did nothing to change the presumption that both types of aliens would continue to be found only within United States territory."

The Court concluded that the U.N. Protocol, like the relevant section of the act, is "completely silent with respect to the Article's possible application to actions taken by a country outside its own borders." In spite of the "moral weight" of arguments that a nation be prevented from repatriating refugees to their "potential oppressors," the text and negotiating history of Article 33 "affirmatively indicate that it was not intended to have extraterritorial effect." Those who drafted the U.N. Convention (and provisions of the act) may not have contemplated that a nation would return fleeing refugees "to the one country they had desperately sought to escape." Indeed, Stevens suggested that such actions may even "violate the spirit" of the provisions. But a treaty "cannot impose uncontemplated extraterritorial obligations on those who ratify it through no more than its general humanitarian intent." Justice Blackmun strongly disagreed. The Haitians did not claim a right to admission to the country. In his view, all they sought was the United States to "cease forcibly driving them back to detention, abuse and death. That is a modest plea, vindicated by the Treaty and the statute. We should not close our ears to it."

Importation of "gray-market" goods has been a persistent commercial problem. Gray-market merchandise is manufactured outside the United States, carries a valid trademark, and is brought into the country and sold without consent of the trademark holder. The Tariff Act of 1930 prohibits the importation of such merchandise without the written consent of the trademark owner. The U.S. Customs Service subsequently issued regulations that created exceptions to the ban to permit the entry of foreign-manufactured goods by the "same person" who holds the trademark, someone who is subject to "common control" of the trademark holder, or where a foreign manufacturer has received the trademark owner's authorization to use the trademark. An association of trademark holders challenged the regulation as incompatible with provisions of the Tariff Act. A federal district court upheld the regulations but was reversed by the Court of Appeals for the District of Columbia Circuit. The Supreme Court affirmed in part and reversed in part in *K Mart Corporation v. Cartier, Inc.* (486 U.S. 281: 1988). The basis for judgment is the specific language at issue as well as the "language and design" of the statute as a whole. If a statute is "clear and unambiguous," courts must give effect to congressional intent and "cannot pay deference to a contrary agency interpretation." If, on the other hand, a statute is "silent or ambiguous" on a specific question, a court must defer to an agency's interpretation provided it "does not conflict with the statute's plain meaning." In this instance, the Customs Service "same person" or "common control" regulation was found to be consistent with the applicable provisions of the Tariff Act and thus a permissible construction of the statute designed to resolve ambiguities. When statutory language is ambiguous, an agency is "entitled to choose any reasonable definition" that enables more effective implementation of the law. The "authorized use" regulation, however, was found to conflict with the "unequivocal" language of the Tariff Act and was struck down. Under no "reasonable construction" of the statutory language can goods produced in a foreign country by a foreign manufacturer "be removed from the purview of the statute" because it would deprive the domestic trademark holder from protection under the Tariff Act.

Appointment and Removal

***Weiss v. United States*, 510 U.S. 163, 127 L.Ed. 2d 1, 114 S.Ct. 752 (1994)**
This case arose out of military court-martial proceedings. Eric Weiss and Ernesto Hernandez pleaded guilty to criminal charges in separate proceedings. Weiss and Hernandez pursued two constitutional issues on appeal. First, they claimed that because military officers are not specifically appointed to the position of military judge by the president the Appointments Clause of Article II is violated. Second, they contended that because military judges do not have specified or fixed terms their independence is sufficiently compromised so as to deny military defendants due process of law. The Supreme Court unanimously rejected both contentions. Notwithstanding specification by Congress that military judges possess certain qualifications such as membership in a state or federal bar, the Court did not find indication of congressional intent to create a separate office. Further, none of the relevant sections of the Uniform Code of Military Justice (UCMJ) mentions a separate appointment for military judges. The Court also noted that Congress treated differently those offices, such as chairman of the Joint Chiefs of Staff, that require second appointment of already commissioned officers. The difference, said Chief Justice Rehnquist, negates any inference that Congress intended military judges to receive a second appointment but that in a "fit of absentmindedness [it] forgot to say so." In rejecting the Appoint-

ments Clause claim, the Court suggested that although military judges perform certain "unique and important functions" all military officers "play a role in the operation of the military justice system." Indeed, the Court found that the position of military judge is "less distinct from other military positions than the office of full-time civilian judge is from other officers in civilian society." The fixed-term claim was not based on allegations of bias in the specific cases under review. Rather, Weiss and Hernandez asked the Court to consider the presumption that absence of a fixed term diminishes the level of independence necessary to ensure impartiality. It was the Court's view that "neither history nor current practice . . . supports such an assumption." A fixed term of office is not, said Rehnquist, "an end in itself." It is a means of promoting judicial independence, which in turn helps to ensure impartiality. It was the Court's view that applicable provisions of the UCMJ and corresponding regulations "sufficiently preserve judicial impartiality" by insulating military judges from the effects of command influence. Furthermore, the entire system is overseen by a Court of Military Appeals, which is "composed entirely of civilian judges who serve for fixed terms of 15 years." *See also* APPOINTMENT POWER, p. 581; ARTICLE II, p. 139; *HUMPHREY'S EXECUTOR v. UNITED STATES* (295 U.S. 602: 1935), p. 151; *MYERS v. UNITED STATES* (272 U.S. 52: 1926), p. 1926.

Significance Article II vests the president with the power to nominate ambassadors, federal judges, and "other officers" of the United States. Exercise of the appointment power is generally subject to Senate advice and consent, but appointment of "inferior" as distinct from "principal" officers may occur with Senate confirmation. The appointment of judges to military courts has given the Court two opportunities to examine the process in recent years. *Weiss* was the first. The second case was *Edmond v. United States* (137 L.Ed. 2d 917: 1997). *Weiss* held that appointment as a commissioned officer qualifies a person for subsequent appointment as a military judge. The question in *Edmond* involved appointment of civilians to serve as military judges. Edmond and several others were convicted in court-martial proceedings. They all unsuccessfully appealed to the Coast Guard Court of Criminal Appeals. At least one of the judges was a civilian for each of these appeals. Edmond and the others sought review by the Court of Appeals for the Armed Forces, claiming that their initial appeals had been heard by improperly appointed judges. They argued that *Weiss* could not apply to civilian judges and that a civilian must be specifically nominated to a military judgeship by the president with subsequent confirmation by the Senate. The Court of Appeals for the Armed Forces rejected this argument and affirmed the rulings of the lower court. The Supreme

Court also affirmed. Edmond et al. argued that the secretary of transportation's civilian appointments to the Coast Guard Court of Criminal Appeals are invalid because (1) the secretary lacks authority to appoint members of the court and (2) judges of the military Courts of Criminal Appeals are "principal, not inferior officers within the meaning of the Appointments Clause." Appointment of such principal officers requires Senate confirmation. Justice Scalia said the statutory language "most relevant" to the case provides that the secretary of transportation "may appoint and fix the pay of officers and employees of the Department of Transportation and may prescribe their duties and powers." Edmond et al. did not dispute that these judges are Department of Transportation officers. Thus, although the statutory language does not specifically mention Coast Guard judges, the "plain language appears to give the Secretary power to appoint them." Furthermore, provisions of the Uniform Code of Military Justice (UCMJ) that empowers the Judge Advocate General to establish criminal courts of appeal "conspicuously" omits any discussion about appointment of military judges. Instead, the UCMJ refers to judges who are "assigned" to a court of criminal appeals. The difference between the power to "assign" officers to a particular task and the power to "appoint" those officers "is not merely stylistic." Drawing on *Weiss,* Scalia said that Congress has "consistently" used the word "'appoint' with respect to military positions requiring separate appointment rather than using terms not found within the Appointments Clause, such as 'assign.'" Thus, the pertinent provision in the UCMJ "concerns not the appointment of Court of Criminal Appeals judges, but only their assignment." Scalia agreed that the "default" method for appointing both principal and inferior officers is the same but that there is an "Excepting Clause" contained within the Appointments Clause that empowers Congress to vest appointment of inferior officers with the president, courts, or heads of departments. The language was added for the "obvious purpose [of] administrative convenience," but that convenience was deemed to "outweigh the benefits of the more cumbersome procedure only with respect to the appointment of 'inferior officers.'"

The Court also responded to the contention that judges of the Court of Criminal Appeals are principal rather than inferior officers. Scalia suggested that prior cases had not "set forth an exclusive criterion for distinguishing between principal and inferior officers for Appointment Clause purposes." The argument that these judges are principal officers focused on the importance of their responsibilities. The exercise of "significant authority" pursuant to the laws of the United States marks the line between "officer and non-officer" rather than the line between principal and inferior officers, however. In the context of a clause "designed to preserve political accountability relative to important government assignments," Scalia said, it is "evident" that inferior officers are those whose work is "directed and supervised at some level by others who were appointed by presidential nomination with the advice and consent of the Senate." Generally, the term "'inferior officer' connotes a relationship with some higher ranking officer or officer below the President: whether one is an 'inferior' officer depends on whether [that officer] has a superior." The Court concluded that the judges of the Court of Criminal Appeals have no power "to render a final decision on behalf of the United States unless permitted to do so by other executive officers." As a result, the secretary of transportation may appoint judges of the Coast Guard Court of Criminal Appeals, and such appointment is "in conformity" with the Appointments Clause, since those judges are "inferior" officers within the meaning of that provision "by reason of the supervision of their work exercised by the General Counsel of the Department of Transportation in his capacity as Judge Advocate General and the Court of Appeals for the Armed Forces."

Law Enforcement and Asset Forfeiture

***United States v. X-Citement Video, Inc.*, 513 U.S. 64, 130 L.Ed. 2d 372, 115 S.Ct. 464 (1994)** The Protection of Children Against Sexual Exploitation Act prohibits "knowingly" transporting, receiving, distributing, or reproducing any materials that depict minors engaged in sexually explicit acts. The issue in *United States v. X-Citement Video, Inc.,* was whether the "knowingly" reference required demonstration by the government that the defendant was aware the performers were actually minors. A number of videotapes sold by Rubin Gottesman, the owner of X-Citement Video, featured a performer who was not yet 18 years old at the time the videos were produced. Placement in the statute of the term "knowingly" before transporting could support an interpretation that the act did not require knowledge by the defendant that any sexually explicit material transported included performances by minors. In other words, given the placement of the term "knowingly," did the act only require that the defendant knowingly transported or received such material? It was the view of the Court of Appeals for the Ninth Circuit that the Constitution requires knowledge that "at least one of the performers is under age 18" and that the act was unconstitutional on due process grounds because it did not clearly require proof the defendant had knowledge that any of the performers was a minor. In a 7-2 decision, the Supreme Court concluded that the act is properly read as containing a knowledge requirement on the element of performer age.

Chief Justice Rehnquist suggested that under the Ninth Circuit's reading of the act the word "knowingly" would not modify the elements of a performer's age or the sexually explicit nature of the material. The Court did not think this to be the "end of the matter," however, because of the "anomalies which result" from such an interpretation. Rehnquist also noted "respective assumptions" that some form of scienter (guilty knowledge) is to be implied in a criminal statute even if not expressed and that a statute should be interpreted "where fairly possible" so as to avoid substantial constitutional questions. The government is required to demonstrate that the accused had knowledge of each essential component of any other crime. From this perspective, the Court concluded that knowledge of the age of performers was implicit in the federal child pornography law. Reading the statute as the Ninth Circuit did would produce results that are "not merely odd, but positively absurd," Rehnquist continued. The critical element in separating wrongful conduct from lawful or protected conduct is the age of the performers. Knowledge that at least one performer in sexually explicit material is under the age of 18 thus must be seen as an essential component for the offenses of transporting and distributing child pornography since neither transporting nor distributing sexually explicit material involving adult performers only is criminal. A statute "completely bereft" of a knowledge requirement as to the age of the performers would "raise serious constitutional doubts." Accordingly, it is "incumbent" on the Court to read the statute to eliminate those doubts so long as such a reading is "not plainly contrary to the intent of the Congress." Justices Scalia and Thomas dissented. Scalia suggested that the Ninth Circuit's interpretation of the statute was "quite obviously the only grammatical reading" possible. The dissenters argued that federal law must be applied as written by Congress; it must be interpreted on the basis of the words, not a broader context or perceived legislative intent. They strongly objected to the Court writing in a knowledge requirement that Congress had failed to provide. Rehnquist characterized the Court's interpretative approach in this case as giving the statute its "most natural grammatical reading." Scalia called this "understatement to the point of distortion." *See also* JUDICIAL SELF-RESTRAINT, p. 627; *UNITED STATES v. CAROLENE PRODUCTS COMPANY* (304 U.S. 144: 1938), p. 93.

Significance The 1930s featured an unusually high level of conflict between the Supreme Court and the executive and legislative branches of government. The Court found a number of Franklin D. Roosevelt's New Deal initiatives constitutionally defective until 1937. A change in the use of judicial review became apparent in several important rulings in the late 1930s. In *U.S. v. Carolene Products Company* (304 U.S. 144:

1938), for example, Justice Harlan F. Stone suggested assuming the constitutionality of legislation aimed at economic regulation. Although closer scrutiny of laws affecting individual rights ought to remain, the basis for all other legislative initiatives should be presumptively sufficient. This approach was an extension of the standards discussed by Justice Louis D. Brandeis in *Ashwander v. Tennessee Valley Authority* (297 U.S. 288: 1936) two years earlier. The so-called Ashwander Rules suggested such limits on judicial review as not "anticipating" a question of constitutional law and refraining from passing on a constitutional question if there is some narrower ground on which the case could be resolved. Most germane to the *X-Citement Video* ruling is the Ashwander directive suggesting a "cardinal principle" that the Court try to find a construction of law that avoids, if "fairly possible," finding a constitutional defect. This approach closely reflects the values of the judicial self-restraint orientation. It is most evident in *X-Citement Video* that Chief Justice Rehnquist went to great lengths to find a construction, even one based on implication, that would save the challenged provisions of the Protection of Children Against Sexual Exploitation Act.

***Austin v. United States*, 509 U.S. 602, 125 L.Ed. 2d 488, 113 S.Ct. 2801 (1993)** Ruled that the Excessive Fines Clause of the Eighth Amendment could apply to civil forfeitures. Federal law permits civil forfeiture of any properties used in or acquired with proceeds from illegal activities, most frequently illegal drug transactions. Richard Austin sold two grams of cocaine to an individual working with local police. The buyer had approached Austin at the automobile body shop he owned and operated. Austin left his shop, went to his trailer home, which was located nearby, and delivered the cocaine to the buyer upon returning. Austin eventually pleaded guilty to one state count of drug possession with intent to distribute. Following his sentencing, a federal civil forfeiture proceeding was initiated. Austin's trailer home and place of business were both confiscated without trial on the grounds that these properties had been used in the drug transaction. Austin unsuccessfully argued before the Court of Appeals for the Eighth Circuit that the Excessive Fines Clause of the Eighth Amendment applied to and could limit civil forfeitures. A unanimous Supreme Court held in *Austin v. United States* that the clause could apply. Justice Blackmun said the general purpose of the Excessive Fines Clause is to "limit the government's power to punish." This language specifically limits the government's power to "extract payments, whether in cash or in kind, 'as punishment for some offense.'" According to Blackmun, the issue was not "whether forfeiture was civil or criminal, but rather whether it is punishment." Sanctions frequently serve more than one purpose. It is not necessary to "exclude the possibility that a forfeiture serves remedial purposes to conclude that it is subject to the limitations of the Excessive Fines Clause." All that must be shown is that the forfeiture "serv[es] in part to punish." The Court found the objective of punishment reflected in several ways: in the legislative history of the relevant provisions of the law; in Congress's choice of linking forfeiture directly to drug offenses; and in the inclusion of an "innocent owner defense." Despite arguments by the government that the forfeiture provisions were remedial, the Court ruled that the government failed to show that the civil forfeiture process was exclusively remedial. A civil sanction that "cannot fairly be said *solely* to serve a remedial purpose, but rather can only be explained as also serving either retributive or deterrent purposes, is punishment, as we have come to understand the term." Austin asked the Court to fashion a "multi-factor" test for determining whether a forfeiture is "excessive." The Court refused to do so. Instead, it noted that since the Eighth Circuit had foreclosed such inquiry "prudence dictates that we allow the lower courts to consider that question in the first instance" and remanded the case. *See also* EIGHTH AMENDMENT, p. 596; JUDICIAL REVIEW, p. 627.

Significance The civil forfeiture process has long been available to the government for use against those who profit from criminal conduct. Forfeiture has been employed with increased frequency as part of the current "war" against those who produce and distribute illegal drugs. In the last several years, the Supreme Court has been asked to examine a number of constitutional issues arising from the more frequent use of civil forfeiture. One such case was *Alexander v. United States* (509 U.S. 544: 1993), which involved obscenity rather than illegal drugs. Production and/or distribution of obscenity is one of the offenses that falls under the forfeiture provisions of the Racketeer Influenced Corrupt Organizations Act (RICO). RICO provides that property traceable to persons convicted of two or more obscenity offenses can be confiscated. Ferris Alexander was convicted in 1989 on 18 obscenity counts and three RICO violations. In addition to ordering prison terms, fines, and assessed costs, the trial court ordered Alexander to forfeit his entire business. Under the RICO forfeiture, Alexander lost almost $9 million in cash as well as the property and inventory connected to his business activities. Alexander challenged the RICO forfeiture on two grounds: it constituted a prior restraint on expression protected by the First Amendment; and it was an excessive or disproportionate punishment prohibited by the Eighth Amendment. The Court remanded the Eighth Amendment issue on much the same basis as in *Austin* but rejected his First Amendment claims outright. Alexander contended that the practical effect of the RICO forfeiture order imposed a "complete *ban* on his future expression because of previous unprotected speech." The Court disagreed, concluding that Alexander had "stretch[ed] the term 'prior restraint' well beyond the limits" of previous rulings. The Court did not see the RICO forfeiture as forbidding Alexander from future expressive conduct, nor was he required to obtain prior approval for any expressive activities. Rather, the order deprived him only of particular assets determined to be connected to his RICO convictions. The Court saw no legal impediment to his future expressive activity. Indeed, he was "perfectly free to open an adult bookstore or otherwise engage in the production and distribution of erotic materials." The forfeiture order merely prevented Alexander from financing any such enterprise with assets derived from prior RICO offenses. Alexander also contended that the RICO forfeiture provisions had a "chilling effect" on expression. The Court acknowledged that "cautious" booksellers might practice self-censorship but that the deterrence of the sale of obscenity is a "legitimate end of state anti-obscenity laws." The dissenters contended that the ruling allowed the "destruction" of a book or film business and its entire inventory of legitimate expression for a "single past speech offense." This "ominous, onerous threat undermines free speech and press principles essential to our personal freedom."

A procedural challenge to forfeiture came in *United States v. James Good Real Property* (510 U.S. 43: 1993). James Good pleaded guilty to a drug charge in 1985 and was sentenced to a year of imprisonment and five years of probation. In 1989, the federal government began a civil forfeiture action against Good's property. A federal magistrate determined there was probable cause to believe the property was connected to Good's drug offense and issued a seizure warrant against the property. Good, who was living in Nicaragua at the time, was not notified of the forfeiture action. Furthermore, there was no hearing on the issue of whether the property was forfeitable. A federal district court upheld the seizure, but the decision was reversed by the Court of Appeals for the Ninth Circuit. In *James Good Real Property,* the Supreme Court affirmed the Ninth Circuit ruling. The government argued that because the forfeiture served a law enforcement purpose it only need comply with the Fourth Amendment when seizing property. The Court disagreed. The seizure of property "implicates two explicit textual sources of constitutional protection," the Fourth Amendment and the Due Process Clause of the Fifth Amendment. The proper question in this case was not "which Amendment controls but whether either Amendment is violated." The Court agreed that the Fourth Amendment applies to civil seizures but held that the "purpose and effect" of the government's action in this case went beyond the traditional meaning of search and seizure. The government did not seize the property to preserve evidence of criminal conduct but rather to "assert ownership and control over the property itself." Legal action that can result in loss of property must comply with the Due Process Clause of the Fifth and Fourteenth Amendments. The Court said the right to prior notice and hearing is "central to the Constitution's command of due process." The purpose of this requirement is to protect an individual's use and possession of property from "arbitrary encroachment—to minimize substantively unfair or mistaken deprivations of property. . . ." The Court found Good's right to maintain control over his home without governmental interference of both "historic and continuing importance." Governmental seizure gives the government the right to prohibit sale, evict occupants, modify the property—to generally "supersede the owner in all rights pertaining to use, possession, and enjoyment of the property." These interests are substantial. The Court then found that the practice of ex parte seizure created an "unacceptable risk of error" as well. The intent of drug forfeiture laws is not to deprive innocent owners of property, but the ex parte approach "affords little or no protection to the innocent owner." Finally, the Court did not find a sufficiently important government interest to require asserting control over the property without first affording notice and hearing. To the contrary, postponement of seizure until after an adversary hearing "creates no significant administrative burden." Any harm resulting from the delay is "minimal in comparison to the injury occasioned by erroneous seizure." Unless exigent circumstances exist, the Due Process Clause requires "notice and meaningful opportunity to be heard before seizing real property subject to civil forfeiture."

Finally, the Court considered whether criminal prosecution and a separate property forfeiture based on the same offense constitutes double jeopardy in *United States v. Ursery* and *United States v. $405,089.23* (135 L.Ed. 2d 549: 1996). The government sought to seize Ursery's property by claiming it was used to further unlawful possession and distribution of marijuana. Ursery eventually paid an agreed-upon sum of money instead. He then sought to overturn his criminal conviction on double jeopardy grounds since it occurred after the property forfeiture action. The district court rejected Ursery's contention, concluding that the forfeiture and criminal conviction were part of a "single, coordinated prosecution." The Court of Appeals for the Sixth Circuit, however, reversed, holding Ursery's consent judgment in the civil proceeding was sufficiently similar to a plea agreement in a criminal case and that jeopardy had attached when the forfeiture complaint was filed. In *$405,089.23,* Charles Arlt and James Wren were convicted of several federal drug trafficking and money laundering charges. A civil forfeiture complaint was filed following the indictment of Arlt and Wren but by mutual consent was deferred until the conclusion of the criminal proceedings. Following the defendants' convictions, the government successfully sought summary judgment on the forfeiture complaint. The Court of Appeals for the Ninth Circuit reversed, ruling that the property forfeiture was punishment for the same offenses underlying the criminal convictions. The Supreme Court held, however, that the government can seek criminal penalties and civil forfeiture to seize property without violating the prohibition against double jeopardy. Chief Justice Rehnquist summarized prior double jeopardy rulings and suggested that those cases "did not foreclose" the possibility that in a particular case a civil penalty may be "so extreme and so divorced from the Government's damages and expenses as to constitute punishment." Nonetheless, these prior decisions revealed a "remarkably consistent theme": Civil forfeiture is a "remedial civil sanction," distinct from civil penalties, and "does not constitute a punishment." Further, civil forfeiture is not primarily punitive. In the Court's view, the forfeiture proceedings under challenge in these cases did not demonstrate they were "so punitive in form and effect as to render them criminal." To the contrary, Rehnquist pointed to the "important nonpunitive goals" of federal forfeiture laws, such as "encourag[ing]" property owners to take care in managing their property and ensuring that owners will not "permit that property to be used for illegal purposes." The fact that a forfeiture statute, Rehnquist concluded, "has some connection to a criminal violation is far from the 'clearest proof' necessary to show the proceeding is criminal." Finally, Rehnquist said the Court "declined to import the analysis of *Austin* into our double jeopardy jurisprudence."

Administrative Authority

***Babbitt v. Sweet Home Chapter*, 515 U.S. 687, 132 L.Ed. 2d 597, 115 S.Ct. 2407 (1995)** The Endangered Species Act of 1973 (ESA) makes it a crime for any person to "take" endangered or threatened species. The statute defines the term "take" to mean "harass, harm, pursue, wound, or kill" endangered species. Under the law, the federal government is prohibited from "modifying or degrading" the critical habitats of endangered species. The U.S. Fish and Wildlife Service, an agency in the Department of the Interior, issued regulations that defined the term "harm" to include habitat degradation by private parties on privately owned lands. A number of individuals, businesses, and organizations (the Sweet Home plaintiffs) filed a federal suit, seeking to bar implementation of the regulation on their private property. The district court granted summary judgment for the government, but the Court of Appeals for the District of Columbia Circuit reversed, concluding that the word "harm" referred exclusively to direct use of force against the endangered or threatened animal. The Supreme Court, however, upheld the regulation in a 6-3 decision. The Court found three reasons in the text of the ESA for concluding that the secretary of the interior's interpretation of the statute was reasonable. First, an "ordinary understanding of the word 'harm' supports it." The Sweet Home plaintiffs had argued that the regulation should have limited the purview of "harm" to "direct applications of force against protected species." The dictionary definition of "harm" does not include the word "directly" or suggest "in any way that only direct or willful action that leads to injury constitutes 'harm.'" Second, the "broad purpose" of the ESA supports the secretary's decision to extend protection against activities that "cause the precise harms Congress enacted the statute to avoid." The ESA was described as the "most comprehensive legislation for the preservation of endangered species ever enacted by any nation." Whereas laws enacted in the 1960s had not contained any "sweeping prohibition against the taking of endangered species except on federal lands," the 1973 statute applied to "all land in the United States and to the Nation's territorial seas." Finally, the Court concluded that authorizing the secretary to issue permits for "takings" that the law would "otherwise prohibit" reflected congressional intent to prohibit "indirect as well as deliberate takings." The Court did not decide whether the definition in the law of the term "take" compels the secretary's interpretation of the term "harm," for two reasons: (1) Congress had not "unambiguously manifest its intent" to adopt the challengers' view, and (2) the secretary's interpretation is "reasonable" enough to decide this case. The latitude the ESA gives the secretary in enforcing the statute, together with the "degree of regulatory expertise necessary to its enforcement, establishes that we owe some degree of deference to the Secretary's reasonable interpretation." *See also* ARTICLE II, p. 139; STANDING, p. 655; *UNITED STATES v. STUDENTS CHALLENGING REGULATORY AGENCY PROCEDURES* (412 U.S. 669: 1973), p. 113.

Significance The ease with which "public interest" plaintiffs can establish standing to sue affects the extent to which courts may intervene in a variety of situations. The Court relaxed the direct injury component of standing in *United States v. Students Challenging Regulatory Agency Procedures* (412 U.S. 669: 1973). The plaintiff in *SCRAP* was an environmental group seeking to challenge an Interstate Commerce Commission action it believed would create injury to the public at large through adverse environmental impact. The Court made it clear in *SCRAP* that "aesthetic and environmental" values were sufficiently important to American quality of life to permit them to serve as the basis by which standing was established. As important, the Court said that standing determinations are not to be a function of the number of people affected. As distinct from taxpayer groups, environmental groups generally have been more successful in establishing standing. The Rehnquist Court restricted this access in *Lujan v. National Wildlife Federation* (497 U.S. 871: 1990).

The National Wildlife Federation (NWF) brought suit in federal court, alleging that the Department of the Interior violated the National Environmental Protection Act (NEPA) through its Land Withdrawal Review Program. The program involves review of federal lands with the possibility that protective regulations might be removed and the lands opened for commercial uses. The NWF claimed its members were injured as a result of the department's program. The claim of standing was based on affidavits from NWF members who made recreational use of land "in the vicinity of" lands opened to commercial use under Interior's program. The district court eventually granted summary judgment to the government on the standing issue, but the Court of Appeals for the District of Columbia Circuit reversed and remanded the case for trial. The Supreme Court, however, held that the standing requirement for review under provisions of the Administrative Procedure Act (APA) had not been met. The standing provisions of the APA require that the party claiming the right to sue must identify an "agency action" that affects him or her and show that a "legal wrong" was suffered because of the agency action. It was the Court's conclusion that the facts alleged in the affidavits of the NWF members did not raise a "genuine issue of fact" as to whether they had a right to relief under the APA. There was no showing that the interests claimed by the members were "actually affected" by actions of the Department of the Interior. The affidavits alleged only that the members used unspecified lands "in the vicinity of immense tracts of territory." The court of appeals had erroneously ruled that the trial court must presume specific facts sufficient to support the general allegations of injury. Furthermore, the challengers did not refer to a single agency order or regulation but only to "continuing" operations regarding public lands. The Land Withdrawal Review Program is not an "identifiable agency action," nor is there any "final" action of an agency in this instance. Agency action is not ordinarily ready for judicial review under provisions of the APA, said Justice Scalia, until the "scope of the controversy has been reduced to manageable proportions, and its factual components fleshed out by concrete action that harms or threatens to harm" a complainant. The Court's decision in *Lujan* does not preclude the possibility of judicial review of agency actions by federal courts through the APA, but it clearly makes access to federal courts more difficult for parties who wish to challenge actions of federal administrative agencies.

***United States v. Kokinda*, 497 U.S. 720, 111 L.Ed. 2d 571, 110 S.Ct. 3115 (1990)** Upheld a U.S. Postal Service (USPS) regulation banning solicitation on sidewalks located entirely on USPS property. The Court first determined that the tripartite standard used in reviewing public forum cases would be used. Under this framework, the regulation of speech on government property that has been "traditionally open to the public for expressive activity," such as public streets or parks, is examined under "strict scrutiny." On the other hand, expressive activity where the government has not dedicated its property to First Amendment activity is examined "only for reasonableness." The Court rejected the argument that all sidewalks are a traditional public forum. The "mere physical characteristics" of the property cannot alone determine the forum standard. Rather, the "location and purpose" of a public sidewalk "is critical to determining whether such a sidewalk constitutes a public forum." The sidewalk subject to regulation in this case did not have the "characteristics of public sidewalks traditionally open to expressive activity." Rather, this particular sidewalk was constructed "solely to provide for the passage of individuals engaged in postal business," thus it was not a traditional public forum sidewalk. Even if the sidewalk had some recognized First Amendment uses, "regulation of the reserved nonpublic uses would still require application of the reasonableness test." Under this standard, the regulation must be "reasonable," and it must not be an "effort to suppress expression merely because public officials oppose the speaker's views." Two factors were key to the Court's finding this regulation reasonable. First, Congress had directed the USPS to become self-sufficient and provide "responsive" service to the "needs of the American people." This mission was drawn for the USPS "at a time when the mail service is becoming much more competitive." The Court was thus deferential to regulations designed to facilitate the efficient conduct of USPS business. Second, solicitation is different from other forms of expression. It is "confrontation" and is "inherently more intrusive and intimidating than an encounter with a person giving out information." These factors led the Court to conclude that it is reasonable to limit access to USPS property for solicitation, because solicitation is "inherently disruptive of the Postal Service's business." Because the regulation excludes all groups from engaging in solicitation, it was viewed as content-neutral and could not be regarded as an "effort to suppress expression because officials oppose the views." *See also* ARTICLE II, p. 139; JUDICIAL REVIEW, p. 627.

Significance Use of public property for assemblies has presented several difficult issues for the Court. The Court held in *City Council of Los Angeles v. Taxpayers for Vincent* (466 U.S. 789: 1984), for example, that a municipality could ban the posting of political campaign signs on utility poles. The ban was seen to be content-neutral and directed toward a legitimate aesthetic interest. The purpose of the regulation was "unrelated to the suppression of ideas" and interfered with expression only to the extent necessary to eliminate visual clutter. The Court noted that the ban on posting signs did not impinge on any alternative modes of communication.

Congress passed a law in the late 1930s that made it unlawful to display any sign within 500 feet of an embassy that might bring a foreign government into disrepute or to congregate within 500 feet of an embassy and refuse to disperse upon police order. The law exempted picketing as a result of bona fide labor disputes. This law, now part of the District of Columbia Code, was reviewed in *Boos v. Barry* (485 U.S. 312: 1988) after Boos and others had sought to display signs critical of the Soviet Union and Nicaragua. The Supreme Court upheld the congregating provisions but struck down the provisions applying to displays. Although recognizing the need to shield foreign governments from criticism, the Court found the display provisions to be a content-based regulation on particular expression in a public forum. The Court did not find the restriction narrowly focused enough and suggested that less restrictive alternatives were "readily available." The Court also said that while regulations may permissibly be aimed at "secondary effects," those that focus on the "direct impact of speech on its audience represent a different situation." The "emotive impact of speech on its audience is not a secondary effect." The congregating provision, on the other hand, had been confined by the lower courts to dispersal of those assemblies "directed at an embassy" and only when security was threatened. This construction did not allow the provision to reach a "substantial amount of constitutionally protected conduct." The regulation's reach was limited to security-threatening situations and was specific. Accordingly, the Court ruled that the provision was not overbroad; nor did the provision permit the police too much enforcement discretion.

***Rust v. Sullivan*, 500 U.S. 173, 114 L.Ed. 2d 233, 111 S.Ct. 1759 (1991)** Upheld regulations of Health and Human Services secretary on federal family planning funds. Title X of the Public Health Service Act of 1970 authorizes federal funding for public and private nonprofit agencies providing family planning services. Section 1008 of the act specifies that none of the funds appropriated under Title X can be used for programs where "abortion is a method of family planning." Until 1988, this phrase was interpreted as precluding Title X grantees from actually performing abortions as opposed to providing information about abortion as an option. In 1988, the Health and Human Services secretary issued new regulations that imposed conditions on grant recipients. First, staff people working at Title X–funded projects cannot counsel about abortion or provide referrals for abortions. Instead, pregnant clients must be referred to agencies providing "appropriate" prenatal services. Recipient agencies are explicitly forbidden from referring a client to an abortion provider, even on specific request. Second, a Title X project cannot engage in activities that "encourage, promote or advocate abortion as a method of family planning." Finally, recipient agencies must be organized in such a way as to be wholly independent from any abortion-related activities. Activities supported by federal funds must take place in separate facilities and use personnel independent from any agency personnel involved in abortion services.

A number of Title X grantees and physicians associated with recipient agencies sought to prevent implementation of the new regulations. In *Rust v. Sullivan,* the Supreme Court ruled 5-4 that the secretary's regulations were permitted under terms of the act and that the regulations did not violate the First Amendment or Fifth Amendment rights of recipient agencies or their clients. The constitutionality of abortion as such was not before the Court in this case. Chief Justice Rehnquist spoke for the majority and said the secretary's interpretation of the meaning of section 1008 must be accorded substantial deference not only because his agency administers the statute but also because the evidence as to congressional intent is "ambiguous." In addition, the Court thought the secretary's regulations reflected a "plausible construction" of the statute. The secretary's interpretation was clearly not one that would lead the Court to conclude that Congress had not intended regulations of this kind. Focus was then turned to the First Amendment issue. The principal contention of the challengers was this: Because Title X funds speech in a way that is not "evenhanded with respect to views and information about abortion, it invidiously discriminates on the basis of viewpoint." Rehnquist agreed that the secretary's regulations represented a value choice of preferring childbirth over abortion but said the government may make that policy decision and "implement that judgment by the allocation of public funds." Unequal utilization, however, is not unconstitutional. When government believes it is in the public interest to fund a program to "encourage certain activities but does not fund an alternative program," government has not "discriminated on the basis of viewpoint; it has merely chosen to fund an activity to the exclusion of the other." In the Court's view, the essence of the challengers' argument was "if the Government chooses to subsidize one protected right, it must subsidize analogous counterpart rights." Rehnquist said that proposition had been "soundly rejected" in previous Court decisions. Rather, when the government appropriates public funds to establish a program, it is entitled to define the limits of that program. Furthermore, the regulations do not require Title X recipients to forego abortion-related speech. Instead, the regulations "merely require that the grantee keep such activity separate and distinct from Title X activities." Finally, the Court concluded that the regulations did not violate a woman's Fifth Amendment right of choice. Citing *Webster v. Reproductive Health Services* (492 U.S. 490: 1989), Rehnquist said the government has no "constitutional duty to subsidize an activity merely because the activity is constitutionally protected and may validly choose to fund childbirth over abortion." That funding decision does not create obstacles for the woman wishing to terminate her pregnancy. The woman has the same choices she would have if the government had chosen to fund no family planning services at all. Nor did the Court find the regulations to interfere with the patient-physician relationship or the woman's right to have certain options discussed by her physicians. Access to abortion-related information remained "unfettered outside the context of the Title X project." The conclusion was unaffected by the fact that most Title X clients are precluded by indigence from seeing a physician besides the Title X grantee. Inability of indigent women to "enjoy the full range" of the protected freedom of choice was seen as a product of her indigence and not as restrictions under the regulations. The dissenters, through Justice Blackmun, said the regulation was "viewpoint suppression of speech solely because it imposed on those dependent on the Government for economic support." The purpose and result of the regulations is to "deny women the ability voluntarily to decide their procreative destiny." Justice O'Connor said in dissent that the Court should simply have ruled the regulations were unreasonable under the statute. This would have avoided the need to address any constitutional issues, and it would have returned the question to Congress for clarification of what it intended under the statute. *See also* ARTICLE II, p. 139; JUDICIAL SELF-RESTRAINT, p. 627.

Significance As we have seen in other cases discussed in this chapter, the Court will generally defer to agency judgments whenever that can be done within the provisions of statutes. Further evidence of this judicial preference can be seen in the *Rust* ruling above and *National Labor Relations Board v. Town and Country Electric, Inc.* (516 U.S. 85: 1995). Town and County Electric had refused to interview or retain a number of employees because they were union members intending to try to organize the company if hired or retained. During any period of employment with Town and Country, these employees would have also been compensated by the union. The National Labor Relations Board (NLRB) found that these were "employees" within the meaning of the National Labor Relations Act (NLRA) and that Town and Country had committed an "unfair labor practice" by not hiring or retaining these employees. The NLRB finding was reversed by the Court of Appeals for the Eighth Circuit, which concluded the NLRA does not protect persons who work for a company while also receiving compensation from a union for union organizing activity. The Supreme Court unanimously upheld the NLRB's "broad literal" interpretation of the statutory term "employee." The NLRB definition is entitled to "considerable deference as the interpretation of the agency created by the Congress to administer the Act." In addition, the Court concluded the NLRB interpretation was consistent with purposes of the act such as "protecting employees' right to organize for mutual aid without employer interference and encouraging and protecting the collective-bargaining process."

Another recent example of agency deference is found in *Cisneros v. Alpine Ridge Group* (508 U.S. 10: 1993). Section 8 of the United States Housing Act authorizes the Department of Housing and Urban Development (HUD) to make "assistance payments" to private landlords who rent to low-income tenants. The assistance payments were intended to cover the difference between the tenant's payments and a "contract," or market value–based rent, agreed upon by HUD and the landlords. One provision of the HUD contracts with landlords provided for annual adjustment in contract rents determined by a multifactor formula. The adjustment, however, could not produce "material differences" between the rental charges for assisted units and comparable unassisted units. To determine if the automatic adjustment factors produced materially higher contract rents, HUD began to conduct independent "comparability studies" in selected locations and to use the private market rents to cap assistance payments. Two groups of developers of section 8 housing projects brought separate suits, claiming that section 801 of the Department of Housing and Urban Development Reform Act of 1989, which authorized limiting future rent adjustments based on these comparability studies, violated the Due Process Clause of the Fifth Amendment by depriving them of automatically adjusted rent increases. The district court granted summary judgment to each plaintiff, both judgments being affirmed, in a consolidated appeal, by the Court of Appeals for the Ninth Circuit. The Supreme Court unanimously reversed. It was the Court's conclusion that the developers had no contractual right to "unobstructed formula-based rent adjustments." The assistance contracts administered by HUD did not prohibit the use of comparability studies to create adjustment caps. The statutory language mandating that contract rents cannot be adjusted to materially exceed rents charged for comparable unassisted units "clearly envisioned some comparison of assisted and unassisted rents" and provided HUD with sufficient discretion to design and implement such studies as a means to give effect to its mandate. Many of Alpine Ridge's contentions seemed to the Court to "circle back" to the claim that the studies were poorly conceived and conducted. In the Court's view, the integrity with which an agency carries out studies like the comparability studies here is an "entirely different matter from its contractual authority to employ such studies at all."

***Federal Election Commission v. National Rifle Association Political Victory Fund*, 513 U.S. 88, 130 L.Ed. 2d 439, 115 S.C. 537 (1994)** The Federal Election Commission (FEC) brought a civil action against the National Rifle Association Political Victory Fund (the Fund) in an attempt to enforce provisions of the Federal Election Campaign Act (FECA). The FEC alleged that funds were illegally transferred to the Fund by the NRA Institute for Legislative Action (the Institute). A federal district court found for the FEC, assessed civil penalties against the Fund and the Institute, and ordered that no such similar transfers occur in the future. The NRA raised a separation of powers issue on appeal. It was the NRA's contention that members of the U.S. House and Senate could not serve as FEC members, even with nonvoting status. The Court of Appeals for the District of Columbia Circuit reversed the district court. The FEC filed its own petition for a writ of certiorari without first obtaining the solicitor general's authorization. Such authorization did follow, but more than 120 days after the filing deadline had passed. The FEC subsequently filed a brief claiming independent authority to pursue the appeal in this case. Without addressing the separation of powers issue relating to FEC membership, the Supreme Court ruled that although the FEC had authority to litigate this case before the district court, it could not independently file a petition for certiorari with the Supreme Court. Chief Justice Rehnquist said that "sound policy reasons may exist" for providing the FEC with independent litigating authority in the Supreme Court with actions enforcing FECA. Congress's choice of creating the FEC as an independent agency was "undoubtedly influenced" by congressional belief that the Justice Department "might choose to ignore" alleged infractions of the president's own political party. That Congress had this in mind when giving the FEC "independent *enforcement* powers," however, does not demonstrate that it intended to "alter the Solicitor General's statutory prerogative to conduct and argue the Federal Government's litigation in the Supreme Court."

That statutory authority also "represents a policy choice by Congress to vest the conduct of litigation before this Court in the Attorney General." Rehnquist observed that the Court is "well served" by this practice because the "traditional specialization" of that office has led it to be "keenly attuned" to the Court's practice with respect to granting or denying petitions for certiorari. This practice also serves the government well. An individual agency necessarily has a "more parochial view" of the interest of the government in litigation than does the solicitor general, who has a "broader view" of the litigation in which the government is involved throughout the federal and state court systems. Decisions about seeking further appeal depend on a "number of factors which do not lend themselves to easy categorization." The government as a whole "is apt to fare better if these decisions are concentrated in a single official." And though Congress has the authority to "sacrifice the policy favoring concentration of litigating authority" before the Supreme Court, it was the Court's conclusion that Congress has not made such a choice despite the FEC contention that it had represented itself before the Court in previous cases without any questions being raised regarding its authority to do so. The Court also concluded that the permission the solicitor general eventually sent "simply came too late." If the solicitor general was allowed to retroactively authorize otherwise unauthorized agency petitions after the deadline had expired, he would have the "unilateral power to extend the 90-day statutory period for filing certiorari petitions. . . ." Such a practice would result in the "blurring of the jurisdictional deadline." As a result, the Court dismissed the FEC petition for certiorari for lack of jurisdiction. *See also* ARTICLE II, p. 139; CERTIORARI, p. 584; JURISDICTION, p. 629.

Significance The attempts to regulate campaign finance have raised a number of difficult questions. The case *Colorado Republican Federal Campaign Committee v. Federal Election Commission* (135 L.Ed. 2d 795: 1996) is illustrative. The Colorado Republican Party spent in excess of $15,000 for some radio spots and printed material challenging claims made by an incumbent Democratic member of Congress. The question in the Colorado case was whether this ad campaign was an independent or a coordinated expenditure. An independent expenditure is beyond the reach of federal limits, whereas a coordinated expenditure, an expenditure made "in connection" with a candidate's campaign, would be subject to federal spending limits. The Colorado Democrats filed a complaint with the FEC, contending that the ads constituted a coordinated expenditure and that the cost of the ads exceeded the limit for such spending. The FEC agreed and proposed to settle the matter for a minimal civil penalty. The Colorado Republicans declined, and the FEC brought suit in federal district court. The district court concluded that the expenditure was independent rather than coordinated. The Court of Appeals for the Tenth Circuit reversed, ruling that federal campaign law applies to any campaign message that clearly identifies a candidate even if the message does not clearly advocate that candidate's defeat. The Supreme Court reversed the Tenth Circuit, ruling that party expenditures may not be restricted unless there is direct evidence that the spending was coordinated with an individual candidate's campaign. Although the ruling was 7-2 in favor of lessening restrictions on party expenditures, the Court was divided on several substantial points.

Justice Breyer announced the Court's judgment and offered an opinion joined by Justices O'Connor and Souter. Breyer reviewed prior decisions involving federal regulation of campaign financing and identified two relevant propositions: Restrictions on independent expenditures impair political advocacy and do not relate directly to preventing political corruption. It was Breyer's view that limits on a party's independent expenditures cannot "escape the controlling effect" of these prior rulings. Indeed, the independent expression of a party's views is "core First Amendment activity no less than is the independent expression of individuals, candidates, or other political committees." The Court, said Breyer, was not aware of any "special dangers of corruption associated with a political party's independent expenditures to tip the constitutional balance in another direction." The absence of "prearrangement" and "coordination" does not eliminate but helps diminish any danger that a candidate will understand the spending as an "effort to obtain a quid pro quo." In other words, the diminished risk of corruption could not justify the "burden on basic freedoms" produced by the party expenditure restriction. Indeed, Breyer continued, an expenditure made possible by a donation, but "controlled and directed" by a party rather than the donor, would seem "less likely to corrupt than . . . [an] independent expenditure made directly by that donor." This prevents the Court from "assuming, absent convincing evidence to the contrary, that the limitation on political parties' independent expenditures is necessary to combat a substantial danger of corruption of the electoral system." Finally, Justice Breyer rejected the "conclusive presumption" of the FEC that all party expenditures are "coordinated," that the party and its candidates are "identical." Noting that a party's coordinated expenditures share some "constitutionally relevant features" with its independent expenditures, the Court remanded the question for further examination. The Court also chose not to respond to the contentions of the two major parties that any regulation of party expenditures, independent or otherwise, is barred by the First Amendment. The dissenters, Chief Justice Rehnquist and Justices Scalia, Kennedy, and

Thomas, fully embraced that proposition and would have freed parties from any expenditure regulation. Rehnquist would have gone even farther. He called for the overturning of *Buckley v. Valeo,* 424 US 1 (1976), and said the regulation of contributions are as burdensome on political speech and association as are expenditure restrictions. Justices Stevens and Ginsburg dissented. Stevens pointed to an important governmental interest in "leveling the electoral playing field" and urged the strengthening of regulations on party finances, both income and spending.

Executive Immunity

Clinton v. Jones, **__U.S.__, 137 L.Ed. 2d 945, 117 S.Ct. 1636 (1997)** A sexual harassment suit was filed in federal court in 1994 by Paula Jones, who alleged misconduct by President Clinton while he was governor of Arkansas. Clinton sought to have the case delayed until he left the presidency. The U.S. district court delayed the trial but permitted pretrial discovery to proceed during Clinton's term as president. A divided Court of Appeals for the Eighth Circuit ruled that the trial need not be postponed until Clinton leaves office. The issue before the Supreme Court in *Clinton v. Jones* involved timing exclusively: Is a sitting president immune from civil claims until he completes his term of office? The Supreme Court ruled that the Constitution does not afford the president even temporary immunity from civil damages litigation arising out of events that occurred before his taking office. Justice Stevens said that the rationale for providing immunity from suits seeking money damages stemming from official acts is "inapplicable to unofficial conduct." Immunity serves the public interest in "enabling such officials to perform their designated functions effectively without fear that a particular decision may give rise to personal liability." The Court's "central concern" in previous executive immunity cases, said Stevens, was to "avoid rendering the President unduly cautious in the discharge of his official duties." The "sphere of protected action," he continued, must be "closely related to the immunity's justifying purposes." Although immunity must extend to official acts at the "outer perimeter of his authority," no official, including the president, has immunity that extends beyond the "scope of any action taken in an official capacity." The Court concluded that the president was not entitled to special status in this regard. Immunities are grounded in the "nature of the function performed, not the identity of the actor who performed it."

Clinton's contention that his immunity claim based on the text and structure of the Constitution—separation of powers grounds—was regarded by the Court as his "strongest argument." Clinton argued that the presidency is a "unique" office with powers and responsibilities "so vast and important that the public interest demands that he devote his undivided time and attention to his public duties." Given the nature of the office, the doctrine of separation of powers places limits on the "authority of the Federal judiciary to interfere with the executive branch that would be transgressed by allowing this action to proceed." Stevens said the Court "had no dispute with the initial premise of the argument" but found it does not necessarily follow that separation of powers principles would be violated by allowing this case to proceed. Clinton had claimed that allowing this case to go forward would "hamper performance of his official duties." The Court said this "predictive judgment" was not supported by history or the "relatively narrow compass" of the issues raised in this case. Finding that only three sitting presidents had been subjected to suits for their private actions, Stevens said that if the "past is any indicator, it seems unlikely that a deluge of such litigation will ever engulf the Presidency." If this case is "properly managed" by the district court, it appeared "highly unlikely" to the Court that this case would "occupy any substantial amount" of Clinton's time. The Court rejected Clinton's presumption that interactions between the judicial and executive branches, even "quite burdensome interactions, necessarily rise to the level of constitutionally forbidden impairment of the executive's ability to perform its constitutionally mandated functions." Stevens offered two broad categories of constitutionally permissible interactions that may result in limiting presidential power. First, official actions of presidents are subject to judicial review, and occasionally such review may find that a president has exceeded constitutional authority, as in the case of President Truman's seizure of the steel mills. Second, the Court found it "also settled" that the president is "subject to judicial process in appropriate circumstances." President Nixon's obligation to comply with a subpoena in the Watergate case represents an interaction of this kind. Accordingly, the Court concluded that the separation of powers doctrine does not "bar every exercise of jurisdiction over the President." If the courts, Stevens continued, may "severely burden the executive branch" by reviewing the legality of official conduct" and if the courts may "direct appropriate process" to the president himself, it "must follow that the Federal courts have power to determine the legality of his unofficial conduct." The burden on a president's time and energy that is a "mere by-product of such a review surely cannot be considered as onerous as the direct burden imposed by judicial review and the occasional invalidation of his official actions." The Court did suggest that while separation of power principles do not preclude this case from proceeding, the potential burdens on the president are "appropriate matters" for the trial court to evaluate in its management of this case.

Further, the "high respect" that is owed the office, though not justifying "categorical immunity, is a matter that should inform the conduct of the entire proceeding, including the timing and scope of discovery." Stevens concluded his opinion by commenting on two issues "discussed at length" in the briefs: (1) the risk that allowing this case to proceed before Clinton leaves office will generate much politically motivated "harassing and frivolous litigation"; (2) and the danger that "national security concerns might prevent the President from explaining a legitimate need for a continuance." The Court found neither of these risks to be "serious." Most "frivolous and vexatious litigation" is terminated at the pleading stage or on summary judgment with "little if any personal involvement" by the defendant. Further, the Court found no reason to assume that district courts will be either unable to accommodate a president's needs or "unfaithful to the tradition, especially in matters involving national security, of giving the utmost deference to Presidential responsibilities." The Court was confident that federal judges could effectively deal with both of these concerns but indicated that Congress could legislate additional protection if it felt such a measure necessary. The Court agreed with the Eighth Circuit that the federal district court possesses jurisdiction to decide this case and that Paula Jones, like every other citizen who properly invokes that jurisdiction, has a "right to an orderly disposition of her claims." *See also* EXECUTIVE IMMUNITY, p. 601; EXECUTIVE PRIVILEGE, p. 603; *NIXON v. FITZGERALD* (457 U.S. 731: 1982), p. 155; SEPARATION OF POWERS, p. 56; *UNITED STATES v. NIXON* (418 U.S. 683: 1974), p. 153.

Significance Executive immunity shields a sitting president from criminal prosecution while in office and from civil suits brought against a president for official conduct. The Court has never examined the question of criminal immunity, but it was assumed that President Richard Nixon was protected from prosecution while still in office for acts associated with the Watergate scandal. That criminal immunity, of course, ends once a president leaves office. Immunity from civil suits applies as well. In *Nixon v. Fitzgerald* (457 U.S. 731: 1982), the Court ruled that a president is absolutely free from civil claims for damages from official actions taken during his tenure. Such immunity was seen as a "functionally mandated incident of the President's unique office," a protection rooted in the separation of power principle. The *Fitzgerald* decision extended broad immunity, concluding that it encompassed the "special nature" of the presidency and its functions, even those reaching only the "outer perimeter of official responsibility." The *Clinton* case differs, however, from previous cases in that it involves alleged misconduct that took place prior to the beginning of his tenure as president, a point the Court made clear as it confined *Fitzgerald* to official acts. The *Clinton* case is interesting for two issues not taken up by the Court. First, the claim of immunity was asserted in a federal court and relied heavily on the separation of powers doctrine. The Court did not consider whether a "comparable claim might succeed in a state tribunal." If this case had been heard in a state court, Clinton "presumably" would have advanced federalism and comity concerns among others. Whether those concerns "present a more compelling case for immunity," said Justice Stevens, "is a question that is not before us." Second, the Court's decision to allow the case to proceed did not require the Court to address the question of whether a court "may compel the attendance of the President at any specific time or place." It was the Court's assumption in *Clinton* that the president's testimony for discovery or trial use could be taken at the White House at a time that will "accommodate" his schedule. If the case progressed to the trial stage, there would be "no necessity for the President to attend in person, though he could elect to do so."

3. Legislative Power

Independent Counsel and Criminal Sentencing

***Morrison v. Olson*, 487 U.S. 654, 101 L.Ed. 2d 569, 108 S.Ct. 2597 (1988)** Upheld the federal independent prosecutor statute. The authorization for appointment of independent counsel came in the Ethics in Government Act, which requires the attorney general to conduct preliminary investigations of particular high-level executive officers alleged to have engaged in criminal misconduct. If there is cause to believe "further investigation is warranted," the attorney general is obligated to refer the case to the U.S. Court of Appeals for the District of Columbia Circuit. The federal appellate court then appoints independent counsel. Once appointed, an independent counsel may be removed by the attorney general only for "good cause," a decision subject to judicial review. The dispute in *Morrison v. Olson* began in 1982 as Congress sought certain documents from the Environmental Protection Agency concerning the "Superfund" toxic waste law. At the suggestion of Justice Department counsel, the documents were withheld. Olson, an assistant attorney general in the Office of Legal Counsel, testified before the House Judiciary Committee, which was investigating the matter. The committee issued a report sometime later suggesting, among other things, that Olson had given false testimony during the inquiry. The committee chair requested independent counsel to look into the actions of Olson and two other officials. Morrison was appointed following the preliminary investigation of the attorney general. As part of the inquiry into whether a conspiracy to obstruct the Judiciary Committee investigation had occurred, subpoenas were issued by a grand jury to obtain testimony and documents from Olson and the others. Olson, in turn, sought to quash the subpoenas, asserting that Morrison had no authority to proceed because the independent counsel law was unconstitutional. The law was upheld by a federal district court, but the Court of Appeals for the District of Columbia Circuit found for Olson. The court of appeals ruled that the law violated the separation of powers principle by encroaching on executive prerogatives. Over the single dissent of Justice Scalia, the Supreme Court reversed.

Chief Justice Rehnquist began the Court's opinion by considering the Appointments Clause of Article II. Under the clause, the president shall nominate various "principal officers" of the government; Congress has the authority to appoint "inferior" officers. Although the line between principal and inferior officers is "far from clear," the independent counsel "clearly falls on the 'inferior side' of that line." Rehnquist offered several reasons in support of this conclusion. First, Morrison was subject to removal by the attorney general, an indication she was "inferior in rank and authority." Second, the special prosecutor is empowered to "perform only certain, limited duties." Although counsel has the authority to exercise "all investigative and prosecutorial functions and powers" of the Justice Department, counsel has no authority to "formulate policy" nor administrative duties "outside those necessary to operate her office." Third, the office is "limited in jurisdiction" and has "limited tenure." Rehnquist then moved to the contention that the Appointments Clause did not permit "inter-branch" appointments, that is, Congress cannot place the authority to appoint an inferior officer outside the executive branch. In the Court's view, Congress possesses "significant discretion" to empower courts to make such appointments. Such power is not unlimited, however. Congress could not, for example, vest the courts with power to appoint officers where "incongruity" exists between the "functions normally performed by the courts and the performance of their duty to appoint." The Court concluded there is no "inherent incongruity" about a court having the power to appoint prosecutorial officers. When Congress created the office of independent counsel, it was concerned with conflicts of interest that could occur when the executive branch was called upon to investigate its own officials. If it was necessary to remove the appointing authority from the executive branch, the "most logical place to put it was the Judicial Branch." Nor did the Court find that the law was incompatible with Article III provisions assigning the courts judicial functions. A court's role in the independent counsel process is "passive," with the court having no supervisory power over the special prosecutor's performance. Specifically, a court is not entitled to approve or disapprove the content of any report or finding of either the attorney general or special counsel. Finally, the Court ruled that the law did not improperly encroach on executive power. While the independent counsel cannot be removed at will, the Court did not find this factor decisive. The executive retained "sufficient control" over independent counsel to support the conclusion that Congress had not "unduly" interfered with the president's executive power. Important to the Court's finding was its observation that the law did not represent an attempt by Congress to "increase its own powers at the expense of the Executive Branch." *See also* APPOINTMENT POWER, p. 581; DELEGATION OF LEGISLATIVE POWER, p. 591; SEPARATION OF POWERS, p. 56.

Significance The *Morrison* ruling says Congress can establish processes for investigations within the executive branch, but the Court did not give Congress unlimited authority to designate areas subject to investigation by special counsel. Nonetheless, independent prosecutors have been used in several high-profile cases, such as the prosecution of Reagan advisers Lyn Nofziger and Michael Deaver, the inquiry into the Iran-Contra affair, and, of course, the Whitewater investigation of alleged improprieties involving Bill and Hillary Clinton.

An analogous separation of powers issue was reviewed by the Court in *United States v. Mistretta* (488 U.S. 361: 1989). Troubled by "serious disparities" produced under the federal indeterminate criminal sentencing system, Congress passed the Sentencing Reform Act of 1984. Among other things, the act created the U.S. Sentencing Commission as an independent entity within the judicial branch. The commission was empowered to promulgate binding sentencing guidelines, creating a range of determinate sentences for all federal crimes. Mistretta, who was sentenced under the guidelines, claimed Congress had delegated excessive authority to the commission and that the commission was established in violation of the separation of powers principle. The Supreme Court disagreed. The Court first addressed Mistretta's claim that the commission possessed "excessive legislative discretion" producing a violation of the nondelegation doctrine. The Court said the determination of whether delegation is excessive is "driven by a practical understanding" that, given the complexity of problems facing Congress, it "cannot do its job absent an ability to delegate power under broad general directions." The Court ruled that delegation is not forbidden so long as Congress sets forth an "intelligible principle" upon which a body must base its action. In establishing the sentencing commission, Congress offered three broad but well-defined goals it wanted criminal sentencing to achieve and mandated the technique of a guideline system to be used to regulate sentencing. Further, Congress directed the commission to consider a number of specific factors as it developed categories of both offenses and offender characteristics and forbade consideration of factors such as race, sex, national origin, creed, and socioeconomic status or factors that might serve as their proxy. In short, the Court concluded the act set forth "more than merely an 'intelligible principle.'" Although the commission "enjoys significant discretion in formulating guidelines," the Court had "no doubt" the criteria supplied by Congress were "wholly adequate for carrying out the general policy and purpose of the Act."

The Court then turned to the separation of powers claims. The Court embraced Madison's "flexible understanding" of separation of powers. There is a "degree of overlapping responsibility" among the three branches, and the greatest security against accumulation of excessive authority in a single branch "lies not in a hermetic division" between the branches but in a "carefully crafted system of checked and balanced power within each branch." Placement of the commission, an independent body that does not exercise judicial power as such, within the judicial branch made it a "peculiar institution," but separation of powers is not violated, said the Court, by "mere anomaly." Congress's decision to create an independent rulemaking body under the judicial branch is not unconstitutional unless Congress vested in the commission "powers that are more appropriately performed by other branches or that undermine the integrity of the Judiciary." It was argued by Mistretta that the requirement that three commission members be federal judges undermined the integrity of the judicial branch by diminishing its independence and impartiality (or appearance of impartiality). The Court disagreed, concluding that inclusion of the federal judges, who serve voluntarily, "does not of itself" threaten the integrity of the judiciary. Nor does participation by judges on the commission undermine public confidence in judicial impartiality. Judges' participation in the promulgation of guidelines "does not affect their . . . ability to impartially adjudicate sentencing issues." Finally, the Court considered the presidential control issue—the matter of selection and removal of commission members. The Court dismissed as "fanciful" the contention that the president's power to appoint federal judges to the commission gives him inappropriate influence over the judicial branch or interferes with the performance of its functions. Presidential appointment power for positions that may be attractive to judges does not, in itself, corrupt the integrity of the judiciary. The opinion concluded by saying that in creating the commission, an "unusual hybrid in structure and authority," Congress did not excessively delegate legislative power nor "upset the constitutionally mandated balance of powers among the Coordinate Branches." The Constitution does not prohibit Congress from delegating to an "expert body located within the Judicial Branch the intricate task of formulating sentencing guidelines with such significant statutory direction as is present here." Nor, said the Court, does the checks and balances system prohibit Congress from "calling upon the accumulated wisdom and experience" of the judicial branch in "creating policy on a matter uniquely within the ken of judges."

The Supreme Court in *Mistretta* approved the process by which Congress chose to formulate judicial sentencing guidelines. The guidelines are an approach to reducing disparities in criminal sentences, provide direction to judges as they make sentencing decisions, and act to confine judicial discretion. Most guidelines provide sets of sentence ranges that vary by seriousness of the offense and prior criminal record of the offender. In most jurisdictions, guidelines are not binding. Rather, judges may impose a greater or lesser sentence than is suggested by the guidelines but must offer a written rationale for departing from the guidelines. Sentencing guidelines have been adopted by a number of states as well as the federal courts. Guidelines may be mandated either legislatively, as in the Sentencing Reform Act, or by state supreme courts in the exercise of their supervisory function in state judicial systems. *Mistretta* makes clear that procedures for developing these guidelines are generally immune from successful challenge on delegation or separation of powers grounds. In many ways, this conclusion parallels the Court's response to the separation of powers issue presented in *Morrison.*

Apportionment and Voting Rights

***United States Department of Commerce v. Montana*, 503 U.S. 442, 118 L.Ed. 2d 87, 112 S.Ct. 1415 (1992)** Upheld use of the method of "equal proportions" for apportioning congressional seats to the states. Congress adopted the "equal proportions" formula by statute in 1941, and it has been used ever since to distribute the 435 seats in the U.S. House of Representatives. The U.S. Bureau of the Census, located within the Department of Commerce, used the formula to determine the apportionment of seats following the 1990 census. The population changes that occurred during the ten years before the 1990 census resulted in several states gaining congressional seats while other states lost seats. Montana was one of the states to lose a seat, and the state filed suit, challenging the constitutionality of the "equal proportions" formula. A three-judge district court ruled 2-1 that the federal law embracing this formula was unconstitutional because the variance between the population of the single district and the "ideal" population size could not be justified against the "one person–one vote" standard. Had Congress chosen an alternative method for apportioning seats, Montana would have retained both seats. On direct appeal, the Supreme Court unanimously reversed the lower court and upheld the apportionment method used since 1941. Justice Stevens said the provision of Article I, Section 2, that representatives be apportioned across the states "according to their respective numbers," is "constrained" by three requirements: the number of representatives shall not exceed one for every 30,000 persons; each state must have at least one representative in the U.S. House; and district boundaries may not cross state lines. These requirements make it impossible to have interstate equivalence of district populations. Stevens reviewed the previous efforts by Congress to address this matter. Among other things, he referred to the report from a special committee convened by the National Academy of Sciences in 1929, which favored the equal proportions method over several other options. The Court concluded that none of the alternative measures of population variance yielded a "substantive principle of commanding constitutional significance." Indeed, the "polestar" of equal protection does not provide "sufficient guidance to allow us to discern a single constitutionally permissible course." The constitutional requirement that every state have at least one representative "inexorably compels a significant departure" from any national "ideal" district population. The need to allocate a fixed number of representatives among states of varying populations makes it "virtually impossible to have the same size district in any pair of States, let alone all 50." Although "common sense" supports a test requiring a good-faith effort to produce precise population equality within each state, the constraints imposed by Article I, Section 2 "make that goal illusory for the Nation as a whole." The constitutional framework that made it necessary to compromise interests among the states in the apportionment process "must also delegate to Congress a measure of discretion that is broader than that accorded to the States in the much easier task of determining district sizes within State border." The decision of Congress to adopt the equal proportions method was made after "decades of experience, experimentation, and debate" about the method to be used to apportion U.S. House seats. This history, Stevens said, "supports our conclusion that Congress had ample power to enact the statutory procedure in 1941 and to apply the method of equal proportions after the 1990 census." *See also* APPORTIONMENT, p. 582; *BALDRIDGE v. SHAPIRO* (455 U.S. 345: 1982), p. 212.

Significance The apportionment of congressional seats has raised issues beyond the comparability of district populations. Generally, the Court defers to the judgment of the secretary of commerce in a manner similar to the deference shown Congress in *United States Department of Commerce v. Montana.* The question in *Franklin v. Massachusetts* (505 U.S. 788: 1992), for example, was whether the Census Bureau properly counted federal employees stationed overseas as residents of states for apportionment purposes. These citizens, mostly members of the military, were not included in the 1980 census. The effect of this change caused Massachusetts to lose one of its congressional seats. A three-judge panel had found the Census Bureau policy to be "arbitrary and capricious." A unanimous Supreme Court disagreed, saying the decision to include the overseas workers "does not hamper the underlying constitutional goal of equal representation. . . ." Indeed, the Court said the change may "actually promote equality" to the extent overseas employees may retain ties to their home states.

Wisconsin v. City of New York (517 U.S. 1: 1996) reviewed the decision of the secretary of commerce not to revise 1990 census counts in a number of large, urban areas. The census has historically suffered from undercounts of some population subgroups. The secretary of commerce refused to engage in a statistical estimation technique fashioned to reduce the effect of any undercount in the 1990 census. At stake in this case were the allocation of congressional seats and federal funding distributed to state and local units of government through population-based formulas. A U.S. district court found the secretary's decision not to adjust the original counts was neither arbitrary nor capricious. The U.S. Court of Appeals for the Second Circuit reversed, however, finding the secretary had not made a good-faith effort to obtain the most accurate count of population. The Supreme Court unanimously reversed. Chief Justice Rehnquist pointed to the text of the Constitution that "vests Congress with virtually unlimited discretion" in conducting the census. The Census Act, in turn, delegated broad authority over the census to the secretary of commerce. So long as the secretary's conduct of the census is consistent with the "constitutional language and the constitutional goal of equal representation" it does not violate the Constitution. Because the Constitution broadly grants authority to Congress, the secretary's decision not to adjust the census needs to bear "only a reasonable relationship to the accomplishment of the actual enumeration of the population. . . ." The Court's deference to the secretary's judgment, said Rehnquist, was not based on the "highly technical" character of the decision but rather on the "wide discretion bestowed by the Constitution upon Congress, and by Congress upon the Secretary." Regardless of the secretary's "statistical expertise," it is he or she "to whom Congress has delegated its constitutional authority over the Census." The Court also ruled that the secretary's decision was not subject to heightened judicial scrutiny. It was the Court's view that the strict scrutiny, "one person–one vote" standard used by the Second Circuit should not apply here. The "good-faith effort" to achieve population equality required when a state undertakes intrastate redistricting "does not translate into a requirement that the federal Government conduct a Census that is as accurate as possible."

***Chisom v. Roemer*, 501 U.S. 380, 115 L.Ed. 2d 348, 111 S.Ct. 2354 (1991)** The question in *Chisom* was whether the "results test" contained in the 1982 amendments to the Voting Rights Act protects the right to vote in state judicial elections. In a 6-3 decision, the Court ruled that judicial elections are covered by the act as amended. Prior to 1982, section 2 of the act was not violated without a showing of discriminatory intent. The

1982 amendment substituted the results standard. Congress established that a violation would occur if portions of the electorate had less opportunity than others to "participate in the political process and elect representatives of their choice." The question in *Chisom* rested on whether judges are "representatives." The Court concluded that they are. Justice Stevens began by noting that the Voting Rights Act had been enacted for the "broad remedial purpose" of eliminating racial discrimination in voting. Accordingly, the act should be interpreted in a manner that provides the "broadest possible scope in combatting racial discrimination." The Court pointed to the "extensive legislative history" of the 1982 amendment. Had Congress intended to exclude judicial elections from the coverage of the act, such intent would have been made explicit. Furthermore, Congress had replaced the term "legislators" with the word "representative" in the amendment. This substitution indicated "at the very least," said Stevens, "that Congress intended the amendment to cover more than legislative elections." Finally, the Court felt the "fundamental tension between the ideal character of the judicial office and the real world of electoral politics cannot be resolved by crediting judges with total indifference to the popular will while simultaneously requiring them to run for elective office." When each of several judges of a court must live in separate districts and be elected by voters of those districts, it "seems both reasonable and realistic to characterize the winners as representatives of that district." Justice Scalia issued a dissent that was joined by Chief Justice Rehnquist and Justice Kennedy. He was critical of the Court's interpretation of the amendment that judges are representatives. Scalia said the act is not "some all-purpose weapon for well intentioned judges to wield as they please in the battle against discrimination." The Court's construction of the act disregarded the language of the act and instead, said Scalia, began with an "expectation about what the statute must mean" and interpreted the words accordingly. Scalia saw the term "representative" as going beyond popular election to include the notion of acting on behalf of the people. A prosecutor, for example, acts on behalf of "the People" and a judge represents "the Law." Judges often must rule against the "People" in upholding the "Law," which is why "we do not ordinarily conceive of judges as representatives." *See also* FIFTEENTH AMENDMENT, p. 606; *SOUTH CAROLINA v. KATZENBACH* (383 U.S. 301: 1966), p. 197.

Significance A second case involving Louisiana judicial elections was also before the Court in 1991. A number of changes in election practices had occurred in Louisiana following passage of the Voting Rights Act of 1965. Some of these changes were approved in advance (precleared) by the Justice Department pursuant to section 5 of the act, but others were not. A class-action suit was filed, challenging those changes that had not been precleared. Prior to the 1990 elections, the plaintiffs unsuccessfully sought to stop all judicial elections that involved unapproved changes. In denying injunctive relief, the three-judge district court said that a number of the unapproved changes had been implicitly approved when other changes in the judicial districts had been subsequently precleared. The Supreme Court ruled unanimously in *Clark v. Roemer* (500 U.S. 646: 1991) that preclearance could not occur "by implication." Indeed, it was the Court's view that preclearance of current proposed changes could not retroactively approve earlier changes without "subvert[ing] the efficacy of administrative preclearance under Section 5." Accordingly, the Court ruled that the elections in the affected judicial districts should not have taken place.

Section 2 of the Voting Rights Act prohibits use of a voter qualification or a "standard, practice, or procedure that abridges the right to vote on the basis of race or membership in a language minority." Dilution of the voting strength of one or more minorities violates section 2. The test for determining whether minority voting strength is illegally diluted was set forth in *Thornburg v. Gingles* (478 U.S. 30: 1986). Section 2 is violated if a minority group can demonstrate that its voters are "sufficiently numerous and compact" that they would constitute a majority in a district of a multimember body. There are two other *Gingles* preconditions: that whites vote as a bloc in a "manner sufficient to defeat the black preferred candidate" and that blacks are "politically cohesive." *Holder v. Hall* (512 U.S. 874: 1994) considered whether the *Gingles* criteria apply to single-official electoral situations. Bleckley County, Georgia, operated a form of government in which a single commissioner possessed all legislative and executive authority. In 1985, the state legislature authorized the county to move to a five-member commission, but the proposal was defeated in a referendum. Black voters filed an action, claiming that the single-commissioner system was maintained to limit the political influence of the minority population (77 percent of the county's population was white). A federal district court found no violation, but the Court of Appeals for the Eleventh Circuit reversed and ordered the design of a five-member commission with one district created to facilitate the election of a minority member. In a 5-4 decision, the Supreme Court reversed.

The Court held that the size of a governing body is not subject to a vote dilution challenge under section 2 of the Voting Rights Act. Before a court can find a section 2 violation, it must determine whether the *Gingles* preconditions, supported by a totality of other circumstances, are met. Beyond that, a court must find a "reasonable alternative practice as a benchmark against which to measure the existing voting practice." There is no "objective and workable standard," said Justice Kennedy, in cases where the "challenge is brought to the size of a governing authority; there is no reason why one size should be selected over another." In this case, the challengers to the single-commissioner structure offered no convincing reason why the benchmark should be a five-member commission. Neither the fact that a five-member commission is most commonly found in use in Georgia counties nor that Bleckley County was authorized to expand up to a five-member commission constituted convincing evidence in the Court's view. Justices Thomas and Scalia also voted to overturn the lower court. Their reasoning, expressed in Justice Thomas's lengthy concurring opinion (almost 60 pages), differed substantially from that of Justice Kennedy. They felt that the size of a governing body was not a "standard, practice, or procedure" within the meaning of section 2. Rather, section 2 covers only those practices that affect ballot access by minority voters; districting systems and election processes that affect the "weight" given a vote are "simply beyond the purview of the Act." They urged that *Gingles* be overruled because it interprets section 2 as reaching vote dilution. By allowing consideration of dilutive electoral practices, federal courts have become "immersed" in a "hopeless project of weighing questions of political theory." "Worse," Thomas continued, the Court has devised remedial mechanisms that "encourage federal courts to segregate voters into racially designated districts to ensure minority electoral success." In doing so, the Court has "collaborated on what might be called the racial 'balkanization' of the Nation." Thomas said he no longer supported a reading of the Voting Rights Act that has produced "such a disastrous misadventure in judicial policymaking." Justices Blackmun, Stevens, Souter, and Ginsburg dissented. They concluded that the single-commissioner system had the effect of diluting minority voting strength. It was their view that the Voting Rights Act had to be interpreted to effectively confront "subtler, more complex means of infringing minority voting strength." The dissenters expressed strong opposition to that view.

***Shaw v. Reno*, 509 U.S. 630, 125 L.Ed. 2d 511, 114 S.Ct. 2581 (1993)** Congressional districts were apportioned following the 1990 census. The process resulted in a gain of one congressional seat for North Carolina in the U.S. House of Representatives. The North Carolina General Assembly fashioned a plan establishing 12 congressional districts. The plan, containing a single majority-black district, was submitted to the Justice Department for preclearance as required under section 5 of the Voting Rights Act. A section 5 objection was made by the Justice Department on the grounds that the plan still underrepresented minority voting strength in the state. In response to the objection, the North Carolina General Assembly revised the plan by adding a second majority-black district. The Justice Department approved the revised plan that contained the two majority-black districts, and African-Americans were subsequently elected in both districts in November 1992. A challenge to the revised plan was brought by the North Carolina Republican Party and several white voters residing in the state. They claimed the plan was based on unconstitutional political gerrymandering. The political gerrymander claim was dismissed, but a second claim was heard by a three-judge district court on the grounds that North Carolina had unlawfully gerrymandered on the basis of race. The district court rejected the challengers' contention that race-conscious redistricting "to benefit minority voters is per se unconstitutional." In addition, the district court upheld the North Carolina plan containing the two black-majority districts. Direct appeal was taken to the U.S. Supreme Court, which reversed in a 5-4 decision.

It was the Court's conclusion in *Shaw* that the challengers' claim was one for which Equal Protection Clause relief could be granted. The case was remanded to allow the white voters an opportunity to demonstrate that the districting plan was an unconstitutional gerrymander (which they did in *Shaw v. Hunt* [135 L.Ed. 2d 207: 1996], below). Justice O'Connor said it was "unsettling how closely the North Carolina plan resembles the most egregious racial gerrymanders of the past." The challengers did not claim dilution of white voting strength. Rather, their claim focused the constitutional right to "participate in a 'color-blind' electoral process." Their objection to the redistricting plan is that it is so "extremely irregular on its face" that it can be viewed "only as an effort to segregate the races for purposes of voting, without regard for traditional districting principles and without sufficiently compelling justification." In the Court's view, the Equal Protection Clause could provide relief in such a situation. O'Connor referred to such traditional principles as compactness, contiguity, and political subdivision boundaries as "objective factors" that might provide the basis for setting aside claims of racial gerrymandering. Apportionment is an area where, said O'Connor, "appearances do matter." A reapportionment plan that includes in a district individuals of one race, who are otherwise "widely separated by geographical and political boundaries, and who may have little in common with one another but the color of their skin, bears an uncomfortable resemblance to political apartheid." Racial classifications of "any sort pose the risk of lasting harm to our society." Such classifications reinforce the belief that individuals should be judged on the basis of their race. Racial classifications with respect to voting "carry particular dangers." Racial gerrymandering, even for remedial purposes, "may balkanize us into competing racial factions; it threatens to carry us further from the goal of a political system in which race no longer matters. . . ." Justices White, Blackmun, Stevens, and Souter dissented. Justice White observed that members of the white majority cannot "plausibly argue that their influence over the political process has been unfairly canceled or that such had been the State's intent." Similarly, it was Blackmun's view that no Equal Protection Clause violation exists unless the redistricting plan has the effect of unduly minimizing a particular group's voting strength. He found it "particularly ironic" that the Court chose a case to recognize an "analytically distinct" constitutional claim that was a challenge by white voters to a plan under which North Carolina "has sent black representatives to Congress for the first time since Reconstruction." Justice Stevens discounted the "bizarre" shape of the districts, saying that there is "no independent constitutional requirement of compactness or contiguity." He also saw drawing districts for the purpose of facilitating the election of a second black member of Congress as justifiable. The difference between constitutional and unconstitutional gerrymanders has nothing to do with whether they are based on assumptions about the groups they affect but whether their purpose is to "enhance the power of the group in control of the districting process at the expense of any minority group, and thereby to strengthen the unequal distribution of electoral power." *See also* APPORTIONMENT, p. 582; FIFTEENTH AMENDMENT, p. 606; *SOUTH CAROLINA v. KATZENBACH* (383 U.S. 301: 1966), p. 197.

Significance The Court held in *Shaw v. Reno* that a redistricting plan must be subject to strict scrutiny when it contains a minority-majority congressional district of highly "bizarre" shape that it obviously apportions voters on the basis of race. That means the plan is permissible only if the government can show a compelling interest and that the plan has been tailored as narrowly as possible in the pursuit of that interest. *Shaw v. Reno* did not categorically rule out the creation of majority-minority districts but remanded the North Carolina plan to the district court for further consideration. A number of cases followed *Shaw*. The first to come before the Court was *Miller v. Johnson* (515 U.S. 900: 1995), which involved a challenge to the plan adopted by the Georgia legislature and approved by the Justice Department. Prior to 1990, one of Georgia's ten districts was a majority-minority district. The 1990 census showed sufficient population growth to entitle Georgia to one additional seat in the U.S. House of Representatives. An 11-district plan was drawn that contained three majority-minority districts. The plan was challenged, and a three-judge district court found "overwhelming" evidence of the state legislature's intent to "racially gerrymander" at least one of the new districts (the 11th). Because race was the "predominant" factor in drawing the new 11th District, the panel struck down the plan. Zell Miller, the governor of Georgia, filed direct appeal with the Supreme Court. In a 5-4 ruling, the Court affirmed. It was Georgia's contention that *Shaw* required more than a showing of deliberate classification of voters by race. Regardless of purpose, it must also be shown that a district's "shape is so bizarre that it is unexplainable other than on the basis of race." Justice Kennedy suggested that Georgia's view of a constitutional violation "misapprehends our holding in *Shaw*" and the Equal Protection Clause decisions upon which *Shaw* was based. *Shaw* recognized a claim "analytically distinct" from a vote-dilution claim. The latter asserts that the state purposefully sought to "cancel out" the voting potential of racial or ethnic minorities. An equal protection claim, on the other hand, occurs when the state uses race as the basis for separating voters into districts. Just as the state may not otherwise segregate (parks, schools, and the like) on the basis of race, neither may it separate citizens into voting districts on the basis of race. The idea, said Kennedy, is a "simple one: At the heart of the Constitution's guarantee of equal protection lies the simple command that the Government must treat citizens as individuals, not simply as components of a racial, religious, sexual, or national class." When a state assigns voters on the basis of race, it engages in the "offensive and demeaning assumption that voters of a particular race, because of their race, think alike, share the same political interests and will prefer the same candidates at the polls." The observations in *Shaw* about the consequences of racial stereotyping were not meant to suggest that a district "must be bizarre on its face as a threshold condition of a constitutional violation." Shape is relevant "not because bizarreness is a necessary element of a constitutional wrong," Kennedy continued, but because it "may be persuasive circumstantial evidence that race for its own sake, and not other districting principles, was the Legislature's dominant and controlling rationale in drawing its district lines." The Court concluded the lower court finding that race was the "predominant" factor motivating the creation of the 11th District was "not clearly erroneous." Although the shape of the 11th District may not seem "bizarre on its face," when its shape is considered along with its racial and population densities, the "story of racial gerrymandering" seen by the district court "becomes much clearer."

The Court then subjected the Georgia plan to strict scrutiny, a standard that requires the state to show that a districting scheme is narrowly tailored to achieve a compelling interest. The Court had "little doubt" that Georgia's "true interest" in designing the 11th District was to design a third majority-black district in order to satisfy preclearance requirements of the Justice Department under section 5 of the Voting Rights Act. Compliance with federal antidiscrimination laws could not, in the absence of an interest in remedying past discrimination, provide the necessary compelling interest. Kennedy suggested that trying to achieve equal opportunity to gain public office is a worthwhile objective, but that end is "neither assured nor well served . . . by carving electorates into racial blocs." Justice O'Connor provided the critical fifth vote in *Miller.* She offered a concurring opinion that possibly narrowed the scope of this ruling. The standard announced in this case, she said, "does not throw into doubt the vast majority of the Nation's 435 congressional districts" where states have established the district lines using "customary" districting principles. That is true even though race "may well have been considered in the redistricting process." Application of the new standard gives effect to *Shaw*'s basic objective of making "extreme instances of gerrymandering subject to meaningful judicial review." Justice Ginsburg issued a dissent joined at least in part by Justices Stevens, Souter, and Breyer. It was their view that in *Shaw* virtually every factor other than race was excluded. The record in this case did not demonstrate that race "similarly overwhelmed traditional districting practices in Georgia." She contended that district homogeneity had value: "Ethnicity itself can tie people together." Ginsburg said a state can no longer avoid federal judicial oversight by giving "genuine and measurable consideration" to traditional districting practices. Instead, a federal case can be pursued whenever a plaintiff can plausibly allege that other factors "carried less weight than race."

Shaw v. Reno (hereafter *Shaw I*) held that congressional districts created on the basis of "racial gerrymandering" violate the Equal Protection Clause. The Court remanded in *Shaw I* to allow North Carolina to justify the intentional use of race in drawing new congressional district boundaries. The three-judge U.S. district court concluded that North Carolina's interest was compelling and that the plan was sufficiently narrowly tailored to survive strict scrutiny. The Supreme Court disagreed in *Shaw v. Hunt* (135 L.Ed. 2d 207: 1996) (hereafter *Shaw II*). *Shaw II* was a narrower case than *Bush v. Vera* (see below) because the Court's review was limited to application of the strict scrutiny standard as mandated by *Shaw I.* The fact situation remained the same, with only the state's justifications for the plan under review. The ruling, however, was confined to challenged District 12; since no plaintiffs in *Shaw II* lived in District 1, standing did not exist to pursue a challenge of that district. In order to meet the *Shaw I* standard under strict scrutiny, North Carolina had to demonstrate that the plan with two minority-majority districts both pursued a "compelling" state interest and did so in a "narrowly tailored" way. North Carolina sought to sustain the plan by asserting three compelling interests: to eradicate the effects of past discrimination and to comply with sections 2 and 5 of the Voting Rights Act. Eradication of the effects of past racial discrimination may only rise to the "compelling" level if the discrimination is "identified" as such. A generalized assertion of past discrimination is insufficient. Further, the institution that distinguishes the specific from the generalized assertion of discrimination must have a "strong basis in evidence" that remedial action is required. It was the Court's conclusion that an interest in "ameliorating past discrimination did not actually precipitate the use of race in the redistricting plan." Chief Justice Rehnquist then turned to the justifications stemming from North Carolina's duty to comply with the Voting Rights Act. Section 5 requires the Justice Department to "preclear" any changes in election laws. Although the Justice Department urged creation of the second minority-majority district, the second district was not required under a "correct reading of Section 5." Citing *Miller,* Chief Justice Rehnquist said North Carolina's first plan was sufficiently ameliorative; the second minority-majority district was not required notwithstanding the Justice Department's "preclearance demands." North Carolina also asserted that District 12 was created to avoid liability under section 2 of the act. Section 2 prohibits the "dilution" of minority group voting strength. Rehnquist said that section 2 liability is contingent on the "geographical compact[ness]" of the minority group. The Court concluded that such a "geographically compact population of any race" did not reside in District 12, thus it could not serve as a remedy for any potential section 2 violation. Rehnquist suggested that a district drawn "anywhere" would not remedy a section 2 violation. The vote-dilution injuries suffered by members of a minority are "not remedied by creating a safe majority-black district somewhere else in the State." Justice Stevens, in dissent, took issue with the conclusion that race was the "predominant" factor underlying the plan. Legislative decisions are often the "product of compromise and mixed motives." Stevens characterized such mixed motives as "endemic to the endeavor of political districting." He urged deference to the congressional objective of "assuring fair and effective representation to minority voters," a policy contained in the Voting Rights Act. The Court, he continued, should also "respect North Carolina's conscientious effort to conform to that congressional determination." The Court should not intervene in a process through which federal and state actors are trying to resolve "difficult questions of politics and race that have long plagued North Carolina."

Texas gained three congressional seats as a result of population increases measured in the 1990 census. The postcensus redistricting plan drawn by the Texas legislature created some "irregularly" shaped majority-minority districts. In addition to enhancing the prospect of electing minorities to Congress, the plan had nonrace-based objectives, including the protection of incumbent members of Congress. A three-judge U.S. district court ruled the three new majority-minority districts were unconstitutional under the Supreme Court's decision in *Shaw I*. *Bush v. Vera* (135 L.Ed. 2d 248: 1996) gave the Court an opportunity to further develop criteria applying to redistricting cases where race plays a prominent but not exclusive role. The Court struck down the Texas plan in a 5-4 ruling, although the majority was split on the rationale. Justice O'Connor spoke for Chief Justice Rehnquist and Justice Kennedy. She saw no need to "revisit" the discussion from *Shaw I* but rather focused on the particulars of the Texas plan and whether it met the requirements of that framework. The Constitution does not "mandate regularity of district shape," O'Connor said, and the "neglect of traditional districting criteria is merely necessary, not sufficient." In her view, the decision to create a majority-minority district is not in itself unconstitutional. In order for strict scrutiny to apply, traditional districting criteria must be "*subordinated to race.*" O'Connor saw evidence of subordinating other factors to race. One component of that evidence was the decision to create minority-majority districts. Another component was the use of a computer program that was "significantly *more* sophisticated with respect to race than with respect to other demographic data." Taken together, the trial court had substantial evidence that race led to the "neglect of traditional districting criteria. . . ." The strict scrutiny standard, on the other hand, does not apply to districting plans where "traditional considerations predominated over racial ones." Political gerrymandering, for example, is not subject to strict scrutiny. Similarly, protecting incumbents has been recognized as serving a "legitimate state goal." If district lines "merely correlate" with race as a result of basing the lines on party affiliation that also correlate with race, then there is "no racial classification to justify. . . ." And if the goal is otherwise constitutional political gerrymandering, O'Connor continued, the state may freely use a range of political data, such as precinct voting patterns, to achieve its objective "regardless of its awareness of its racial implications . . . and that it does so in the context of a majority-minority district." On the other hand, if race becomes a "proxy for political characteristics, a racial stereotype requiring strict scrutiny is in operation." If the nation is to be free of "state-sponsored discrimination," the Court cannot "pick and choose" between the forms of political participation in an attempt to "eliminate unjustified racial stereotyping by government actors." It was O'Connor's conclusion that the district court had ample grounds in this case to find that "racially motivated gerrymandering had a qualitatively greater influence" on this districting plan than politically motivated gerrymandering and that political gerrymandering was essentially accomplished "by the use of race as a proxy." Despite using the racial data in "complex ways" and for "multiple objectives, [it] does not mean that race did not predominate over other considerations." Indeed, the trial court record reflects "intensive and pervasive" use of race both as a "proxy to protect the political fortunes of adjacent incumbents, and for its own sake in maximizing the minority population [in one of the three districts] regardless of traditional districting principles." O'Connor termed the district's (District 30, in this instance) combination of a "bizarre, noncompact shape" and evidence the shape was "essentially dictated" by racial considerations in one form or another "exceptional." That combination of characteristics led the Court to subject District 30 to strict scrutiny. The Court came to similar conclusions about the other challenged districts (18 and 29).

As in other recent cases of this kind the Court was fragmented, and several strongly held and divergent views were represented in separate opinions. Justices Scalia and Thomas concurred separately; they agreed that the three Texas districts were unconstitutional but were of the view that race could never be constitutionally taken into consideration, a possibility the O'Connor opinion left open. Justices Stevens, Souter, Ginsburg, and Breyer dissented. It was their view that in determining whether to apply strict scrutiny to the Texas plan the Court improperly ignored the "complex interplay" of political and geographical factors that led to the creation of these particular districts. Instead, the majority focused exclusively on the "role race played in the State's decision to adjust the shape of its districts." Stevens characterized the Court's course as one that "struck out into a jurisprudential wilderness that lacks a definable constitutional core and threatens to create harms more significant than any suffered by the individual plaintiffs challenging these districts." Stevens noted the "irrational[ity]" of assuming that a person is not qualified to vote simply because of skin color or other physical characteristics. At the same time, it is neither "irrational nor invidious" to assume a black resident of a particular community is a Democrat "if reliable statistical evidence discloses that 97 percent of the blacks in that community vote in Democratic primary elections." For that reason, Stevens felt it reasonable for those drawing the district lines in Texas to sometimes use racial data as a proxy for making political judgments as in assuming that "wealthy suburbanites . . . are more likely to be Republicans than communists." Requiring the state to ignore the association between race and party affiliation would be "no more logical," in Stevens's view, than it would be to "prohibit the Public Health Service from targeting African-American communities in an effort to increase awareness regarding sickle-cell anemia." He concluded that the Court-imposed barriers confining the shape of the district "will interfere more directly with the ability of minority voters to participate in the political process than did the oddly shaped districts the Court has struck down in recent cases." The Court will remain heavily engaged with this issue for at least the near future.

Broadcast Regulation

***Turner Broadcasting v. Federal Communications Commission*, 512 U.S. 622, 129 L.Ed. 2d 497, 114 S.Ct. 2445 (1994)** Congress passed the Cable Television Consumer Protection and Competition Act in 1992. Among other things, the act required in sections 4 and 5 that most cable systems use one-third of their cable capacity to retransmit local broadcast channels. These provisions are referred to as the "must-carry" rules. The cable industry argued that the act prevents it from carrying the content it wishes in violation of the First Amendment. Broadcasters, on the other hand, contended that cable systems are essentially local monopolies and, as such, are subject to regulations designed to protect broadcasters from unfair competition. Passage of the act brought immediate challenge from Turner Broadcasting System and a number of cable programmers. A special three-judge district court upheld the law. Under terms of the act, the Supreme Court reviewed the case on direct appeal, in *Turner Broadcasting System v. FCC* (*Turner I*). In a 5-4 decision, the Court held that the First Amendment does not broadly insulate the cable industry from federal regulations and that the must-carry provisions are content neutral. At the same time, the Court concluded there were "genuine issues of material fact still to be resolved on the record" and that the lower court had erred in granting summary judgment to the government. The case was remanded to the three-judge court to enable further fact-finding on the government's contention that without the must-carry requirements cable systems would bring about the demise of broadcast stations. Justice Kennedy began the opinion of the Court by indicating that the must-carry provisions must be evaluated by using a heightened or intermediate level of First Amendment scrutiny. Cable technology has virtually none of the characteristics, for example, a finite number of frequencies, that provides the rationale for extensive regulation of broadcasters. At the same time, the majority found the must-carry provisions justified by the "special characteristics of the cable medium: the bottleneck monopoly power" exercised by cable operators and the "danger this power poses to the viability of broadcast television." Cable's position as a "bottleneck" was controlling, in the majority's thinking. By virtue of its "ownership of the essential pathway for cable speech," said Kennedy, a cable operator can "prevent its subscribers from obtaining programming it chooses to exclude." The "potential for abuse," he continued, of this private power "over a central avenue of communication cannot be overlooked." The First Amendment prohibits governmental interference with free speech, but it does not "disable the Government from taking steps to insure that private interests not restrict, through physical control of a critical pathway of communication, the free flow of information and ideas." The Court also rejected the contention of the cable industry that the must-carry regulations were not content-neutral, which would require compelling justification by the government. The "overriding objective" of Congress in enacting the must-carry requirement was "not to favor programming of a particular subject matter, viewpoint or format" but rather, said Kennedy, to "preserve access to free television programming" for those Americans without cable service. Justice O'Connor offered a dissent that was joined by Justices Scalia, Thomas, and Ginsburg. It was their view that the must-carry provisions were an unconstitutional restraint on the cable operators' "editorial discretion as well as on the cable programmers' speech." The dissenters also concluded the regulation was based on content. No matter how praiseworthy the objective of maintaining access and diverse sources of information, said O'Connor, the regulation here is "directly tied to the content of what speakers are likely to say." In the dissenters' view, no governmental interest could justify that kind of interference with free speech. *See also* COMMERCE CLAUSE, p. 291.

Significance Congress has regulated broadcasting since the 1920s. In 1934, Congress created the Federal Communications Commission to implement legislative policy. The government's authority to regulate broadcast is based on the industry's use of the public airwaves to operate. Since broadcasting frequencies are finite, the government must regulate their use to protect the public interest. Generally, the Court has deferred to the actions of the FCC. The advent of cable technology changed the industry and raised new questions, as seen in *Turner I.* Two recent rulings illuminate this point. The Court ruled in *Turner I* (see above) that review of the FCC's must-carry regulations should be conducted at the intermediate scrutiny level. Applying that standard, the Court placed the burden of demonstrating that the requirement advanced important governmental interests in the least restrictive way on the FCC. The Court then remanded the case for further consideration of whether the must-carry requirement actually met this test. On remand, a three-judge district court upheld the provisions by a 2-1 vote. The cable industry unsuccessfully pursued direct appeal to the Supreme Court in *Turner Broadcasting System, Inc. v. FCC* (137 L.Ed. 2d 369: 1997, *Turner II*); the Court split 5-4, as in *Turner I.* Justice Kennedy spoke for a somewhat unusual combination of justices that included Chief Justice Rehnquist and Justices Stevens, Souter, and Breyer (in large part). He began "where the plurality ended" in *Turner I*, with the application of intermediate scrutiny standards. A content-neutral regulation can withstand First Amendment review if it advances an "important" governmental interest "unrelated to the suppression of free speech" and does not "burden substantially more speech than necessary" to further those interests. Three interrelated interests were identified in *Turner I* as served by the must-carry requirements: preservation of local broadcast television carried over the air; promotion of multiple-source information dissemination; and promotion of fair-market competition for television programming. The Court reaffirmed that each constituted an important governmental interest.

Kennedy then turned to the conclusions drawn by Congress that justified the must-carry regulations. Congress, said Kennedy, was under "no illusion" that broadcast television would completely disappear without the must-carry regulation. Congress was concerned, however, that "significant numbers of broadcast stations [would] be refused carriage on cable systems" and that those broadcast stations denied carriage would either "deteriorate to a substantial degree or fail altogether." Congress was also concerned that without regulatory action there would be a reduction in the number of "media voices available to consumers." Indeed, Congress identified a specific interest in "ensuring continuation" of the local origination of broadcast programming. Congress's "evident interest" in preserving the existing structure of the broadcast industry "discloses a purpose to prevent any significant reduction in the multiplicity of broadcast programming sources available to noncable households." Kennedy then examined the two propositions underlying the government's contention that the "economic health of local broadcasting is in genuine jeopardy and in need of the protections afforded" by must-carry: that a significant number of broadcast stations will be refused carriage on cable systems and that those stations denied carriage will "deteriorate" substantially. Kennedy suggested that when courts determine whether laws like this are constitutional they must accord "substantial deference to the predictive judgments of Congress." Such deference is appropriate because Congress is institutionally "far better equipped" than the courts to "amass and evaluate" the large quantity of data bearing on the legislative question. The deference to Congress is like the deference given to administrative agencies "because of their expertise." Given this perspective, Kennedy said the Court had "no difficulty" in recognizing a substantial basis to support Congress's conclusion that a "real threat justified enactment of the must-carry provisions." Among the supporting conclusions: (1) cable operators had "considerable and growing market power over local video programming markets"; (2) cable operators possess a local "monopoly" over cable households; (3) the "structure" of the cable industry gave cable operators "increasing ability and incentive to drop local broadcast stations from their systems or reposition them to a less-viewed channel"; and (4) many broadcast stations had either "fallen into bankruptcy" or had suffered lost operating revenue resulting from "adverse carriage decisions by cable systems." In short, it was the Court's view that Congress had "ample basis" to conclude that without legislative action the free local broadcast systems were "endangered."

The evidence assembled on remand "confirm[ed] the reasonableness of the congressional judgment." Turner Broadcasting found in the record evidence it claimed could support the contrary conclusion that the must-carry regulation was not necessary to protect the economic viability of the broadcast system. Kennedy said Turner Broadcasting's assertion "misapprehends the relevant inquiry." The question is not whether Congress was correct to determine that must-carry is necessary to prevent "significant financial hardship" for local broadcast stations. Rather, the question is whether the legislative conclusion "was reasonable and supported by substantial evidence in the record before Congress." Although some evidence could have supported the opposite conclusion, a "reasonable interpretation" was that expansion in the cable industry was "causing harm" to broadcasting. It was for Congress, said Kennedy, "to determine the better explanation" of the assembled data. The Court is "not at liberty to substitute [its] judgment for the reasonable conclusion of a legislative body." Congress is "allowed to make a rational prediction" of the effects of either regulating or taking no action to advance governmental interests. The Court found it apparent that the must-carry regulation serves the government's interests in a "direct and effective way." The next question was whether must-carry is "broader than necessary" to achieve governmental objectives—to consider the "fit between the asserted interests and the means chosen to advance them." The Court saw the must-carry provisions as potentially interfering with protected speech in two ways: They restrain the editorial discretion of cable operators, and they make it more difficult for cable programmers to "compete for carriage" on the limited number of remaining channels. The Court compared the number of broadcast stations that gained carriage as a result of the must-carry provisions. This number was less than 20 percent of the number of broadcast stations carried voluntarily. The Court saw the burden imposed by must-carry as "congruent to the benefits it affords" and concluded that the requirement was "narrowly tailored to preserve a multiplicity of broadcast stations for the 40 percent of American households without cable." Kennedy concluded his lengthy opinion by reiterating the extent to which the Court should defer to Congress's judgment. Determination of how "competing economic interests are to be reconciled in the complex and fast-changing field of television are for Congress to make." Those judgments cannot be "ignored or undervalued" simply because a First Amendment challenge is lodged. The challenge to must-carry in this case reflects "little more than disagreement over the level of protection broadcast stations are to be afforded." The justices cannot "displace" Congress's judgment about content-neutral regulations "with our own [judgment], so long as its policy is grounded on reasonable factual findings supported by evidence that is substantial for a legislative determination." It was the Court's judgment that those requirements were met in this instance. Justice O'Connor issued a dissent joined by Justices Scalia, Thomas, and Ginsburg. O'Connor said that the Court "misapplie[d] the intermediate scrutiny framework" in its review, and she disputed strength of evidence used to justify the must-carry regulation. She termed "entirely mythical" the claim that the entire broadcast industry was at risk. Rather, the only broadcast stations that would not be carried by cable systems were the "marginal" stations. Congress had acted, in O'Connor's estimation, using "unquestionably outdated" information about an industry whose technology is rapidly changing. The recent growth of direct-broadcast satellite television, for example, diminishes the argument that cable operators possess monopolistic strength in the industry. The dissenters were concerned as well that the First Amendment aspects of this case had been subordinated or "trivialize[d]" by the Court's deference to a "highly dubious economic theory."

Congress sought to protect minors from objectionable content available on the Internet by enacting the Communications Decency Act of 1996 (CDA). Among its other provisions, the act prohibits the knowing transmission of "indecent communications" to minors. More generally, the act prohibits the transmission or display of obscene material. The case of *Reno v. ACLU* (138 L.Ed. 2d 874: 1997) presented two questions for the Supreme Court. The first focuses on the manner in which the government might protect minors from indecent communications—how adults and minors are to be effectively separated. The act suggests that Internet users who make a "good-faith" effort to prevent access by minors do not violate the act, for instance, persons who restrict access through such devices as access codes or identification numbers. The issue is whether the act is narrowly tailored enough to pass First Amendment scrutiny. The second issue is whether such terms as "indecency" and "patently offensive" are defined clearly enough in the act. Upon passage of the act, actions were filed in federal district court to prevent implementation of the law. One suit was commenced by a wide range of groups, including the ACLU, online user groups, service providers, and nonprofit organizations. A second suit was filed by such groups as the American Library Association, American Booksellers Association, and a number of major Internet access providers, such as America Online and Microsoft. These two cases were consolidated as *Reno v. ACLU.* A three-judge district court found the act unconstitutional on its face because the language of the statute was vague and because age verification is too expensive and technologically unfeasible. The Supreme Court agreed.

The Court's focus was on the terms "indecent" and "patently offensive." Notwithstanding the "legitimacy and importance" of protecting minors from harmful materials, the Court concluded that the terms were sufficiently vague and ambiguous to render the CDA "problematic" for purposes of the First Amendment. The "absence of definition" of either term will "provoke uncertainty among speakers about how the two standards relate to each other and just what they mean." Justice Stevens suggested that the vagueness of the CDA was of "special concern" for two reasons. First, the act is "content-based regulation of speech." The vagueness of such a regulation has an "obvious chilling effect on free speech." Second, the CDA is a criminal statute. The CDA not only brings disgrace and the stigma of criminal conviction but contains penalties of imprisonment for up to two years for each violation. The "severity of criminal sanctions may well cause speakers to remain silent rather than communicate even arguably unlawful words, ideas, and images." The objective of denying access of minors to potentially harmful material "effectively suppresses a large amount of speech that adults have a constitutional right to receive and to address to one another." This burden on adult expression is unacceptable if "less restrictive alternatives would be at least as effective in achieving the legitimate purpose the statute was enacted to serve." Previous decisions on the expressive rights of adults make it "perfectly clear that sexual expression which is indecent but not obscene is protected by the First Amendment." The government had argued that adult communication was not diminished, but the Court found the claim to be based on the "incorrect factual premise" that prohibiting transmissions when one of its recipients is a minor would not interfere with communication among adults. The Court agreed with the trial court finding that the existing technology does not currently include any "effective method for a sender to prevent minors from obtaining access to its communications on the Internet without also denying access to adults." The breadth of the content-based regulation of expression imposes an "especially heavy burden" on the government to explain why a "less restrictive provision would not be as effective as the CDA." The government "ha[d] not done so," in the Court's view, and the CDA is "not narrowly tailored if that requirement has any meaning at all." Finally, Justice Stevens responded to the government contention that it has an "equally significant interest" in fostering the growth of the Internet. The government "apparently assumes," said Stevens, "that the unregulated availability of indecent and patently offensive material on the Internet is driving countless citizens away from the medium because of the risk of exposing themselves or their children to harmful material." The Court found this contention "singularly unpersuasive." The "dramatic expansion" of this new medium "contradicts the factual basis of this contention." Stevens pointed to the continued growth of the Internet as "phenomenal." In the absence of evidence to the contrary, the Court presumed that government regulation of the content of speech is "more likely to interfere with the free exchange of ideas than to encourage it." Justice O'Connor wrote a separate concurring opinion and suggested that the attempt to create "adult zones" on the Internet were different from those created for sexual content found in the "physical world." She saw this physical world as having two characteristics that make it possible to create "adult zones": geography and identity. A minor needs to actually enter establishments to obtain adult material, and if such an attempt is made, the minor will be unable to "conceal completely his identity (or, consequently, his age)." The "twin characteristics" of geography and identity enable a proprietor to prevent minors from entering an establishment while at the same time maintaining adult access. The electronic world, on the other hand, is "fundamentally different." Cyberspace allows both speakers and listeners to conceal their identities, at least for the time being. O'Connor acknowledged that the prospects for eventual zoning of the Internet "appear promising," but the constitutionality of the CDA must be evaluated "as it applies to the Interest as it exists today." Until effective gateway technology is available, the only way for a speaker to avoid liability under the CDA is "to refrain completely from using indecent speech." Previous regulations restricting what adults may say to minors "in no way restricts the adult's ability to communicate with other adults." When a minor enters an Internet chat room otherwise occupied by adults, the CDA "effectively requires the adults in the room to stop using indecent speech." The CDA is "therefore akin to a law that makes it a crime for a bookstore owner to sell pornographic magazines to anyone once a minor enters his store."

Environmental Regulation

***General Motors Corp. v. United States*, 496 U.S. 530, 110 L.Ed. 2d 480, 110 S.Ct. 2528 (1990)** The Clean Air Act of 1970 was aimed at diminishing air pollution from stationary sources. One of the regulatory devices in the act is the State Implementation Plan (SIP). SIPs are programs developed at the state level intended to meet national air quality standards. The act authorized the U.S. Environmental Protection Agency to review and approve initial state plans and any subsequent revisions to them. In 1980 the EPA approved a SIP submitted by Massachusetts regulating ozone emissions from automobile-painting operations. The plan required General Motors to fully comply with emission limits by the end of 1985 but allowed the automobile manufacturer to reach full compliance incrementally. In June 1985, General Motors sought an 18-month extension. Massachusetts agreed and revised the SIP accordingly. The revision was then submitted to the EPA a day before the original full compliance deadline. The EPA did not reject the proposed revision until late 1988 but, in the meantime, filed an enforcement action against General Motors in U.S. district court. The court ruled that the Clean Air Act required EPA to review revisions to approved plans within four months. Since EPA had failed to do so, the court concluded that EPA could not enforce the original plan from the end of the four-month period until EPA took action on the proposed revision. The Court of Appeals for the First Circuit reversed, however, ruling that failure to meet the four-month deadline did not prevent EPA from enforcing the original plan. The Supreme Court ruled the Clean Air Act neither required review of proposed revisions within four months nor precluded enforcement of the original plan, even if proposed revisions were not reviewed in a timely fashion. It was the Court's view that the deadlines contained in the act were intended to assure that "some form of pollution-control requirements were put in place quickly." The deadlines, however, were directed at review of the original plan and "did not impose such a time restraint on EPA review of a . . . revision." Even though the EPA was not bound by the four-month deadline when reviewing proposed revisions to previously approved plans, the EPA must still act "within a reasonable time" under terms of the Administrative Procedure Act (APA). General Motors contended that a delay in excess of four months to review plan revisions was categorically unreasonable and that, as a result, EPA could not bring an action to enforce a previously approved plan if there was unreasonable delay in acting on proposed revisions. The Court disagreed. The Clean Air Act permits the EPA to bring action whenever there is a "violation of any requirement of an applicable implementation plan." The previously approved plan remains the "applicable implementation plan even after the State has submitted a proposed revision." Furthermore, there is no provision in the Clean Air Act that limits EPA enforcement authority to any case where there has been no unreasonable delay. In the absence of a "specific provision suggesting that Congress intended to create an enforcement bar, we decline to infer one." *See also CHEMICAL WASTE MANAGEMENT, INC. v. HUNT* (504 U.S. 334: 1992), p. 181 (Supp.); *FEDERAL ENERGY REGULATION COMMISSION v. MISSISSIPPI* (456 U.S. 742: 1982), p. 362; *NEW YORK v. UNITED STATES* (505 U.S. 144: 1992), p. 118 (Supp.).

Significance Federal environmental initiatives have occasionally come into conflict with policies at the state and local levels. Such conflicts raise basic questions about federalism by focusing on the limits of the federal government's power to regulate interstate commerce or its power to tax and spend. Two examples will illustrate. The city of Chicago owned and operated a facility that burned solid waste and recovered the energy produced by the incinerating process. The process, however, left waste in the form of ash. The city disposed of this ash at landfills that were not licensed to accept hazardous waste. The Environmental Defense Fund filed a complaint under the Resource Conservation and Recovery Act (RCRA), alleging violations under the act as well as of EPA regulations. The city did not dispute that it had not complied with provisions of the act covering hazardous wastes but argued that the ash that remained after incineration was excluded from the hazardous waste provisions of the act. The federal district court agreed and granted the city's motion for summary judgment, but the Court of Appeals for the Seventh Circuit reversed. While the matter was pending the EPA directed its personnel to treat ash from municipal incineration operations as exempt from the hazardous waste provisions of the act. The Supreme Court vacated the appellate ruling in *Chicago v. Environmental Defense Fund* (511 U.S. 328: 1994) and returned the issue to the circuit court for further consideration. The Seventh Circuit reinstated its previous opinion, concluding that the language of the act was clear notwithstanding the EPA directive. The Supreme Court affirmed the Seventh Circuit and held that ash from the city's incineration facility was not exempt from regulation under the act as hazardous waste. The Court's judgment was based on its "plain meaning" interpretation of the exemption language of RCRA. As long as a municipal facility recovers energy by incineration of appropriate wastes, the facility is not subject to regulation as a facility that "treats, stores, disposes of, or manages hazardous waste." The language of RCRA does not, on the other hand, "contain any exclusion for the *ash itself.*" To the contrary, the "waste the facility produces (as opposed to that which it receives) is not even mentioned" in the act, thus it cannot qualify for a "waste stream exemption." The language of the statute provided the Court with "authoritative expression" of the law; the language "prominently *omits* reference to [waste] generation." As a result, the text of the statute "requires rejection" of the plea for deference to the EPA's interpretation, which goes "beyond the scope of whatever ambiguity" that might be found in the law.

The second example is *C & A Carbone, Inc. v. Clarkstown* (511 U.S. 383: 1994). The town allowed a private solid waste disposal company to construct a transfer station to separate items that could be recycled from those that could not. To offset the cost of building the transfer station, the town guaranteed a minimum volume of waste coming to the station for which the contractor could charge a fee. The method the town chose was "flow control," which required all nonhazardous waste gathered within the town be taken to the transfer station. Recyclers like Carbone were prohibited under the ordinance from shipping nonrecyclables and were instead required to bring such nonrecyclable material to the transfer station. Clarkstown became aware that Carbone was shipping nonrecyclable waste out of state and filed suit in state court, seeking an order compelling Carbone to use the transfer station. The state court found the ordinance constitutional and granted summary judgment to the town. The Supreme Court reversed, concluding that the ordinance regulates interstate commerce and had economic effects that were interstate in character. The Court saw the "article of commerce" not as the nonrecyclable waste but the service of processing and disposing of it. The ordinance thus prevented any operator except the designated local contractor from engaging in waste separation and disposal of nonrecyclable residue. By favoring a single local contractor, the ordinance also "squelched competition" in the waste-processing business. Thus, even in the absence of conflicting provision of federal legislation, the Court found the local ordinance in conflict with the congressional commerce power nonetheless.

Social Security and Medicare

***Bowen v. Georgetown University Hospital*, 488 U.S. 204, 102 L.Ed. 2d 493, 109 S.Ct. 468 (1988)** The Health and Human Services secretary is authorized to determine which costs are "reasonable" and reimbursable to health care providers under the Medicare program. In 1972, the secretary was authorized to establish cost-limit rules that would prospectively cap reimbursable costs; the cost limits would be distributed to providers such that each would know reimbursement ceilings before the rendering of medical services. The secretary devised various indexes or formulas by which to establish cost limits. A change was made, however, in the method for calculating wage cost indexes in

1981 by excluding wages paid at federal hospitals. In other words, the wage cost indexes for 1981 were only based on wages paid at state, local, and private hospitals. Local providers in areas with federal hospitals were disadvantaged by this change because it tended to lower cost limits from what they might have been had wages paid at federal facilities been included. A group of hospitals including Georgetown University Hospital successfully challenged the 1981 regulations in the U.S. District Court for the District of Columbia on the grounds that the secretary had failed to comply with the notice and comment provisions of the Administrative Procedures Act. On the basis of this ruling, the providers were reimbursed on the basis of a formula that included wages from federal hospitals. The secretary reissued the 1981 cost-limit rule in 1984 and recovered the funds paid to the providers under terms of the 1983 district court decision. The providers returned to court, claiming the retroactive application of the earlier cost-limit rule was invalid under the Medicare Act. Summary judgment was granted for the providers, and the Court of Appeals for the District of Columbia Circuit affirmed. The Supreme Court unanimously affirmed as well. Justice Kennedy said it is "axiomatic" that an administrative agency's power to fashion regulations is "limited to the authority delegated by Congress." The question in this case, then, was whether Congress had authorized retroactive rulemaking in the Medicare Act. As a general rule, retroactivity is "not favored in the law," and enactments will not be read as having retroactive effect "unless their language requires this result." Similarly, a statutory grant of rulemaking authority will not be "understood to encompass the power to promulgate retroactive rules unless that power is conveyed by Congress in express terms." Even where some "substantial justification" for retroactive rulemaking is presented, courts should be "reluctant to find such authority absent an express statutory grant." Although the Medicare Act provides "some form of retroactive action," this authority is confined to making "case-by-case adjustments" to reimbursement payments where the "regulations prescribing computation methods do not reach the correct result in individual cases." The "structure and language" of the Medicare Act "require the conclusion that the retroactivity provision applies only to case-by-case adjudication, not to rulemaking." The Court also rejected the argument that the secretary's action is entitled to judicial deference. Such deference is not applicable, said Kennedy, to agencies "litigating positions that are wholly unsupported by regulations, rulings, or administrative practice." Deference to what "appears to be nothing more than an agency's convenient litigating position would be entirely inappropriate." The Court did not consider the weight the secretary's arguments might have in other contexts. Rather, the Court was satisfied that this case could be resolved by the particular statutory language itself. The Court's interpretation of the Medicare Act, said Kennedy, "compels the conclusion that the Secretary has no authority to promulgate retroactive cost-limit rules." *See also STEWARD MACHINE COMPANY v. DAVIS* (301 U.S. 548: 1937), p. 391.

Significance The courts have developed general ground rules for reviewing legislative enactments. As in *General Motors* (see above), retroactive application of statutory language will generally not occur unless expressly mandated. Similarly, exceptions to legislative requirements are not presumed from ambiguity. To the contrary, exceptions are typically read narrowly to allow the primary objective(s) of legislation to be reached. Medicare is one of a number of programs tied either directly or indirectly to the Social Security Act. Indeed, many other federal initiatives are aimed at government services and the conditions under which such services are delivered. For example, the Fair Housing Act (FHA) as amended in 1988 prohibits housing discrimination against handicapped persons, among others. The FHA includes in its definition of discrimination the refusal to make "reasonable accommodation in rules, policies, practices, or services when such accommodations may be necessary to afford [handicapped] persons equal opportunity to use and enjoy a dwelling." The FHA contains language in section 3607(b)(1), however, exempting federal, state, and local regulations that deal with the maximum numbers of people "permitted to occupy a dwelling." The zoning code of Edmonds, Washington, provides that occupants of single-family dwellings must compose a "family." A family is defined as persons related by "genetics, adoption, or marriage." The code does not establish a maximum number of family members who may occupy a single-family dwelling. No more than five persons, however, who do not meet the definition of family may reside together in a single-family dwelling. Oxford House, Inc., runs a group home in Edmonds for adults recovering from alcoholism and drug addiction. The home is located in a single-family residential zone, and it typically houses about a dozen unrelated persons. Edmonds cited Oxford House for zoning code violations, and Oxford House contested the citation on the grounds that the FHA prevented enforcement of this provision. A federal district court ruled that the exemption covered the Edmonds ordinance, but the Court of Appeals for the Ninth Circuit reversed, finding the exemption to be inapplicable in this case. The Supreme Court affirmed the Ninth Circuit's ruling in *City of Edmonds v. Oxford House, Inc.* (514 U.S. 725: 1995). Justice Ginsburg delivered the opinion of the Court on behalf of a six-justice majority. It was the Court's view that the defining provision at issue in this case "describes who may compose a family unit." Prescriptions of a "family-defining kind" are designed primarily to "foster the family character of a neighborhood." The question before the Court, said Ginsburg, was whether the Edmonds "family composition rule qualifies as a restriction regarding the maximum number of persons permitted to occupy a dwelling." Exceptions to a general statement of policy ought to be "sensibly read narrowly," Ginsburg continued, in order to "preserve the primary operation of the [policy]." Congress was fully aware of an "evident distinction" between municipal land use restrictions and maximum occupancy restrictions when it enacted the FHA. Limiting land use to single-family residences requires the definition of the term "family." Family composition rules are, as a result, an "essential component of single-family residential use restrictions." Maximum occupancy restrictions, on the other hand, cap occupancy in relation to such factors as floor space or number of rooms. Such restrictions "apply uniformly to all residents in all dwelling units." The Court found the zoning code provisions at issue here to be "classic examples" of a use restriction and complementing the family composition rule. As such, they did not fall within the section 3607(b)(1) exemption.

Remedial Authority to Protect Civil Rights

***Harris v. Forklift Systems*, 510 U.S. 17, 126 L.Ed. 2d 295, 114 S.Ct. 367 (1993)** Title VII of the Civil Rights Act of 1964 prohibits discrimination in the workplace on the basis of factors such as race and gender. The Supreme Court ruled in *Meritor Savings Bank, FSB v. Vinson* (477 U.S. 57: 1986) that actions can be brought under Title VII if sexual harassment is sufficiently severe as to "alter the conditions of the victim's employment and create an abusive working environment." Theresa Harris filed a sexual harassment claim against her employer but was unsuccessful in the lower courts because she had not demonstrated that she suffered psychological injury as a result of her employer's conduct. The Court granted review in *Harris v. Forklift Systems* to determine whether proof of psychological injury was required to bring a sexual harassment claim under Title VII. A unanimous Court reaffirmed the standard from *Meritor*, which takes a "middle path between making actionable any conduct that is merely offensive and requiring the conduct to cause a tangible psychological injury." Justice O'Connor sought to clarify the *Meritor* standard in *Harris*. Conduct that is not pervasive enough to create an "objectively hostile work environment," or an environment that a "reasonable person would find hostile or abusive," is outside the reach of Title VII. Similarly, if the victim does not "subjectively perceive the environment to be abusive," there is no conduct that has actually altered the victim's working conditions and no Title VII violation. On the other hand, said O'Connor, Title VII "comes into play before the harassing conduct leads to a nervous breakdown." An abusive workplace environment, even one that does not "seriously [affect] employees' psychological well-being," can and often will "detract from employees' job performance, discourage employees from remaining on the job, or keep them from advancing in their careers." Even without regard to what O'Connor characterized as "tangible effects" of workplace discrimination, conduct that is so severe as to create an abusive workplace environment "offends Title VII's broad rule of workplace equality." The Court said the lower courts erred in Harris's case by "needlessly focus[ing] the fact-finder's attention on concrete psychological harm," an element not required under Title VII. Certainly conduct that seriously affects an employee's psychological well-being violates Title VII, but the statute, said O'Connor, "is not limited to such conduct." As long as the workplace environment is reasonably perceived as hostile or abusive, there "is no need for it also to be psychologically injurious." O'Connor acknowledged that there is no "mathematically precise" test to apply to claims of sexual harassment. Determination of whether a workplace environment is hostile or abusive requires examination of "all the circumstances." Psychological harm, like any other relevant factor, may be taken into account, "but no single factor is required." Justice Scalia concurred but expressed concern about the imprecision of the standard contained in O'Connor's opinion. As a practical matter, he suggested, the ruling "lets virtually any unguided jury decide whether sex-related conduct engaged in (or permitted by) an employer is egregious enough to warrant an award of damages." He favored an inquiry that would focus more attention on job performance but agreed that Title VII cases should not be confined to that consideration. He joined the majority because he knew of "no alternative to the course the Court has taken today." *See also* *BOWEN v. GEORGETOWN UNIVERSITY HOSPITAL* (488 U.S. 204: 1988), p. 87 (Supp.); *HEART OF ATLANTA MOTEL v. UNITED STATES* (379 U.S. 241: 1964), p. 343.

Significance Federal statutory law often provides a more promising basis for legal challenges to discriminatory practices than does the Equal Protection Clause of the Constitution. This is true because these laws can more readily reach private discrimination than constitutionally based claims. Furthermore, federal civil rights laws usually require only a showing of differential treatment. Proof of discriminatory intent is seldom required, which heightens the plaintiff's chance for winning the lawsuit. The matter of sexual harassment and whether such conduct falls within the scope of Title VII is illustrative. *Meritor Savings* was the first ruling on this very question. After working four years for Meritor, Mechelle Vinson was discharged for abusing the bank's sick-leave policy. Vinson subsequently brought suit, claiming she had been subjected to harassment through her four years of employment. The bank argued that workplace discrimination covered under Title VII was confined to "tangible" economic loss. The Court disagreed. Instead, the Court recognized a congressional intent to "strike at the entire spectrum of disparate treatment of men and women" in the workplace. The Court also pointed to guidelines issued by the Equal Employment Opportunity Commission as fully supporting the view that "harassment leading to noneconomic injury can violate Title VII." Sexual misconduct of the type suffered by Vinson constitutes prohibited harassment where the behavior has the purpose or effect of "creating an intimidating, hostile, or offensive working environment." The Court also addressed the lower court conclusion that no actionable conduct occurred if the employee voluntarily participated in an "intimate or sexual relationship." The fact that sex-related conduct was "voluntary, in the sense that the complainant was not forced to participate against her will, is not a defense to a sexual harassment suit." Rather, the essence of any sexual harassment claim is that the alleged sexual advances were "unwelcome."

The question in *Landgraf v. USI Film Products* (511 U.S. 244: 1994) was whether the provisions of the Civil Rights Act of 1991 apply retroactively to cases already existing prior to the effective date of the law. Under Title VII of the 1964 Civil Rights Act, victims of job discrimination were able to obtain job reinstatement and back pay or an order prohibiting future discriminatory conduct. The 1991 act added trial by jury in employment discrimination cases, and it provided the opportunity to obtain compensatory and punitive damages. Barbara Landgraf brought a Title VII action, claiming she had been forced from her job as a result of unlawful sexual harassment. The trial court found that her employer had taken sufficient corrective action so that Landgraf's resignation was unrelated to any unlawful harassment. The act became law while Landgraf's case was on appeal. The Court of Appeals for the Fifth Circuit rejected the contention that Landgraf was entitled to benefit from the provisions of the new law. Over the lone dissent of Justice Blackmun, the Supreme Court agreed. Justice Stevens said the Court starts with a "presumption against statutory retroactivity." The presumption is "deeply rooted in our jurisprudence, and embodies a legal doctrine centuries older than our Republic." There is, however, no conflict between the Court's presumption and statutory language that "unambiguous[ly]" provides for retroactivity. The presumption will be set aside only if there is "clear evidence" that Congress intended retroactive application. Absent such clear evidence to that effect, the Court has no legal basis except to apply statutory language prospectively. Requiring clear evidence of intent ensures that Congress has "affirmatively considered the potential unfairness of retroactive application and determined that it is an acceptable price to pay for the countervailing benefits." No such clear evidence of congressional intent for retroactivity was found here. The Court also compared the language of the 1991 act with language from the civil rights bill that passed both houses of Congress the preceding year. The 1990 bill explicitly called for application of many of its provisions to cases arising before its effective date. The bill was vetoed by President Bush, at least in part because of the "unfair retroactivity rules." Congress failed to override the veto. When the 1991 bill was introduced, it did not contain comparable retroactivity language. It is possible, suggested Stevens, that because Congress "was unable to resolve the retroactivity issue with clarity in the 1990 legislation, Congress viewed the matter as an open issue to be resolved by the courts." The Court also rejected Landgraf's textual arguments. Given the "high stakes" of the retroactivity question, Stevens said, it would "be surprising for Congress to have chosen to resolve the question through negative inferences drawn from [the] two provisions [asserted by Landgraf] of quite limited effect."

***Gregory v. Ashcroft*, 501 U.S. 452, 115 L.Ed. 2d 410, 111 S.Ct. 2395 (1991)** Upheld Missouri constitutional provision requiring the retirement of state judges who reach the age of 70. The Court upheld the mandatory retirement provisions against challenges brought by a number of state judges who were subject to the requirement. The judges asserted that the requirement violated the Age Discrimination in Employment Act (ADEA) and the Equal Protection Clause. The Court centered its ruling on the Tenth Amendment. Justice O'Connor spoke for the majority and said that the authority of the people of a state to set qualifications of government officials "lies at the heart of representative government." Making such a decision is one of the "most fundamental sort for a sovereign entity." Because congressional interference with Missouri's decision would "upset the usual constitutional balance of federal and state powers," courts must be certain that congressional intent to do so is "unmistakably clear." No such level of certainty existed here. The Court also rejected the challenge based on the Equal Protection Clause. In order to overturn the mandatory retirement provision, it must be demonstrated that the classification is so unrelated to a legitimate objective that it is irrational. The Court said it is quite rational that the people of a state could conclude that the risk of mental and/or physical deterioration at age 70 is sufficiently great to justify mandatory retirement. The Court saw the interest in maintaining a capable judiciary as not only legitimate but "compelling." *See also* FEDERALISM, p. 29.

Significance Age discrimination cases have appeared with some regularity before the Court. Generally, the Court has upheld application of federal statutes such as ADEA. Departure from this pattern emerges when the age discrimination claim is compounded by considerations of federalism. In such situations, the Court has seldom used the Fourteenth Amendment to set aside mandatory retirement initiatives of state and local governments, especially for elected officials as shown in *Gregory*. Similarly, the Court upheld a mandatory retirement age for uniformed police officers in *Massachusetts Board of Retirement v. Murgia* (427 U.S. 307: 1976). The review of challenged schemes of classification involves application of different evaluative standards. The least stringent of these is the rationality test. This test would invalidate classifications only if they are arbitrary and have no demonstrable justification. The rationality test is typically used in reviewing age-based classifications. In *Murgia,* a provision of state law required that uniformed police officers retire at age 50. Key to the Court's holding in this case was determining the standard by which to assess the mandatory retirement policy. Murgia argued that age classification is "suspect" and entitled to "strict" or "close" scrutiny. Such strict scrutiny is a more stringent review than that associated with the rationality test. The Court disagreed and held that Murgia did not belong to a suspect class. His claim was then reviewed under the rationality standard. In a 7-1 decision, the Court upheld the mandatory retirement law. The rationality test reflects the view that classification is peculiarly and unavoidably a legislative function. The legislature's actions are presumed to be valid under this approach, and "perfection in making the necessary classification is neither possible nor necessary." In this instance, the legislature sought to "protect the public by assuring the physical preparedness of its uniformed police." Given that physical ability generally declines with age, the Court found the mandatory retirement policy rationally related to the state's objective. The Court concluded by saying Massachusetts needed to find the best or most just and humane system to implement their mandatory retirement policy. Under the rationality test, the policy did not deny equal protection. Justice Marshall dissented from use of the less demanding rationality test because of its inability to sufficiently protect equal protection interests. He would have preferred a flexible standard that would have more carefully examined the means chosen by Massachusetts.

Not long after *Murgia,* the Court upheld a mandatory retirement policy for Foreign Service officers in *Vance v. Bradley* (440 U.S. 93: 1979).

Again, the Court found a retirement policy rationally related to the legislative goal of assuring the professional capacity of persons holding critical public service positions. In this case, Foreign Service officers have to undergo special rigors associated with overseas duty. Not all age discrimination suits have been unsuccessful, however. For example, in *Trans World Airlines, Inc. v. Thurston* (469 U.S. 111: 1985), the Court unanimously held that an airline's policy of not permitting the automatic transfer of age-disqualified captains to other positions within the company was a violation of the same discrimination at issue in *Gregory*. The *Thurston* decision was soon followed by two other important rulings involving ADEA. In *Western Air Lines, Inc. v. Criswell* (472 U.S. 400: 1985), the Court unanimously held that an airline could not require mandatory retirement of flight engineers at age 60. Unlike the situation of pilots and copilots, where age was considered a bona fide occupational qualification, the Court held that flight engineers could be individually assessed rather than subjected to blanket early retirement rules. In *Johnson v. Baltimore* (472 U.S. 353: 1985), a unanimous Court also refused to permit a municipality to require mandatory retirement of firefighters at age 55. Key to this decision was the Court's rejection of Baltimore's contention that Congress had approved mandatory retirement when it retained such a policy for federal firefighters at the time it amended the statute in 1978. The Court held that retention of the provision was only for expediency and did not reflect a legislative judgment that youth was a bona fide qualification for the job. Finally, in *EEOC v. Wyoming* (460 U.S. 226: 1983), the Court ruled that state and local governments are not wholly immune from provisions of the ADEA. The Court made it clear, however, that the judgment did not compel a state to abandon policies that can demonstrate age as a bona fide occupational qualification. Central to the decisions in both *Murgia* and *Bradley* was the view that compulsory retirement would better ensure good job performance by limiting the age of employees.

***Adarand Constructors, Inc. v. Pena*, 515 U.S. 200, 132 L.Ed. 2d 158, 115 S.Ct. 2097 (1995)** The Surface Transportation and Uniform Relocation Assistance Act of 1987 provides that not less than 10 percent of the funds appropriated under the act "shall be expended with small business concerns owned and controlled by socially and economically disadvantaged individuals." At issue in *Adarand Constructors, Inc. v. Pena* was the "subcontractor compensation" language that gives preference in the form of a monetary bonus to prime contractors in federal highway construction projects who subcontracted at least 10 percent of the work to "disadvantaged business enterprises (DBEs)." A prime contractor for a highway project was awarded the bonus because it chose a DBE to perform guardrail work even though Adarand submitted the lowest bid for the work. Adarand is owned and operated by a white male and thus does not qualify as a DBE. Adarand filed suit, claiming that the preference given DBEs violated the Equal Protection Clause. The lower federal courts concluded that Congress may use race-based preference in federal construction projects. In a 5-4 decision, the Supreme Court reversed.

The central question in this case was the standard or scrutiny level that should be applied to remedial race-conscious actions of the federal government. The Court had ruled in *Richmond v. J.A. Croson Co.* (488 U.S. 469: 1989) that strict scrutiny is required when race-based programs are initiated by state or local governments. *Croson,* however, did not establish the standard for review required under the Fifth Amendment for action taken by the federal government. Nonetheless, Justice O'Connor noted three instructive themes about governmental racial classifications from *Croson:* skepticism—any preference based on racial or ethnic criteria must "necessarily receive a most searching examination"; consistency—all racial classifications reviewable under the Equal Protection Clause or Due Process of the Fifth Amendment "must be strictly scrutinized"; and congruence—equal protection analysis under the Fifth and Fourteenth Amendments "is the same." Taken together, O'Connor suggested, these themes lead to the conclusion that a person of whatever race "has the right to demand that any governmental actor subject to the Constitution justify any racial classification subjecting that person to unequal treatment under the strictest judicial scrutiny. . . ." Following *Croson,* two distinct standards applied to racial classifications depending on the level of government initiating the policy; the federal government had to meet a less demanding standard. By using intermediate scrutiny as the test for "Congressionally mandated 'benign' racial classifications," the Court created a double standard that "turned its back" on the proposition that strict scrutiny of "all governmental racial classifications is essential." The purpose of strict scrutiny, said O'Connor, is to "'smoke out' illegitimate uses of race by assuring that the legislative body is pursuing a goal important enough to warrant use of a highly suspect tool." Further, this dual approach failed to pursue the objective of congruence between the criteria applicable to federal and state/local racial classifications. All governmental action based on race should be subjected to "detailed judicial inquiry to insure that the personal right to equal protection of the laws is not infringed." Holding "benign" state and federal racial classifications to different standards "does not square" to this principle. A society whose institutions are founded on the concept of equality "should tolerate no retreat from the principle that government may treat people differently because of their race only for the most compelling reasons." The Court concluded that all race-based classifications, imposed by "whatever Federal, state or local governmental actor, must be reviewed under strict scrutiny." Race-based classifications are constitutional only if they are "narrowly tailored measures that further compelling governmental interests." Requiring strict scrutiny was seen as the best way to ensure that courts will give race-conscious classifications the detailed review the Constitution demands, both as to ends and means. In conclusion, O'Connor noted that the "unhappy persistence" of discrimination against minorities is an "unfortunate reality," and government is "not disqualified from acting in response to it." When race-based action is necessary to further a compelling interest, such action is within constitutional limits if it satisfies the "narrow tailoring" test set out by the Court.

Justices Scalia and Thomas concurred separately. It was Scalia's view that government can "never have a 'compelling interest' in discriminating on the basis of race in order to 'make up' for past racial discrimination in the opposite direction." He suggested that individuals who have been victimized by unlawful discrimination should be "made whole," but under the Constitution there can be no such thing as either a "creditor or a debtor race." Pursuit of racial entitlement even for the most "admirable and benign of purposes is to reinforce and preserve for future mischief the way of thinking that produced slavery, race privilege and race hatred." Justice Thomas directed his concurring opinion to the premise "underlying" affirmative action initiatives as represented in the dissenting opinions of Justices Stevens and Ginsburg, that there is a "racial paternalism exception to the principle of equal protection." He saw a "moral" and "constitutional equivalence" between laws intended to "subjugate a race" and those that attempt to allocate benefits on the basis of race "in order to foster some current notion of equality." In Thomas's view, so-called benign discrimination is destructive. It conveys to the majority that because of "chronic and apparently immutable handicaps, minorities cannot compete with the majority without their patronizing indulgence." *See also* COMMERCE CLAUSE, p. 291; FOURTEENTH AMENDMENT, p. 612.

Significance Recent decisions suggest that race-based affirmative action programs violate the Equal Protection Clause unless they are designed to promote a "compelling state interest." Use of strict scrutiny, requiring all levels of government to demonstrate a "compelling" interest where race-conscious policies are at issue, significantly restricts legislative latitude in pursuing preferential initiatives. The only interest that has been compelling enough to justify race-preference initiatives is remediation of demonstrated past discrimination. The Public Works Employment Act of 1977 contained a minority business enterprise section that required at least 10 percent of federal moneys designated for local public works projects to be set aside for businesses owned by minorities. Implementation of the policy was designed to come through grant recipients, who were expected to seek out MBEs and provide whatever assistance or advice that might be necessary to negotiate bonding, bidding, or any other historically troublesome process. The policy was challenged by a number of nonminority contractors but was upheld by the Supreme Court in *Fullilove v. Klutznick* (448 U.S. 448: 1980). Chief Justice Burger said the MBE section must be considered against the background of ongoing efforts directed toward deliverance of the century-old promise of equality of economic opportunity. The chief justice noted that a program using racial or ethnic criteria, even in a remedial context, calls for close examination, "yet we are bound to approach our task with appropriate deference." The Court's analysis involved two steps: the constitutionality of Congress's objectives and the permissibility of the means chosen to pursue the objectives. The Court ruled that Congress had ample evidence to conclude that minority businesses impaired access to public contracting opportunities, that their impaired access had an effect on interstate commerce, and that the pattern of disadvantage and discrimination was a problem national in scope. Thus, Congress had the authority to act. The Court then turned to the means chosen by Congress. Racial or ethnic criteria may be used in a remedial fashion as long as the program is narrowly tailored to achieve the corrective purpose. The Court rejected the view that in developing remedies Congress must act in a wholly color-blind fashion. No component of government has a more comprehensive remedial power than Congress. Where Congress can prohibit certain conduct, "it may, as here, authorize and induce state action to avoid such conduct." The Court recognized that some nonminority contractors who may not have acted in a discriminatory manner themselves may lose some contracts. Such a result, outside of the legislative purpose, is an unfortunate but incidental consequence. As Congress attempts to effectuate a limited and properly tailored remedy to cure the effects of prior discrimination, such a sharing of the burden by innocent parties is permissible.

Fullilove upheld the use of set-asides or reserved funds for minority business enterprises as a method of remedying past discrimination in the construction industry. A year before *Fullilove,* the Court approved a preferential employment training program in *United Steelworkers of America v. Weber* (443 U.S. 193: 1979). The plan, a component of a collective bargaining agreement, was designed to reduce racial imbalances in a corporation's skilled or craft workforce. The plan gave preference to unskilled black employees over more senior white employees in admission to training programs that taught the skills needed to become a craft worker. In a 5-2 decision, the Court held that Title VII of the Civil Rights Act of 1964 did not categorically preclude private and voluntary affirmative action plans. To prohibit such plans would produce a result inconsistent with the intent of the Civil Rights Act. It would be ironic if Title VII, "triggered by a nation's concern over centuries of racial injustice," was interpreted as the "legislative prohibition of all voluntary, private, race-conscious efforts to abolish traditional patterns of racial segregation and hierarchy." *Fullilove* and *Weber* together adopt the proposition that equal protection allows compensatory policies for groups that have demonstrably been disadvantaged in the past.

A decade after *Weber,* the Court reviewed an affirmative action plan adopted by the city of Richmond, Virginia, requiring prime contractors receiving city construction contracts to subcontract at least 30 percent of the dollar value of the contract to businesses owned or controlled by one (or more) of a number of specified minorities. The plan was designed to "promote wider participation by minority business enterprises in the construction of public projects" and was characterized by the city council as "remedial." The Court disallowed the plan in *Richmond v. J.A. Croson Co.*(488 U.S. 469: 1989). The principal defect was that Richmond failed to show past discrimination in the city's contract-letting practices or in the conduct of prime contractors toward minority subcontractors. Rather, the city had relied on data that showed that whereas the city's population was 50 percent black less than 1 percent of the large construction projects had been awarded to minority businesses. The Court viewed claims based on such data as "generalized" and "amorphous" and ruled that these data could not justify the use of an "unyielding" race-based quota approach. The plan was aimed, said the Court, at remedying the effects of discrimination in the entire construction industry. The data on which the plan was based provided "no guidance for a legislative body to determine the precise scope of the injury it seeks to remedy"; it has no "logical stopping point." Using these kinds of data to define "identified discrimination" would allow local governments "license to create a patchwork of racial preferences based on statistical generalizations about any particular field of endeavor." The Court also refused to defer to the city's own designation of the plan as remedial. "Mere recitation of a 'benign' or legitimate purpose for a racial classification is entitled to little or no weight." Racial classifications are "suspect," meaning that "legislative assurances of good intentions cannot suffice" in themselves. Two other aspects of the *Croson* decision must be noted. First, the Court emphasized that this decision does not preclude state and local governments from "taking action to rectify the effects of identified discrimination. Second, the Court made it clear that striking down the Richmond plan had absolutely no effect on the federal set-aside law upheld in *Fullilove* (upon which the Richmond plan had been fashioned). The Court made clear that a different standard applies to congressional action. And though the Fourteenth Amendment bars state and local units from discriminating on the basis of race, Congress has a "specific constitutional mandate to enforce the dictates of the Fourteenth Amendment."

The Court maintained the dual standard in *Metro Broadcasting, Inc. v. FCC* (497 U.S. 547: 1990), ruling that Congress may mandate "benign" minority preference policies even if those measures "are not 'remedial' in the sense of being designed to compensate victims of past governmental or societal discrimination." At issue in *Metro Broadcasting* were two policies of the Federal Communications Commission. The first allows the FCC to consider minority ownership as a factor in licensing decisions. Consideration of this factor enhances minority chances of obtaining new licenses. The second gives minority owners preference in situations where current license holders were likely to lose their licenses—so-called distressed sale situations. Of "overriding" significance in cases such as this, said Justice Brennan, is that these minority preference programs "have been specifically approved—indeed mandated—by Congress." The Court's decision followed directly from *Fullilove.* Under *Fullilove,* the Court need not use the strict scrutiny standard when reviewing affirmative action initiatives of the federal government. Rather, minority preference programs established by Congress need serve "important governmental" interests and be "substantially related" to achievement of those objectives. The Court reviewed the need for federal regulation of the "unique medium" of broadcast. The "safeguarding of the public's right to receive a diversity of views and information" over the airwaves was seen as an "integral component of the FCC's mission." On that basis, the Court concluded that "enhancing broadcast diversity is, at the very least, an important governmental objective and therefore a sufficient basis for the commission's minority ownership policies."

4. Federalism

Case	***Concept***	***Page***
BURDICK v. TAKUSHI (504 U.S. 428: 1992) *Norman v. Reed* (502 U.S. 279: 1992) *Timmons v. Twin Cities Area New Party* (137 L.Ed. 2d 589: 1997) *McINTYRE v. OHIO ELECTIONS COMMISSION* (514 U.S. 334: 1995) *Burson v. Freeman* (504 U.S. 191: 1992) *U.S. TERM LIMITS, INC. v. THORNTON* (514 U.S. 779: 1995)	Voting Regulations	105
SUPREME COURT OF VIRGINIA v. FRIEDMAN (487 U.S. 59: 1988)	Privileges and Immunities of Citizenship	115
UTAH DIVISION OF STATE LANDS v. UNITED STATES (482 U.S. 193: 1987) *Phillips Petroleum v. Mississippi* (482 U.S. 469: 1988)	Equal Footing Doctrine	117
NEW YORK v. UNITED STATES (505 U.S. 144: 1992) *Printz v. United States* and *Mack v. United States* (138 L.Ed. 2d 914: 1997)	Environmental Protection	118
ANDERSON v. EDWARDS (514 U.S. 143: 1995) *Puerto Rico Department of Consumer Affairs v. Isla Petroleum Corp.* (485 U.S. 495: 1988) *Gade v. National Solid Wastes Management Association* (505 U.S. 88: 1992) *Goodyear Atomic Corp. v. Miller* (486 U.S. 174: 1988)	Preemption Doctrine	121

Vacco v. Quill (138 L.Ed. 2d 834: 1997)
Washington v. Glucksberg (138 L.Ed. 2d 772: 1997)

Voting Regulations

***Burdick v. Takushi*, 504 U.S. 428, 119 L.Ed. 2d 245, 112 S.Ct. 2059 (1992)**
The Court ruled in *Burdick* that a state ban on write-in voting imposed only a "very limited burden" on the right to vote. The Court first rejected the argument that a law that imposes "any burden" on voting rights must be subject to strict scrutiny. Although voting is of the "most fundamental significance" in our political system, it does not follow that the right to vote "in any manner" and the right to associate for "political purposes through the ballot are absolute." Election laws will "invariably impose some burden upon individual voters." Subjecting every voting regulation to strict scrutiny would "tie the hands of States seeking to assure that elections are operated equitably and efficiently." The rigor of the Court's inquiry into the propriety of state election laws depends on the "extent to which a challenged regulation burdens" First Amendment rights. When a state election law imposes only "reasonable, nondiscriminatory restrictions" on the First Amendment, a state's important regulatory interests are "generally sufficient to justify the restrictions." Citing several different ways party or independent candidates may appear on Hawaii's ballot, the Court concluded that the restriction on write-in voting did not unreasonably "interfere with the rights of voters to associate and have candidates of their choice placed on the ballot." The Court also rejected the contention that a voter is entitled to both cast and have counted a "protest vote." The function of the election process, said Justice White, is to "winnow out and finally reject all but the chosen, not to provide means of giving vent to 'short-range political goals, pique, or personal quarrels.'" The Court concluded that Hawaii was within its rights to reserve the general election ballot for "major struggles" and not serve as a "forum for continuing intraparty feuds." The prohibition on write-in voting is a "legitimate means of averting divisive sore-loser candidacies." Further, the Court said that there are "other means available . . . to voice such generalized dissension from the electoral process." As a result, the Court saw "no adequate basis for [its] requiring the State to provide and to finance a place on the ballot for recording protests against its constitutionally valid election laws." Justices Kennedy, Blackmun, and Stevens saw the ban on write-in voting as preventing voters dissatisfied with choices

available to them "from participating in Hawaiian elections in a meaningful manner." *See also* FEDERALISM, p. 29; *OREGON v. MITCHELL* (400 U.S. 112: 1970), p. 199.

Significance The Supreme Court has generally deferred to state regulation of the election process. For example, the Court upheld a state law limiting general election ballot access to those candidates receiving at least 1 percent of the primary vote total in *Munro v. Socialist Workers Party* (479 U.S. 189: 1986). The state of Washington established a two-step process for minor party candidates seeking to get on the general election ballot. Any such candidate must first secure the convention nomination of his or her party. As the nominee, the candidate would appear on the primary election ballot. In order to access the general election ballot, the candidate needed to receive at least 1 percent of all votes cast for that office in the primary election. Candidate Dean Peoples was placed on the primary election ballot as the nominee of the Socialist Workers Party. Peoples received only 596 of the 681,690 votes cast in the primary, or .09 percent. Accordingly, his name was not placed on the general election ballot. Action was brought in federal court by Peoples, the party, and two registered voters claiming abridgment of rights secured by the First Amendment. In a 7-2 decision, the Supreme Court upheld the restrictions on ballot access. Justice White established a general framework at the outset by indicating that restrictions on ballot access for political parties impinge on the rights of individuals to associate for political purposes and the rights of qualified voters to cast their votes efficaciously. Such rights are not absolute, however, and are necessarily subject to qualification if elections are to be run fairly and effectively. In reviewing restrictions of this type, White said it is clear that states may condition access to the general election ballot by minor party or independent candidates upon a showing of a modicum of support among the potential voters for the office. Generally, deference will be extended to state regulations in this area. When states attempt to justify access restrictions, there is no requirement of a "particularized showing of the existence of voter confusion, ballot overcrowding, or the presence of frivolous candidates prior to the imposition of reasonable restrictions." To require actual proof of these conditions would invariably lead to lengthy disputes over the sufficiency of the evidence offered by a state in support of the restriction. In addition, such a requirement would necessitate that a state's electoral processes sustain some level of damage before the legislature could act. The Court preferred that legislatures be able to respond to potential deficiencies with foresight rather than hindsight as long as the response is reasonable and does not significantly impinge on protected rights.

The Court addressed a different ballot-access issue in *Norman v. Reed* (502 U.S. 279: 1992). Illinois law required that new political parties wishing to run candidates for office within a political subdivision must obtain signatures of 5 percent of the voters from the last election in the subdivision, or 25,000 voters, whichever is less. Another provision of the statute required the same minimum number of signatures to qualify a candidate running for statewide office. If the political subdivision is divided into separate districts, the signature requirement must be met in each of the districts. Another statute prohibited new parties from using the same name as an established party. The Harold Washington Party (HWP), named after the late mayor of Chicago, was established in 1989. Its candidate in the 1989 mayoral election in Chicago received more than 40 percent of the vote. The 40 percent support level established the party for ballot-access purposes in the city. The following year, a group of people sought to expand the party throughout Cook County. The Cook County Board elects members from two districts: the city district and the suburban district. As an established party within the city, the HWP was able to run candidates in Chicago for countywide office and the city district board. The party was not permitted, however, to run candidates for the suburban district seats because it had not met the 25,000-signature requirement in the district outside the city. The Supreme Court ruled that the signature requirement for the suburban district was not unduly burdensome under the specific facts of the case.

Justice Souter said that citizens have a constitutional right to "create and develop" new political parties. As a result, a state must demonstrate a "sufficiently weighty" interest in order to justify an access limitation for new parties. The state has such a weighty interest in preventing misrepresentation caused by unaffiliated groups from using the name of an established party. But the Court saw the categorical bar preventing candidates from one political subdivision from even using the name of a party established only in another as broader than necessary to protect against misrepresentation. The Court said that simply requiring candidates to obtain formal authorization to use the name of an established party would be "simply expedient for fostering an informed electorate without suppressing the growth of small parties." The Court then ruled that the requirement of 25,000 signatures per district was excessive. This number of signatures would qualify a candidate to run statewide. Further, there was no requirement for a candidate to demonstrate a distribution of support across the state. Qualification for the countywide ballot, on the other hand, required such distribution of support while also requiring twice as many signatures as a statewide candidate—25,000 for the city district and another 25,000 for the suburban district. Put another way, organizers of a new party could access the statewide ballot with 25,000 signatures from the city of Chicago yet fail to qualify for the Cook County ballot in the suburban district. Souter said if the state "deems it unimportant" to require new statewide parties to demonstrate any distribution of support, it "requires elusive logic to demonstrate a serious state interest in demanding such a distribution for new local parties." Souter then turned to the specific claim that the signatures collected in the city should qualify HWP candidates for all races within the county. Absent a claim that the county could not be legally divided into districts, the Court could only examine the signature requirement as applied to the suburban district. Twenty-five thousand signatures represented a support level of only "slightly more" than 2 percent of suburban voters, a "considerably more lenient restriction" than others previously upheld by the Court. Souter concluded: "Just as the State may not cite the Party's failure in the suburbs as reason for disqualifying its candidates in urban Cook County, neither may the Party cite its success in the city district as a sufficient condition for running candidates in the suburbs."

Most states prohibit candidates for public office from appearing on the ballot as the nominee of more than one political party. Minnesota has such an "antifusion" candidacy law, and it prevented the Twin Cities Area New Party from nominating a state legislative candidate who was already the candidate of one of the two major parties in the state. The fusion or cross-nomination strategy is often important to the viability of minor parties that would have no realistic chance of electing candidates on their own. The Twin Cities Area New Party unsuccessfully brought suit in federal district court, but the decision was reversed by the Court of Appeals for the Eighth Circuit. The Eighth Circuit held that the law violated New Party members' First Amendment right to associational expression. The Supreme Court reversed in *Timmons v. Twin Cities Area New Party* (137 L.Ed. 2d 589: 1997). Chief Justice Rehnquist said that the First Amendment protects the right of citizens to "associate and to form political parties for the advancement of common political goals and ideas." At the same time, "it is also clear that States may, and inevitably must, enact reasonable regulations of parties, elections, and ballots to reduce election and campaign-related disorder." The states have been granted "broad power" to prescribe the time, place, and manner of elections for federal offices, a power "matched by state control over the election process for state offices." When deciding whether a state election law violates associational rights, said Rehnquist, the Court must "weigh the 'character and magnitude' of the burden the State's rule imposes on those rights against the interests the State contends justify that burden." Regulations that impose "severe burdens" must advance a compelling interest and be narrowly tailored. Lesser burdens "trigger less exacting review," however, and a state's "important regulatory interests" are typically sufficient to justify "reasonable, nondiscriminatory restrictions." Rehnquist called the New Party's right to select its own candidates "uncontroversial," yet a party was not "absolutely entitled to have its nominee appear on the ballot as that party's candidate." The Minnesota law did not regulate the party's "internal affairs or core associational activities." Rather, it simply kept one party's candidate from appearing on the ballot "as that party's candidate, if already nominated by another party." The Minnesota law, in the Court's view, neither directly precluded minor political parties from "developing and organizing" nor "excluded a particular group of citizens, or a political party from participation in the election process." Thus, the New Party remains free to "endorse whom it likes, to ally itself with others, to nominate candidates for office, and to spread its message to all who will listen." The Court agreed that the ban on fusion candidacies did prevent the New Party from using the ballot to "communicate" its support of a particular candidate who is already another party's nominee. The Court was unpersuaded, however, by the party's claim that it has a right to use the ballot itself to "send a particularized message" to its candidates or voters. Ballots serve "primarily to elect candidates, not as fora for political expression." Even with the ban, the party retained "great latitude" to communicate ideas to voters through its participation in the campaign. In short, the Court concluded that the Minnesota ban did not restrict the ability of the party and its members to "endorse, support, and vote for anyone they like." The law was silent on the parties' "internal structure, governance, and policy-making," and the fusion ban did not directly limit ballot access by the party. The burdens imposed on the party's association rights, "though not trivial, are not severe." The Constitution, said Rehnquist, does not require that Minnesota "compromise the policy choices embodied in its ballot-access requirements to accommodate the New Party's fusion strategy." Minnesota possesses a valid interest in making sure that minor parties who are granted ballot access are "bona fide and actually supported, on their own merits, by those who have provided the statutorily required petition or ballot support." The states also possess a strong interest in the "stability of their political systems." These interests enable the states to enact reasonable election regulations that may, "in practice, favor the traditional two-party system." As a result, states "need not remove all the many hurdles third parties face in the American political arena today." Justice Stevens, in dissent, characterized the premises upon which the Court's conclusions were based as "dubious." It was Stevens's view that although the ballot is not primarily a forum for individual expression of political sentiment through the act of voting, it still serves an expressive function. Stevens saw a legitimate state interest in preventing political factionalism, but he suggested that the activity banned by the Minnesota policy was coalition formation, not the "division and dissension of 'splintered parties and unrestrained factionalism.'" Justice Ginsburg joined Stevens's dissent. Justice Souter also dissented but suggested he could uphold the ban on fusion tickets if it could be shown that such tickets undermined the two-party system.

***McIntyre v. Ohio Elections Commission*, 514 U.S. 334, 131 L.Ed. 2d 426, 115 S.Ct. 1511 (1995)** An Ohio statute required that the name and address of the person(s) or organizations(s) appear on any material designed to influence the outcome of the election. The Ohio Elections Commission found that Margaret McIntyre had violated the law by distributing unsigned campaign literature opposing a local tax initiative. McIntyre was fined $100 for the violation. The law and McIntyre's fine were eventually upheld by the Ohio Supreme Court. The U.S. Supreme Court, however, declared the Ohio law unconstitutional in *McIntyre.* An author's decision to remain anonymous, said Justice Stevens, like other decisions concerning publication content, is "an aspect of the freedom of speech protected by the First Amendment." Anonymity provides a way for a writer who may be "personally unpopular" to ensure that the readers will not prejudice a message "simply because they do not like the proponent." Ohio sought to justify the regulation as a means of preventing dissemination of untruths. The Court was unpersuaded, however, noting that the Ohio statute contained no language limiting its application to fraudulent, false, or libelous statements. Instead, the category of speech regulated by Ohio, said Stevens, "occupies the core of the protection afforded by the First Amendment." Discussion of political issues must be afforded the broadest constitutional protection in order to ensure the fullest possible debate. The views conveyed by McIntyre's leaflets were viewed as the "essence of First Amendment expression." Indeed, Stevens suggested that "no form of speech is entitled to greater constitutional protection." And though deterrence of misleading or false statements was regarded as a legitimate state interest, the Court was satisfied that Ohio had other means of protecting that interest without the "extremely broad" prohibition on anonymous expression. The state's interest of informing the public was also seen as insufficient to justify the ban on anonymous speech. The identity of a speaker is "no different from other components of [a] document's content that the author is free to include or exclude." The simple interest in providing voters with additional relevant information "does not justify a state requirement that a writer make statements or disclosures she would otherwise omit." Anonymous pamphleteering, Stevens concluded, is "not a pernicious, fraudulent practice, but an honorable tradition of advocacy and of dissent." Anonymity is a "shield from the tyranny of the majority." The right to remain anonymous "may be abused when it shields fraudulent conduct," but political speech inherently has "unpalatable consequences." And although Ohio can attempt to regulate fraud directly, it cannot seek to punish fraud indirectly by "indiscriminately outlawing a category of speech, based on its content, with no necessary relationship to the danger sought to be prevented." One would be "hard pressed" to think of a better example of the "pitfalls of Ohio's blunderbuss approach than the facts of the case before us." Justice Thomas preferred an approach that examined whether the Free Speech Clause, as "originally understood," protected anonymous leafleting. He concluded that it did and voted to strike down the Ohio law. Justice Scalia, joined by Chief Justice Rehnquist, dissented. They were troubled by the use of the First Amendment to erode decisionmaking authority of the states. Scalia also suggested that there was little reason to believe that a "right to be unknown while engaging in electoral politics" reflected society's views at the times the First and Fourteenth Amendments were ratified. Scalia then turned to three conclusions he regarded as essential to deciding the case. First, protection of the election process is a most compelling interest, one that "justifies limitations upon speech that cannot constitutionally be imposed generally." Second, a "right to anonymity" was not seen as a prominent value in our constitutional system that even protection of the electoral process cannot be purchased at its expense." Finally, Scalia and Rehnquist were convinced that the ban on anonymous campaigning was effective in protecting democratic elections. A person who is required to put his or her name on a document is "much less likely to lie than one who can lie anonymously." The Ohio law, Scalia suggested, not only deters campaign falsehoods but also promotes a "civil and dignified level of campaign debate—which the State has no power to command, but ample power to encourage by such undemanding measures as a signature requirement." *See also* FEDERALISM, p. 29.

Significance The Court has upheld restrictions on electioneering near polling places and write-in voting. In *Burson v. Freeman* (504 U.S. 191: 1992), a five-justice majority permitted a state to ban political activities, including the distribution of political campaign materials, within 100 feet of a polling place on election day. Upon examination of the history of election regulations, the Court found a "wide-spread and time-tested consensus that some restricted zone is necessary to serve the States' compelling interest in preventing voter intimidation and election fraud." The regulation had been challenged as both over- and underinclusive. The Court concluded that the law was neither. Less-inclusive regulations reach only the "most blatant and specific attempts to impede elections." The underinclusive argument focused on the content-based character of the restriction: It only regulated political expression around polling places. Justice Blackmun said that failure to regulate all speech does not "render the statute fatally underinclusive." The Court found no evidence that political candidates "have used other forms of solicitation or exit polling to commit such electoral abuses [as voter intimidation or fraud]." Blackmun focused on the secret ballot as an integral effort to curb electoral abuses. The only way to preserve the secrecy of the ballot, he argued, "is to limit access to the area around the voter." The dissenters saw the law as a restriction of speech based on content. As such, the law "somewhat perversely disfavors speech that normally is accorded greater protection than the kinds of speech that the statute does not regulate." Creation of campaign-free zones may protect orderly access to the polls but, at the same time, prevents last-minute campaigning. It was the dissenters' view that this regulation unnecessarily "hindered" the latter.

***U.S. Term Limits, Inc. v. Thornton,* 514 U.S. 779, 131 L.Ed. 2d 881, 115 S.Ct. 1842 (1995)** By 1995, 23 states had adopted some form of term limits on members of Congress. The voters of Arkansas adopted a constitutional amendment in 1992 (Amendment 73) effectively limiting membership in the U.S. House of Representatives to three terms (six years) and that in the U.S. Senate to two terms (12 years). Specifically, Amendment 73 prohibited placing on the ballot the name of an otherwise qualified candidate for Congress if that candidate had already served three terms in the House or two terms in the Senate. The amendment did permit incumbents who reached the term limits to run and be reelected through write-in campaigns. Suits were filed in an Arkansas court, challenging the constitutionality of Amendment 73. There were a number of plaintiffs, including Congressman Ray Thornton. Various organizations supporting term limits, including U.S. Term Limits, Inc., intervened as defendants. An Arkansas circuit court found that Amendment 73 was unconstitutional because it was incompatible with language in Article I, Section 2 of the U.S. Constitution, which establishes qualifications for members of Congress. The Arkansas Supreme Court affirmed. In a 5-4 decision in *U.S. Term Limits, Inc. v. Thornton,* the U.S. Supreme Court also ruled against Amendment 73. Justice Stevens, speaking for the majority, said the constitutionality of Amendment 73 "depends critically" on the resolution of two issues. The first was whether the Constitution prohibits states from adding to or altering the qualifications "specifically enumerated" in Article I. Second, if the Constitution does forbid such change, the issue of whether Amendment 73 was a ballot-access restriction rather than an "outright disqualification" of otherwise qualified incumbents must be resolved. The Court was substantially guided by the Court's ruling in *Powell v. McCormack,* (395 U.S. 486: 1969). The issue in *Powell* was whether Congress's power to judge the qualifications of its own members included the power to impose qualifications other than those enumerated in Article I. The Court concluded in *Powell* that it did not. The Court recognized that the ratification debates "confirmed that the framers understood the qualifications in the Constitution to be fixed and unalterable by Congress." The Court also noted in *Powell* that allowing Congress to impose additional qualifications "would violate that fundamental principle of our representative democracy . . . that the people should choose whom they please to govern them." Indeed, Stevens suggested that the relevant historical materials "compelled" these conclusions. The Court also rejected the argument that because *Powell* dealt with the House's power to exclude a member it did not control the more general question of whether Congress has the power to add qualifications. *Powell,* said Stevens, is "not susceptible to such a narrow reading." *Powell,* however, does not reach the question of whether the Constitution prohibits additional qualifications imposed by states.

The supporters of term limits argued that in the absence of an explicit constitutional prohibition the reserved powers of the Tenth Amendment should allow states to add such qualifications. The Court was unpersuaded for two reasons. First, historical materials show that the framers drew a basic distinction between the powers of the newly created national government and the powers retained by the preexisting states. Contrary to the assertions of those supporting Amendment 73, the power to add qualifications is not part of the original powers of sovereignty that the Tenth Amendment reserved to the states. Petitioners' Tenth Amendment argument, said Stevens, "misconceives the nature of the right at issue because [the Tenth] amendment could only 'reserve' that which existed before." Second, even if states had some original power on this subject, the Court concluded that the Framers intended the Constitution to be "the exclusive source of qualifications for members of Congress" and that the framers "divested" states of any power to add qualifications. When the framers decided to create an entirely new national government at the Constitutional Convention, they "envisioned a uniform national system, rejecting the notion that the nation was a collection of states, and instead creating a direct link between the national Government and the people of the United States." The framers recognized that electing representatives to the national legislature was a "new right" arising from the Constitution itself. The Tenth

Amendment thus provided no basis for concluding that the states had authority to add qualifications beyond those fixed in Article I. Rather, any power states might have to set congressional membership qualifications must derive from the delegated powers of national sovereignty. In the absence of explicit delegation of such power to states, states' power to add qualifications does not exist. Further, permitting states to fashion diverse qualifications for members of Congress, said Stevens, would result in a "patchwork of state qualifications, undermining the uniformity and the national character that the framers envisioned and sought to ensure. . . ." Stevens suggested that the issue of term limits has been debated, because the framers unanimously rejected such restrictions; he indicated that it is not the Court's "province to resolve this longstanding debate." The Court further concluded that allowing states to adopt term limits for Congress would "effect a fundamental change in the constitutional framework." A change of that kind cannot come from legislation adopted by either Congress or the states but must come through the amendment procedures set out by the Constitution in Article V.

Justice Thomas issued a lengthy dissent that was joined by Chief Justice Rehnquist and Justices O'Connor and Scalia. He began by pointing out the irony of the Court's recognition of the people's right to freely choose their representatives—yet not allowing elected legislatures or the people themselves through ballot initiatives to "prescribe any qualifications for those representatives." It was the dissenters' view that nothing in the Constitution bars the people of each state the power to establish eligibility requirements for candidates. When the Constitution is "silent" on an issue, it "raises no bar to action by the states or the people." Thomas also disputed the Court's concept of "reserved" powers. The people of the states, he suggested, "need not point to any affirmative grant of power in the Constitution in order to prescribe qualifications for their representatives." Where the Constitution does not speak explicitly or implicitly about the exercise of a particular power, the "Federal Government lacks that power and the states enjoy it." Thomas also disagreed with the Court's conclusion that states could not "reserve" any powers that they did not control at the time the Constitution was written. It was not the state governments that were "doing the reserving." Rather, the Constitution derives its authority from consent of the people of the states. Thomas called it "incoherent" to contend that the people of the states could not "reserve any powers that they had not previously controlled." Finally, Thomas suggested that the Court had made more of the Qualifications Clauses than was appropriate. The clauses restrict state power only in that they keep states from ignoring or abolishing "all eligibility requirements for membership in Congress." Historical evidence is "simply insufficient" to warrant the Court's conclusion that the

Article I provisions on qualifications mean "any more than they say." The Qualifications Clauses give the people of other states no basis to complain if the people of Arkansas elect a new representative in preference to a long-term incumbent. Similarly, it is "hard to see why the rights of the people of other states have been violated when the people of Arkansas decide to enact a more general disqualification of long-term incumbents." As long as the candidate sent to Congress meets the age, citizenship, and inhabitancy requirements of Article I, the "people of Arkansas have not violated the Qualifications Clauses." *See also* FEDERALISM, p. 29; TENTH AMENDMENT, p. 229.

Significance The Supreme Court defined the course federal terms limits advocates must pursue in the *Thornton* ruling. The question in Thornton was whether state-initiated term limits on federal representatives come under the Qualifications Clauses of Article I, Section 2. One view is that a member of Congress can be disqualified from office only on the basis of age, citizenship, or residency and that a term limit is an additional disqualifying factor. Proponents of term limits respond by arguing that states may regulate as they wish so long as that regulation is consistent with the qualifying requirements set forth in Article I. Those subscribing to this view argue that term limits regulate the election of federal officials and not the qualifications of those seeking federal office. The Supreme Court ruled that term limits add a qualification to those enumerated in Article I. As a qualification, it can only take effect if formally adopted as an amendment to Article I, Section 2. The chances of establishing term limits through the constitutional amendment process are limited. The issue of term limits was before Congress as part of the Republican "Contract with America" in 1995. Notwithstanding public support for term limits, congressional incumbents were not enthusiastic. No amendment resolution emerged from the debate because it was impossible to assemble the necessary two-thirds vote on any specific proposal. The only other way an amendment can be initiated is by application of the legislatures of two-thirds of the states. No amendment has been initiated in this way, and history suggests it is unlikely to happen on the question of term limits.

Privileges and Immunities of Citizenship

***Supreme Court of Virginia v. Friedman*, 487 U.S. 59, 101 L.Ed. 2d 56, 108 S.Ct. 2260 (1988)** Virginia Supreme Court Rule 1A:1 allowed attorneys admitted to practice in another state to be admitted to the Virginia bar without taking the state's bar examination provided the applicant was a permanent resident of Virginia. Myrna Friedman practiced law from her employer's Virginia place of business. She was denied application for admission to the Virginia bar because she was a Maryland resident. The Court ruled that a nonresident's interest in practicing law "on terms of substantial equality with those enjoyed by residents" is protected by the Privileges and Immunities Clause of Article 4, Section 2. The clause was designed to place the citizens of each state "upon the same footing with citizens of other States." When reviewing claims that a citizenship or residency classification violates the clause, the Court undertakes a "two-step" inquiry. First, the activity must be "sufficiently basic to the livelihood of the Nation" in order to come under the purview of the Privileges and Immunities Clause. Second, if the challenged regulation "deprives nonresidents of a protected privilege," it will be invalidated only if the Court concludes it is not "closely related to the advancement of a substantial State interest." The clause does not "preclude disparity in treatment" where substantial reasons exist for such disparity and the "degree of discrimination bears a close relation to such reasons." In reviewing the latter question the Court has considered whether "within the full panoply of legislative choices otherwise available to the State, there exist alternative means of furthering the State's purpose without implicating constitutional concerns." Virginia asserted that the residency and full-time practice requirements would help "assure that attorneys admitted the integrity and standards of the bar." The question, however, is whether lawyers who are admitted in other states and then seek admission in Virginia are "less likely to respect the bar and further its interests solely because they are nonresidents." The Court concluded this was not the case. The Court referred to Friedman's Maryland residence as of "scant relevance" and found "indisputable" that she had a "substantial stake in the practice of law in Virginia." The Court also rejected the residency restriction as necessary to aid the enforcement of the full-time practice requirement. A requirement that an applicant maintain an office in Virginia "facilitates compliance" with the full-time practice requirement in "nearly the identical manner that the residency restriction does, rendering the latter restriction largely redundant." The office requirement furnishes an alternative to the residency requirement that is "not only less restrictive, but also is fully adequate to protect whatever interest the State might have in the full-time practice restriction." *See also* FEDERALISM, p. 29; *HICKLIN v. ORBECK* (437 U.S. 518: 1978), p. 453; PRIVILEGES AND IMMUNITIES CLAUSES, p. 647; TENTH AMENDMENT, p. 229.

Significance The Privileges and Immunities Clauses of Article IV and the Fourteenth Amendment protect benefits flowing from one's status as a citizen. The basic purpose of these clauses was to ensure that out-of-state citizens receive the same treatment as a state's own citizens. Put another way, the clauses were designed to establish a "norm of comity" that protects basic equality of treatment. This equality of treatment is not absolute. If a state can show "substantial reason," it may introduce certain policies that give advantage to state residents. Higher nonresident tuition rates at state universities is an example. Generally, however, differential treatment is unconstitutional. In *Hicklin v. Orbeck* (437 U.S. 518: 1978), the Court struck down a state law that attempted to reserve jobs in the gas and oil development industry for qualified state residents. The Court found that the resident preference violated the Commerce Clause and Equal Protection Clause in addition to the Privileges and Immunities Clause. These clauses were seen as having a "reinforcing" relationship with respect to limiting state authority under particular circumstances.

Equal Footing Doctrine

***Utah Division of State Lands v. United States*, 482 U.S. 193, 96 L.Ed. 2d 162, 107 S.Ct. 2318 (1987)** Ruled that Utah obtained title to lake bed beneath navigable water upon admission to the Union. The federal government issued oil and gas leases in 1976 for land under Utah Lake, a navigable body of water in Utah. The state brought suit, asserting that under the "equal footing" doctrine it had acquired title to this land when it became a state in 1894. The Supreme Court agreed. A law had been passed in 1888 that authorized the U.S. Geological Survey to "select sites for reservoirs and other hydraulic works necessary for the storage and utilization of water for irrigation." The lower courts had ruled that the federal government had "reserved" all the land that might have been designated for this purpose. Utah contended that the federal government could not create a federal reservation in this way and could only "defeat a State's title to land under navigable waters" by conveying the land to a third party. The Property Clause of Article IV gives Congress plenary power to "regulate and dispose of land within the Territories." It was Utah's view that although the federal government could create a reservoir site by granting title to Utah Lake to a "private entity" it could not "accomplish the same purpose by a means that would keep Utah Lake under federal control." The Court concluded that the 1888 law did not "make sufficiently clear either a congressional intent to include the bed of Utah lake within the reservation or an intent to defeat Utah's claim to title under the equal footing doctrine." Justices Brennan, Marshall, and Stevens disagreed with the Court. It was their view that Congress has the power to reserve land for an appropriate public purpose and did so with the 1888 statute. *See also* ADMISSION OF NEW STATES, p. 575; FEDERALISM, p. 29.

Significance It has been the case since the inception of our constitutional history that states automatically obtained title to land underlying all navigable waters upon admission to the United States. This practice is derived from the "equal footing" doctrine, which provides that any state entering the Union does so on an "equal footing" with the original states. The original 13 states had title to such land, and the equal footing doctrine says that new states should possess the same ownership rights. The doctrine is not always easily applied. There are many areas, such as tidal lands or coastal wetlands, that are not navigable or were not at the time states were admitted to the Union. The issue in *Phillips Petroleum v. Mississippi* (482 U.S. 469: 1988) was whether states acquired title to land under nonnavigable waters under the equal footing doctrine. In a 5-3 decision, the Court ruled that all land under water "subject to the ebb and flow of the tide" was passed to the states as a public trust upon their entry into the Union, regardless of whether such waters are navigable. The effect of this decision was to reaffirm the "public trust" doctrine, which underlies many environmental protection policies at the state level. The Court was careful to point out in *Phillips Petroleum* that the decision "does nothing to change ownership rights in States which previously relinquished a public trust claim to tidelands" such as those at issue in this case.

Environmental Protection

***New York v. United States*, 505 U.S. 144, 120 L.Ed. 2d 120, 112 S.Ct. 2408 (1992)** Struck down the Low-Level Radioactive Waste Policy Act of 1980. At issue in this case was the "take-title" provisions of the act as amended in 1985, which required states to either enact laws providing for the disposal of such waste generated within their borders or to take title to the waste, "effectively requiring the states either to legislate pursuant to Congress's directions, or to implement an administrative solution." The Court concluded that Congress "could require the state to do neither." Congress may not simply "commandeer the legislative processes of the States by directly compelling them to enact and enforce a federal regulatory program." The Court acknowledged that Congress has the ability to "encourage" the states to regulate in a particular way. Justice O'Connor mentioned the spending power and interstate commerce power as specific means through which such encouragement might occur. Accountability was a critical consideration. Where Congress encourages rather than compels, state governments remain "responsive to the local electorate's preferences" and state officials "remain accountable to the people." On the other hand, when the federal government compels states to regulate, the "accountability of both state and federal officials is diminished." Where the federal government directs the states to regulate, it may be the state official who "bears the brunt of public disapproval," whereas the federal officials who devised the regulatory program may remain "insulated from the electoral ramifications of their decisions." Accountability is thus diminished when, "due to federal coercion," elected state officials cannot regulate "in accordance with the views of the local electorate in matters not pre-empted by federal regulation." The United States contended that the ban on congressional directives to state governments can be overcome where the federal interest is "sufficiently important to justify state submission." The Court responded by saying that regardless of how powerful the federal interest involved the Constitution "simply does not give Congress the authority to require the States to regulate." Where a federal interest is strong enough to prompt congressional action, Congress must legislate "directly; it may not conscript state governments as its agents."

The Court responded to an interesting process question in this case. A number of New York officials supported the act and were among those joining the federal government defending the law. The question posed was this: How can a federal law be found unconstitutional due to encroachment of state sovereignty when state officials supported the enactment and representatives of New York voted for the law's adoption? Justice O'Connor suggested the answer "follows from an understanding of the fundamental purpose served by our Government's federal structure." The Constitution does not protect state sovereignty "for the benefit of the States or state governments as abstract political entities, or even for the benefit of public officials governing the States." Rather, divided authority is designed for the "protection of individuals." Accordingly, when Congress exceeds its authority relative to the states, the "departure from the constitutional plan cannot be ratified by the 'consent' of state officials," as state officials cannot authorize the enlargement of congressional powers "beyond those enumerated in the Constitution." The Constitution, O'Connor concluded, "protects us from our own best intentions: It divides power among sovereigns and among branches of government precisely so that we may resist the temptation to concentrate power in one location as an expedient solution to the crisis of the day." O'Connor acknowledged that the shortage of disposal sites for radioactive waste is a "pressing national problem." A judiciary, however, that "licensed extra-constitutional government with each issue of comparable gravity would, in the long run, be far worse." *See also* COMMERCE CLAUSE, p. 291; *FEDERAL ENERGY REGULATORY COMMISSION v. MISSISSIPPI* (456 U.S. 742: 1982), p. 362; FEDERALISM, p. 29; TENTH AMENDMENT, p. 229.

Significance The strongly worded lesson of *New York v. United States* reflects the thinking of a majority of the justices in the mid-1990s. A clear example is found in *Printz v. United States* and its companion case, *Mack v. United States* (138 L.Ed. 2d 914: 1997). Since 1968, the Gun Control Act has required firearm dealers to be licensed by the federal government. The 1968 act also required certification that persons who buy firearms from federally licensed dealers are not, among other things, convicted felons, undocumented aliens, users of controlled substances, or subject to any restraining order based on domestic assault. The Handgun Violence Prevention Act enacted by Congress in 1993 (more commonly known as the "Brady Act" after James Brady, the former presidential press secretary who was severely wounded in the assassination attempted on President Ronald Reagan in 1981) amended the earlier act by passing on some implementation responsibilities to state and local law enforcement officials. Specifically, local authorities were required to conduct background checks on those seeking to purchase handguns, at least for the short term. New technology is supposed to make it possible for gun dealers to immediately and directly check the background of a prospective gun buyer. The Brady check requirement at issue in *Printz* expires in November 1998. In this case, two county sheriffs, one in Montana (Jay Printz) and one in Arizona (Richard Mack), challenged the background-check, arguing that the commerce power could not provide the basis for the provision and that the Tenth Amendment precluded Congress from imposing such requirements on state and local officials. The Supreme Court agreed. Since there is no constitutional text that speaks directly to this question, the answer must be sought in "historical understanding and practice, in the structure of the Constitution, and in the jurisprudence of this Court." Justice Scalia began with the "incontestable" premise that the Constitution established a system of "dual sovereignty"; although the states "surrendered many of their powers to the new Federal Government," they retained a "residuary and inviolable sovereignty."

Scalia relied heavily on the *New York v. United States* ruling for his majority opinion that struck down a law that "unambiguously required the states to enact or administer a Federal regulatory program." Given the decision in *New York v. United States,* the ruling in *Printz* "should come as no surprise," said Scalia. The "cluster of arguments" advanced in support of the Brady Act "might be relevant" if the Court were considering whether the "incidental application" of a federal law of general applicability to the states "excessively interfered with the functioning of state governments." Such "incidental application" does not occur in this case. Rather, the "whole effect" of the law is to "direct the functioning of the state executive, and hence to compromise the structural framework of dual sovereignty." Scalia considered it "inappropriate" to use a balancing approach on a question of this magnitude. It is the "very principle of separate state sovereignty that such a law offends, and no comparative assessment of the various interests can overcome that fundamental defect." The Court "categorically" reaffirmed the principle contained in *New York v. United States* that the federal government "may not compel the states to enact or administer a Federal regulatory program." The mandatory obligation imposed on the chief law enforcement officers at the local level to perform background checks on prospective handgun purchasers "plainly runs afoul of that rule." Congress cannot "circumvent that prohibition by conscripting the state's officers directly." The federal government, Scalia continued, "may neither issue directives requiring the state to address particular problems, nor command the states' officers, or those of their political subdivisions, to administer or enforce a Federal regulatory program." Such commands are "fundamentally incompatible with our constitutional system of dual sovereignty." In a concurring opinion, Justice Thomas expressed the view that the congressional commerce power does not extend to the regulation of "wholly intrastate" transactions. Absent the underlying authority to regulate the intrastate transfer of firearms, "Congress surely lacks the corollary power to impress state law enforcement officers into administering and enforcing such regulations." Justices Stevens, Souter, Ginsburg, and Breyer dissented. Justice Stevens suggested that when Congress exercises the powers assigned it by the Constitution it may "impose affirmative obligations on executive and judicial officers of state and local governments as well as ordinary citizens." If Congress concludes that statutes like the Brady Act will "benefit the people of the nation, and serve the interests of cooperative federalism better than an enlarged Federal bureaucracy, we should respect both its policy judgment and its appraisal of its constitutional power."

Preemption Doctrine

***Anderson v. Edwards*, 514 U.S. 143, 131 L.Ed. 2d 178, 115 S.Ct. 1291 (1995)** Aid to Families with Dependent Children (AFDC) is a federal welfare program created under the Social Security Act of 1935.

The program is jointly funded by federal and state governments. AFDC is administered by participating states under regulations formulated by the states and approved by the federal Department of Health and Human Services. As long as states remain within limits set by federal law, they are generally able to define eligibility requirements and establish benefit levels. The Court considered challenges to two California welfare provisions in *Anderson v. Edwards* and *Anderson v. Green* (513 U.S. 557: 1995). The question in *Edwards* was whether a state can reduce program benefits through the creation of an assistance unit by grouping sibling and nonsibling children living in the same household into a single unit for purposes of determining AFDC benefits. A unanimous Court upheld California's new rule on assistance units. Justice Thomas delivered the opinion of the Court. The issue in this case was whether federal welfare law prohibits a state from grouping all needy children (whether or not they are siblings) living in the same household under the care of one adult into a single "assistance unit" (AU). The consolidation of two or more AUs into a single AU under the California rule decreased the maximum per-capita AFDC benefits for which the affected children are eligible. Ms. Edwards's situation is illustrative. As the caretaker of her granddaughter, Edwards was eligible for maximum aid benefits of $341 monthly. Subsequently, she became caretaker of her two grandnieces (who were siblings). The grandnieces were initially grouped together as a separate AU. The maximum benefits for this two-person AU was $560 monthly. Edwards received the maximum of $901 monthly in AFDC benefits for the three girls since none of the children received any outside income. Under the California rule, the three girls were grouped together into a single AU and eligible for maximum monthly payments of $694, $207 less per month compared to benefit payments received for two separate AUs. The Court must be cognizant of the "cardinal principle," said Thomas, that federal law "gives each State great latitude in dispensing available funds." From this perspective, the Court concluded that California was not precluded from adopting the new rule. Edwards's granddaughter received $341 in monthly benefits prior to the arrival of the grandnieces. After the grandnieces entered her household, the granddaughter's per-capita benefits were reduced to $231.33 (one-third of $694). Edwards argued that the reduction of the granddaughter's per-capita benefits was solely the result of the presence of the grandnieces, children who were "non-legally responsible individuals" in relation to the granddaughter. Thomas dismissed this argument as "simply wrong." The presence of the grandnieces was not solely responsible for the decline in per-capita benefits for the granddaughter. To be sure, the grandnieces were part of Edwards's household. Equally important was that the application for AFDC assistance for the grandnieces came through Edwards. Had the grandnieces not applied for AFDC assistance or applied through a different caretaker relative living in that home, the California rule would not have affected the granddaughter's level of benefits. Thomas suggested in a footnote that California is "simply recognizing the economies of scale" that inhere in multiple recipients sharing the same household. The Court also rejected contentions that the rule violated income "availability" regulations (regulations dealing with income other than AFDC received by one or more members of the AU). California may "rationally assume," said Thomas, that caretakers such as Edwards will "observe her duties to all members of the AU and will take into account the receipt of any outside income by one child when expending funds on behalf of the AU."

Green involved a challenge to a California policy adopted in late 1992 that capped for one year a new resident's benefits to the level of benefits that would have been received had the person remained in his or her former state of residence. Green and others asserted that the requirement discriminated against new residents. A federal court enjoined implementation of the residency requirement on the grounds that it violated the right to freely move from state to state. The Court of Appeals for the Ninth Circuit affirmed. The Supreme Court did not reach the merits of the challenge, however. Rather, the Court ruled that there was no justiciable controversy. The California law provided that the new policy could not take effect without receipt of a waiver from the Secretary of Health and Human Services (HHS). Such a waiver was secured near the end of George Bush's term as president and was in effect when the lower courts ruled in this case. After the court of appeals rendered its judgment, it set aside the HHS waiver in another case on the grounds that the objections to the California policy had not been adequately considered. The Clinton administration did not appeal that ruling, nor did it issue a new waiver in response to California's renewed application. Without a new waiver, California must treat Green and anyone else similarly situated as it treats long-term residents of California. As a consequence, the parties have "no live dispute now, and whether one will arise in the future is conjectural." *See also* FEDERALISM, p. 29; PREEMPTION DOCTRINE, p. 645; STANDING, p. 655; *STEWARD MACHINE COMPANY v. DAVIS* (301 U.S. 548: 1937), p. 391.

Significance The preemption doctrine is derived from the Supremacy Clause in Article IV. It directs that federal laws can supersede or preempt state law in certain policy areas. Although there are guidelines for its application, the Court is periodically required to determine whether federal and state policy may coexist. Some distinctions in how the preemption doctrine applies are illustrated in the several cases that follow.

Congress passed the Emergency Petroleum Allocation Act (EPAA) in 1973. The law required the president to develop regulations for the allocation and pricing of petroleum products. The EPAA expressly preempted state and local allocation and pricing regulations if they were incompatible with the federal regulations. The president's regulatory authority was to end in 1975 but was extended until late 1981. In 1986, the Puerto Rico Consumer Affairs Department issued regulations requiring advance notice of any price increases in petroleum products. Several oil companies brought an action in federal district court, claiming that the regulations were unconstitutional on preemption grounds. The district court agreed and enjoined enforcement of the regulations, finding them preempted by Congress's initial decision to regulate petroleum prices. The Supreme Court reversed in *Puerto Rico Department of Consumer Affairs v. Isla Petroleum Corp.* (485 U.S. 495: 1988). The oil companies argued that the EPAA and subsequent amendments conveyed a federal intent to fully occupy the field of petroleum allocation and price regulation and that the expiration of presidential regulatory authority did not constitute a change from that intent. The Court acknowledged that Congress could mandate free-market control but concluded that state police powers "are not superseded by a federal statute unless that is the clear and manifest purpose of Congress." Since Congress had withdrawn from all "substantial involvement" in petroleum allocation and price regulation, there was no remaining policy that could "create an interference of preemption in an unregulated segment of an otherwise regulated field."

The Occupational Safety and Health Act of 1970 granted the Occupational Safety and Health Administration (OSHA) general authority to develop regulations in furtherance of the objectives of the act. OSHA fashioned regulations pursuant to provisions of the Superfund Reauthorization Act governing the training of workers who handle hazardous waste. Illinois subsequently enacted laws requiring the licensing of workers at hazardous waste sites. Both Illinois laws had the declared purpose of protecting workers and the public safety. The National Solid Wastes Management Association sought to enjoin enforcement of the state laws on preemption grounds. The U.S. district court ruled that the state laws were not preempted because of the declared public safety objective. The Court of Appeals for the Seventh Circuit, however, ruled that the act preempted all state law that "clearly and substantially" regulated worker health and safety without the explicit approval of the secretary of labor. The Supreme Court agreed. In *Gade v. National Solid Wastes Management Association* (505 U.S. 88: 1992) the Court ruled that a state law that "directly and substantially regulates occupational safety" is preempted despite its having another nonoccupational purpose. The Court does not rely exclusively on the legislature's "professed purpose" but on the law's effects as well. Although the Illinois laws had some "saving provisions" that were not preempted by the act, those provisions cannot shield from preemption the other provisions that "affect workplace safety." Any state law, no matter how clearly within a state's "acknowledged power, must yield if it interferes with or is contrary to a federal law." Similarly, the Illinois laws cannot be saved from preemption because they regulate a "precondition" to employment such as training rather than occupational safety as such. The substance of the act demonstrated to the Court that Congress intended to promote occupational health and safety while "avoiding subjecting workers to duplicative regulation."

Goodyear Atomic Corp., a private company, operated the Portsmouth Gaseous Diffusion Plant. The plant is a nuclear production facility owned by the federal government. Esto Miller, an employee of Goodyear Atomic, was injured in an accident at the facility and received benefits under the Ohio workers' compensation laws. Miller claimed that his injury was caused by Goodyear Atomic's violation of a state safety requirement. Under Ohio law, the Ohio Industrial Commission may award additional benefits if an injury was caused by an employer's failure to comply with particular state safety requirements. The commission, however, denied Miller's claim, concluding that Ohio safety regulations did not apply to the nuclear facility on federal preemption grounds. Miller obtained a writ of mandamus from the Ohio Court of Appeals, which ruled that until it was clear that federal preemption covered more than radiation safety regulations Ohio's regulations applied to the nuclear facility. This decision was affirmed by the Supreme Court of Ohio. The U.S. Supreme Court affirmed in *Goodyear Atomic Corp. v. Miller* (486 U.S. 174: 1988). Activities at federal installations are shielded by the Supremacy Clause from direct state regulation unless Congress provides "clear and unambiguous" authorization for such regulation. In *Goodyear,* however, the Court was "not presented with a direct state regulation" of the operation of the Portsmouth facility. Rather, this case involved the "imposition of a supplemental award of workers' compensation," chargeable against Goodyear for an injury caused by its failure to comply with a state safety regulation. In the absence of "affirmative evidence" in the language of applicable federal law, the Court was "unwilling to assume that Congress was ignorant of the substantial number of States to provide additional workers' compensation awards when a state safety regulation was violated by the employer." In fact, it appeared to the Court that Congress recognized the "diversity of workers' compensation schemes when it provided that workers' compensation would be awarded to workers on federal premises in the same way and to the same extent as provided by state law." The Court found it "clear" that Congress intended Ohio's statute and others like it, which were "solidly entrenched" when Congress enacted Federal workers' compensation laws, to apply to federal facilities "to the same extent" that they apply to private facilities within the state. Congress's reluctance to allow direct state regulation of federal projects, the Court concluded, "says little" about whether Congress was likewise concerned with the "incidental regulatory effects arising from the enforcement of a workers' compensation law like Ohio's that provides additional award when the injury is caused by the breach of a safety regulation." The effects of direct regulation on the operation of federal projects are "significantly more intrusive than the incidental regulatory effects of such an additional award provision."

The Airline Deregulation Act of 1978 (ADA) contained a preemption provision that prohibited states from enforcing any laws relating to the "rates, routes, or services" of air carriers. This provision was adopted to prevent states from interfering with the expected benefits of federal deregulation of the airline industry. The Court reviewed two cases stemming from the preemption provisions of ADA. In the first, the Texas attorney general notified several airlines of his intent to apply the state's consumer protection laws against their allegedly deceptive fare advertisements. The airlines filed suit in U.S. district court, seeking to enjoin enforcement of the state laws on preemption grounds. The district court permanently enjoined any state enforcement activity that would limit any aspect of their fare advertising or any other operations involving rates, routes, or services. The Court of Appeals for the Fifth Circuit affirmed. The Supreme Court affirmed in *Morales v. Trans World Airlines, Inc.* (504 U.S. 374: 1992), finding the fare advertising issue to fall within the preemption provisions of ADA. The Court concluded that the advertising restrictions and the disclosures that would have been compelled by intended state action would have a "significant impact on the airlines' ability to market their product, and hence a significant impact upon the fares they charge."

American Airlines, Inc. v. Wolens (513 U.S. 219: 1995) involved consolidated class actions brought in Illinois court challenging retroactive changes American Airlines made in its frequent-flyer program. It was plaintiffs' contention that the retroactive changes to previously credited mileage violated the Illinois Consumer Fraud Act. The class also asserted that the changes constituted a breach of contract. American Airlines argued in response that the ADA preempted the plaintiffs' claims.

The Illinois Supreme Court ruled that the plaintiffs' claims were not affected by the *Morales* ruling because they were only "tangentially related" to rates and that frequent-flyer programs were "peripheral" to American's operations. The Supreme Court decided that although ADA's preemption language generally bars state regulation of air carriers it does allow for court enforcement of contract terms "set by the parties themselves." The ADA does not preclude state court adjudication of "routine breach of contract claims" that exclusively seek recovery for the airline's "breach of its own, self-imposed undertakings."

***City of New York v. Federal Communications Commission*, 486 U.S. 57, 100 L.Ed. 2d 48, 108 S.Ct. 1637 (1988)** The Cable Communications Policy Act of 1984 (CCPA) authorized state and local governments to enfranchise cable systems and specify the facilities and equipment that could be used by franchise holders. The CCPA also authorized the Federal Communications Commission (FCC) to establish technical standards for such facilities and equipment. The FCC set standards for the quality of cable signals and prohibited state or local authorities from imposing more rigorous technical standards. The city of New York sought review in the U.S. Court of Appeals for the District of Columbia Circuit, challenging the scope of the FCC's preemptive authority. As a franchise authority, the city argued it should be able to impose more stringent standards than those set by the FCC. The court of appeals upheld the FCC regulations. The Supreme Court agreed in *City of New York v. Federal Communications Commission* (486 U.S. 57: 1988). Justice White said it has "long been recognized" that many of the responsibilities conferred on federal agencies involve a "broad grant of authority to reconcile conflicting policies." The determination of whether a federal agency has exclusive or preemptive authority in a given area does not necessarily require explicit congressional authorization. Instead, the proper focus is on the agency itself and on the "proper bounds of its lawful authority to undertake such action." If an agency's decision to preempt represents a "reasonable accommodation of conflicting policies committed to the agency's care" under the law, the accommodation "should not be disturbed unless it appears from the statute or its legislative history that the accommodation is not one that Congress would have sanctioned." When the CCPA was enacted in 1984, FCC regulations preempting the field of signal-quality regulation were already in place. Congress acted "against a 10-year background of federal preemption" on this issue and did not indicate any disapproval of the FCC's preemption of local technical standards. To the contrary, Congress was aware of the "difficulties" the FCC had experienced with "inconsistent local standards." Justice White suggested it is "doubtful that Congress would have meant to overturn preemption without discussion or even any suggestion that it was doing so." *See also* FEDERALISM, p. 29; PREEMPTION DOCTRINE, p. 645.

Significance The preemption doctrine does not always lead to the subordination of state interests. It may be the case that the federal government adopts national policy that furthers or accommodates policy choices of the states. The case of *United States & Federal Communications Commission v. Edge Broadcasting Company* (509 U.S. 418: 1993) provides an example. Federal law (Title 18, United States Code, sections 1304 and 1307) prohibits broadcasters located in states that do not allow lotteries from airing lottery advertising, even if their transmissions can be received in states operating lotteries. Edge Broadcasting Company (Edge) is licensed in North Carolina, a nonlottery state. Much of its listening audience resides in Virginia, a lottery state. Edge wished to accept advertising promoting the Virginia lottery and filed a challenge to the regulation. Edge prevailed in the lower courts by asserting a First Amendment right to broadcast advertising since North Carolina residents were already exposed to such content broadcast by Virginia stations. The argument was that because federal law was unable to effectively keep lottery advertising from North Carolina residents there was insufficient governmental interest to justify the First Amendment burden imposed by the regulation. The Supreme Court disagreed in a 7-2 decision. The lottery advertising was seen as commercial speech, a class of expression historically afforded "lesser protection." The two decisive criteria in this kind of commercial expression case are whether a regulation "directly advances" a legitimate governmental interest and the closeness of "fit" between the governmental objective and the means chosen to achieve that end. Instead of favoring either a lottery or a nonlottery policy, Congress chose to defer to the antigambling policy of states like North Carolina by prohibiting stations licensed in those states from broadcasting lottery advertising. At the same time, Congress sought to avoid interference with states sponsoring lotteries by exempting them from the regulation. Stations licensed within lottery states could air lottery advertising even though those advertisements could be heard in nonlottery states. The congressional policy of "balancing the interests" of lottery and nonlottery states was seen by the Court as the substantial government interest required for regulation of commercial speech. White then turned to the question of "fit." The fit between the regulation and the government interest need not necessarily be "perfect, but reasonable." The Court was satisfied that the fit in this instance was a reasonable one. Although more than 90 percent of Edge's audience was in Virginia, its signal reached nine North Carolina counties. To allow Edge to broadcast lottery advertising to listeners in these counties would be "in derogation of the substantial federal interest in supporting North Carolina's laws making lotteries illegal." Applying the restriction to Edge "directly advances" the noninterference policy established by Congress. Finally, White suggested that when reviewing a regulation like this a court must consider the "relation it bears to the overall problem the government seeks to correct," not the interest furthered in the specific case. Here, Congress sought to accommodate policy decisions of both lottery and nonlottery states. The validity of the regulation must be examined in that general context. Justice Stevens, joined by Justice Blackmun, dissented. In their view, the government's "selective ban on lottery advertising unquestionably flunks [the 'reasonable fit'] test." The means chosen, a "ban on speech imposed for the purpose of manipulating public behavior, is in no way proportionate to the Government's asserted interest in protecting the anti-lottery policies of nonlottery States." Stevens said Congress had chosen the "most intrusive and dangerous" form of regulation—"suppressing truthful advertising." It was their judgment that the regulation was "draconian" and "patently unconstitutional."

***Cipollone v. Liggett Group, Inc.*, 505 U.S. 504, 120 L.Ed. 2d 407, 112 S.Ct. 2608 (1992)** Congress enacted the Federal Cigarette Labeling and Advertising Act in 1965. Among other things, the act required that cigarette packages display conspicuous warnings and provided the exact wording such warning labels must contain. The act went on to bar the states from adding to or otherwise changing this language. The 1965 act was amended by the Public Health Cigarette Smoking Act of 1969, which strengthened the warning label and banned cigarette advertising on any medium of electronic communication. The 1969 act amended the preemption provision to say that "no requirement or prohibition based on smoking and health shall be imposed under State law with respect to the advertising or promotion of any cigarettes the packages of which are labeled in conformity with the provisions of this Act."

Rose Cipollone, 40-year smoker, contracted lung cancer. She brought suit in U.S. district court against several cigarette manufacturers, including the Liggett Group. She accused the defendant companies of a number of things, including failure to warn, breach of warranty, and fraudulent misrepresentation. Cipollone died during the course of the litigation, but the case was maintained by her survivors. A jury awarded the family $400,000 damages in 1988. The Liggett Group appealed to the Court of Appeals for the Third Circuit, arguing that personal injury suits like Cipollone's were preempted by the 1965 act as amended; the Third Circuit agreed. The Supreme Court reversed, ruling that the labeling law did not categorically insulate tobacco companies from state personal injury lawsuits. Issues arising under the Supremacy Clause, said Justice Stevens, "start with the assumption that the historic police powers of the States are not to be superseded by Federal Act unless that is the clear and manifest purpose of Congress." The purpose of Congress is the "ultimate touchstone" of preemption analysis. Congressional intent may be explicitly provided in a statute, but in the absence of express language state law may still be preempted if state law actually conflicts with federal law, or if federal law "so thoroughly occupies a legislative field as to make reasonable the inference that Congress left no room for the States to supplement it." In this case, the Court found the preemptive scope of the act as amended was "governed entirely" by expressed provisions of the statutes. The statutory mandate involved here "merely prohibited state and local rulemaking bodies from mandating particular cautionary statements on cigarette labels or in cigarette advertisements." The presumption against preemption of state police power "reinforces the appropriateness of a narrow reading of [section 5 of the 1965 act]." Furthermore, the Court found no "general, inherent conflict between federal preemption of state warning requirements and the continued vitality of state common law damages actions." Cipollone's failure to warn claim asserted that the tobacco companies were negligent in the way they "tested, researched, sold, promoted, and advertised" cigarettes and that the label warnings inadequately communicated the health risks associated with smoking. The Court found this claim preempted to the extent that it was based on state law regulating advertising or promotion. The act, on the other hand, did not preempt claims that relied on "testing or research practices or other actions unrelated to advertising or promotion." The Court also allowed Cipollone's fraudulent misrepresentation arguments to the extent that they were based on a state statutory obligation to disclose material facts "through channels of communication other than advertising or promotion." *See also* FEDERALISM, p. 29; *PENNSYLVANIA v. NELSON* (350 U.S. 497: 1956), p. 244; PREEMPTION DOCTRINE, p. 645; SUPREMACY CLAUSE, p. 227.

Significance The Cigarette Labeling and Advertising Act had two explicit purposes. The first was to inform the public about the health dangers associated with cigarette smoking. The second was to protect the national economy from the "burden imposed by diverse, nonuniform and confusing cigarette labeling and advertising regulations." The Court's ruling in *Cipollone* applied the preemption doctrine in a narrow manner. It ruled the act preempted claims based on a failure to warn and the "neutralization of federally mandated warnings" to the extent those claims were based on "omissions or inclusions" in the tobacco companies' advertising. The effect of this ruling was to strike down only those state regulations of tobacco that pertained specifically to warnings and advertising, thus opening the way for a whole range of state suits unrelated to how cigarette manufacturers promoted their products. The *Cipollone* decision reflects a predisposition of the Rehnquist Court to maintain state police power to the fullest extent possible. The presumption against superseding state police power in the absence of explicit congressional direction has been operative throughout much of our constitutional history. In *Cipollone,* there was express direction from Congress about preemption, but the Court interpreted the preemption mandate narrowly—applicable only to advertising initiatives of tobacco companies. Three criteria set forth in *Pennsylvania v. Nelson* (350 U.S. 497: 1956) have governed recent preemption cases. First, federal regulation must be so pervasive as to allow a reasonable inference that no room is left for the states to act. Second, federal regulation must involve matters where the federal interest is so dominant as to preclude implementation of state laws. Third, the implementation of federal laws must be jeopardized by the conflicting state regulation. Although the *Cipollone* case came near each of these three standards, it was ultimately the Court's judgment that room remained for tobacco companies to be sued for damages in state courts.

Antitrust

***California v. ARC America Corp.*, 490 U.S. 93, 104 L.Ed. 2d 86, 109 S.Ct. 1661 (1989)** Section 4 of the Clayton Act entitles direct purchasers to recover triple damages for overcharges that result from price-fixing practices prohibited under terms of the Sherman Act. A number of states including California brought class actions in federal court, seeking recovery of damages under federal antitrust law for an alleged conspiracy to fix cement prices in violation of state antitrust laws. Unlike federal law, state antitrust laws typically allow indirect purchasers to recover any overcharges passed on to them by direct purchasers. Several cases involving both direct and indirect purchasers were transferred to a U.S. district court for coordinated pretrial proceedings, which ultimately led to a settlement with most of the larger defendants. When California sought payment from the settlement fund for state indirect purchaser claims, a number of the direct purchasers, including ARC America Corp., objected. The district court refused to allow the claims of indirect purchasers on the grounds that state antitrust statutes are preempted by federal antitrust law; its ruling was affirmed by the U.S. Court of Appeals for the Ninth Circuit. A unanimous Supreme Court reversed.

The "path to be followed" in preemption cases, said Justice White, was clearly set out in the Court's prior decisions. It is "accepted" that Congress has the authority, in exercising its Article I powers, to preempt state law. If Congress does not expressly preempt state law, there are "two other bases" for finding preemption. State law is preempted when Congress intends federal law to fully "occupy a given field" or when state law conflicts with federal law to the point that compliance with both is "impossible." In addition, parties such as ARC America must "overcome the presumption against finding preemption of state law in areas traditionally regulated by the States." When Congress legislates in a field traditionally occupied by the states, the Court starts with the assumption that the "historic police powers of the States were not to be superseded" by federal law unless that was the "clear and manifest purpose" of Congress. Given the "long history of state common law and statutory remedies against monopolies and unfair business practices, it is plain that this is an area traditionally regulated by the States." Here, the Court found nothing in *Illinois Brick* (an apposite case; see *Significance* section below) that suggests it would be "contrary to congressional purposes for States to allow indirect purchasers to recover under their own antitrust laws."

The Court also rejected three other conclusions of the Ninth Circuit. First, the Ninth Circuit held that state indirect purchaser statutes "interfere with the congressional purpose of avoiding unnecessarily complicated proceedings on federal antitrust claims." The Court disagreed, concluding that since most state indirect purchaser actions would be heard in state court any complication of federal direct purchaser actions in federal court "would be minimal." Second, the Ninth Circuit believed that allowing state indirect purchaser claims could "reduce the incentives of direct purchasers to bring antitrust actions by reducing their potential recoveries." The Court in *Illinois Brick,* however, was not concerned with the risk that a plaintiff might not be able to recover its entire damages award or might be offered less to settle. Rather, it was concerned that requiring direct and indirect purchasers to apportion recovery under the Clayton Act exclusively would result in no one plaintiff having a "sufficient incentive" to sue under that statute. State indirect purchaser statutes "pose no similar risk" to the enforcement of the federal law. Third, the Ninth Circuit concluded that state indirect purchaser claims might subject antitrust defendants to multiple liability in "contravention of express federal policy condemning multiple liability."

The Court found none of the relevant prior decisions to identify a "federal policy against States imposing liability in addition to that imposed by federal law." When "viewed properly," *Illinois Brick* was a decision considering only the federal antitrust laws, not a decision "defining the interrelationship between the federal and state antitrust laws." As a result, the congressional purposes on which *Illinois Brick* was based "provide no support for a finding that state indirect purchaser statutes are preempted by federal law." *See also* ANTITRUST LAWS, p. 579; PREEMPTION DOCTRINE, p. 645.

Significance The controlling decision on the issue of damages recoverable by indirect purchasers under federal antitrust law is *Illinois Brick Co. v. Illinois* (431 U.S. 720: 1977). The Court in *Illinois Brick* held that only overcharged direct purchasers and not subsequent indirect purchasers were "injured in their business or property" within the meaning of the Clayton Act and that the plaintiff was not entitled to recover under federal law for the portion of overcharge passed on to it. During the several decades following passage of the Sherman Act, state antitrust activity was reduced to relative insignificance. The Burger and Rehnquist Courts have altered that position. Recent rulings of the Rehnquist Court in particular have not interpreted federal antitrust laws as to substantially limit the authority of states. ARC America is a good example. Another example of the Rehnquist Court's predisposition can be seen in *City of Columbia v. Omni Outdoor Advertising, Inc.* (499 U.S. 365: 1991). Omni Advertising, a Georgia corporation, sought to enter the billboard market in Columbia, South Carolina. This was made extremely difficult because another corporation, Columbia Outdoor Advertising, controlled more than 95 percent of the existing billboard market in Columbia. Because of its virtual monopoly over the market, Columbia Outdoor Advertising was able to place severe obstacles in Omni's path, including a number of "anticompetitive" actions such as "offering artificially low rates." Columbia Advertising also enjoyed "close relations" with city officials and was able to get city officials to enact zoning ordinances restricting new billboard construction. After the adoption of these zoning ordinances, Omni brought suit in federal district court, claiming violation of the Sherman Act and South Carolina's Unfair Trade Practices Act. The complaint alleged that the ordinances were the product of an "anticompetitive conspiracy" that removed any immunity to which the City of Columbia might otherwise be entitled. Omni won a jury verdict at trial, but the district court granted the city's motion for judgment (notwithstanding the verdict) on the grounds that their activities were outside the scope of federal antitrust laws. The U.S. Court of Appeals for the Fourth Circuit reversed and reinstated the jury verdict in Omni's favor. In a 6-3 decision, the Supreme Court reversed, ruling that state governments have broad immunity from antitrust liability, even for actions that would constitute an illegal antitrust conspiracy if committed by a private entity. Under *Parker v. Brown* (317 U.S. 341: 1943), there exists a "state-action exemption" that confers antitrust immunity where a restriction of competition by a municipality is an "authorized implementation of state policy" and where the suppression of competition is the "foreseeable result" of what state law authorizes. In this case, South Carolina had "unquestionable" authority to empower a city to regulate the size, location, and spacing of billboards, thus qualifying it for the state-action exemption. The Court also disagreed with the Fourth Circuit's view that when a municipality joins a private party to restrain trade it loses its immunity. There is no "conspiracy exception" to state-action immunity, said Justice Scalia, since it is "both inevitable and desirable" that public officials often agree to do what groups of private citizens urge them to do. A conspiracy exception would "virtually swallow up" the doctrine of state-action immunity, something the Rehnquist Court was not prepared to have occur.

Abortion Regulation

***Planned Parenthood v. Casey,* 505 U.S. 833, 120 L.Ed. 2d 674, 112 S.Ct. 2791 (1992)** The Pennsylvania Abortion Control Act required that a woman seeking an abortion must give "informed consent." To that end, the woman must be provided with certain information at least 24 hours before an abortion. A minor must obtain the informed consent of one of her parents. As in parental-consent requirements upheld by the Court in previous cases, judicial bypass was allowed if the minor did not wish to seek or could not secure parental consent. Further, the act required a married woman to inform her husband of the intended abortion. Finally, the act established certain reporting requirements for facilities that perform abortions. As with several other cases in recent years, most notably *Webster* (an apposite case; see *Significance* section below), this case provided the Court with an opportunity to reconsider the basic questions of whether the right to an abortion is constitutionally protected—in essence, whether to overturn the ruling of *Roe v. Wade.* According to a coalition of five justices—Blackmun, Stevens, O'Connor, Kennedy, and Souter—the "essential holding of *Roe v. Wade* should be retained and once again reaffirmed." These same five justices struck down the portion of the act requiring notification of the husband. Over the dissents of Blackmun and Stevens, the other seven justices upheld the four remaining restrictions contained in the Pennsylvania law. Justices O'Connor, Kennedy, and Souter issued a decisive joint opinion. They identified three underlying principles from *Roe v. Wade* that must be retained. First, women have a right to an abortion at any time before fetal viability and must be free to obtain it "without undue interference from the States." Prior to viability, they said, a state's interests are not strong enough to support a prohibition on abortion or to impose any "substantial obstacle to the woman's effective right to elect an abortion." Second, they confirmed a state's power to regulate abortions after fetal viability as long as the regulation "contains exceptions for pregnancies which endanger a woman's life or health." Thirdly, a state has a legitimate interest in protecting a woman's health and the "life of the fetus that may become a child" from the "outset" of the pregnancy. These principles, they concluded, "do not contradict one another; and we adhere to each." They referred to abortion as a "unique act," and although it is conduct, a state in not entitled to "proscribe it in all instances." This is because the liberty of a woman "is at stake in a sense unique to the human condition and so unique to the law." The right is qualified, however. Women must be able to "make the ultimate decision," although the right to an abortion does not permit her to be "insulated from all others in doing so." As a result, regulations that only create a structural mechanism by which the state, or the parent or guardian of a minor, may "express profound respect for the life of the unborn" are permissible if they do not create a "substantial obstacle to the woman's exercise of the right to choose." Similarly, regulations intended to foster the health of a pregnant woman "are valid if they do not constitute an undue burden." In addition to expressing the justices' agreement with at least the "essence" of *Roe*, the joint opinion argued that *Roe* needed to be retained on stare decisis grounds. To overrule *Roe* in the absence of the "most compelling reason to reexamine a watershed decision would subvert the Court's legitimacy beyond any serious question." Reversal of *Roe*'s essential holding would occur "at cost of both profound and unnecessary damage to the Court's legitimacy, and to the Nation's commitment to the rule of law."

Justice Blackmun expressed strong support for the reaffirmation of *Roe* and acknowledged, as an "act of personal courage and constitutional principles," the position taken by O'Connor, Kennedy, and Souter. At the same time, he expressed a "fear for the darkness as four Justices anxiously await the single vote necessary to extinguish the light." He noted his age (83) and said he and his vote could not "remain on this Court forever. . . ." He predicted a serious confirmation battle for that vote upon his retirement. Chief Justice Rehnquist and Justice Scalia issued dissents. Each signed the dissent of the other, and Justices White and Thomas signed both. Rehnquist said *Roe* was "wrongly decided" and should be overruled. He would have substituted the approach of the plurality in *Webster* (below). Following what he called a "newly minted variation on *stare decisis,*" Rehnquist said the majority had retained only the "outer shell" of *Roe.* In his view, the majority had beaten a "wholesale retreat from the substance of that case." What was left of *Roe,* said Rehnquist, was a "sort of judicial Potemkin Village, which may be pointed out to passersby as a monument to the importance of adhering to precedent." He charged that the Court, behind the "facade" of stare decisis, had resorted to an "entirely new method of analysis, without any roots in constitutional law," to be used when reviewing state abortion regulations. Neither stare decisis nor an interest in judicial legitimacy was well served by such an approach. To Scalia, the question in *Casey* was not whether the "power of a woman to abort her unborn child is a 'liberty' in the absolute sense; or even whether it is a liberty of great importance to many women." Scalia acknowledged both to be true. Rather, he maintained, the "issue is whether it is a liberty protected by the Constitution of the United States." His answer was, "I'm sure it is not." His conclusion was not based on "anything so exalted" as his own concept of existence or the "mystery of life." Instead, it was based on two simple facts: "(1) the Constitution says absolutely nothing about it, (2) the longstanding traditions of American society have permitted it to be legally proscribed." Scalia was also critical of the majority's claim that *Roe* had been a workable response to the abortion controversy. Compromise on the issue had been possible before, he said, but not after *Roe. Roe*'s mandate for "abortion-on-demand destroyed the compromises of the past, rendered compromises impossible for the future, and required the entire issue to be resolved uniformly, at the national level." Furthermore, *Roe* "created a vast new class of abortion consumers and abortion proponents by eliminating the moral opprobrium that had attached to the act." *See also* FEDERALISM, p. 29; STARE DECISIS, p. 656.

Significance The most significant abortion regulation decision prior to *Casey* was *Webster v. Reproductive Health Services* (492 U.S. 490: 1989). *Webster* provided the Court with an opportunity to fully reconsider and possibly overrule the controversial ruling of *Roe v. Wade* (410 U.S. 113: 1973). The Court rendered a decision in *Webster* that substantially modified *Roe* but did not explicitly overrule it. The origin of the case was a Missouri statute enacted in 1986. Several components of the statute were challenged in federal court by a number of doctors and nurses and two nonprofit medical corporations, one of which was Reproductive Health Services (RHS). The challenged provisions included: (1) a preamble that stated that life begins at conception and that the "unborn" have life interests requiring protection; (2) a requirement that before an abortion can be performed on a woman whom a physician has "reason to believe" is 20 or more weeks pregnant, the physician must determine whether the fetus is "viable" by performing specified medical examinations and tests; (3) an informed-consent requirement that included information on abortion alternatives; and (4) prohibitions on use of public funds, public facilities, or public employees in "performing or assisting" an abortion. This last restriction included public employees counseling pregnant women to have nontherapeutic abortions. A federal district court upheld only the viability testing but, in so doing, eliminated many of the viability tests specified in the law. Missouri, through its attorney general, William Webster, challenged each element of the district court decision except for that portion that struck down the informed-consent requirement. The Court of Appeals for the Eighth Circuit affirmed. In a fragmented, 5-4 decision, the Supreme Court allowed the restrictions but did not explicitly reverse *Roe.* The Court did not rule on the preamble. It was seen as an "abstract proposition" rather than an operating regulation. Since the preamble did not restrict the activities of RHS in "some concrete way," the Court concluded RHS had no standing to challenge the preamble language. This ruling was a rejection of RHS's argument that the preamble was an "operative part" of the statute intended to "guide the interpretation of other provisions of the Act." Chief Justice Rehnquist then discussed the ban on the use of public funds, facilities, and employees. The Eighth Circuit had seen this regulation as possibly preventing a woman's doctor from performing an abortion if the doctor did not have privileges in another hospital. Increased costs and possible delay were also attributed to the regulation. The Supreme Court disagreed, using much the same analysis as that found in the Medicaid cases, such as *Maher v. Roe* (432 U.S. 464: 1977) and *Harris v. McRae* (448 U.S. 297: 1980). As in those cases, the Court recognized the state's decision to "encourage childbirth over abortion" and that policy preference "places no governmental obstacle in the path of a woman who chooses to terminate her pregnancy." Missouri's refusal to allow public employees to perform abortions or to allow abortions to be performed in public facilities leaves a pregnant woman "with the same choices as if the State had chosen not to operate any public hospitals at all." Having already ruled (in *Maher* and *Harris*) that state refusal to fund abortions does not violate *Roe v. Wade,* it "strains logic to reach a contrary result for the use of public facilities."

Chief Justice Rehnquist then turned to the most critical aspect of the decision, the viability testing requirements. He said the statute required physicians to perform "only those tests that are useful to making subsidiary findings as to viability." Key, however, was the presumption of viability at 20 weeks, which must be directly rebutted by viability test results before an abortion can be performed. The *Roe v. Wade* decision is based on a concept of trimesters. Under *Roe,* the interests of the fetus are not recognized until the final trimester, which occurs about 24 weeks into the pregnancy. Specification in the Missouri law of methods for determining viability "does superimpose state regulation on the medical determination of viability." This section was struck down by the court of appeals on that basis. The Supreme Court was less convinced that the law was flawed, however. Rather, the problem, said Rehnquist, was the "rigid trimester analysis of the course of a pregnancy enunciated in *Roe.*" The "rigid *Roe* framework is hardly consistent with the notion of a Constitution case in general terms." The Court simply should not function as the "country's *ex officio* medical board with powers to approve or disapprove medical and operative practices and standards. . . ." Thus, the "web of legal rules" developed through application of *Roe* could be loosened. More importantly, the Court did not see "why the State's interest in protecting potential human life should come into existence only at the point of viability" and why there should be a "rigid line allowing state regulation after viability but prohibiting it before viability." The Court acknowledged that the test "increase[s] the expense of abortion and regulate[s] the discretion of the physician in determining the viability of the fetus." Nonetheless, the Court was "satisfied" that the requirement "permissibly furthers the State's interest in protecting potential human life" and is constitutional.

Justice O'Connor agreed that the viability testing requirement was constitutional but came to that conclusion because she did not see the requirement as incompatible with *Roe v. Wade.* Justice Scalia was also among the majority but said that *Roe v. Wade* had been overruled. Indeed, he was critical of Rehnquist for not acknowledging that result. By hanging onto *Roe,* Scalia said, the Court "needlessly prolonged its self-awarded sovereignty over a field where it has little proper business" since responses to most of the critical questions are "political and not juridical." Justices Blackmun, Brennan, Marshall, and Stevens dissented. Blackmun, the author of the *Roe v. Wade* opinion, was most outspoken in criticizing the *Webster* decision. He spoke of the "feigned restraint" of the plurality opinion's claim that it "leaves *Roe* undisturbed." "But this disclaimer is totally meaningless." The plurality opinion, he contended, is "filled with winks, nods, and knowing glances to those who would do away with *Roe* explicitly." Blackmun was very troubled by the viability testing and what it meant to the *Roe* trimester framework. He was even more troubled by Rehnquist's decision to uphold viability testing because it "permissibly furthers the State's interest in protecting potential human life." This "newly minted" standard is "circular and totally meaningless." Whether a challenged regulation "permissibly furthers" a legitimate interest is the "question that courts must answer in abortion cases, not the standard for courts to apply." The standard has no "independent meaning" and consists of "nothing other than what a majority of this Court may believe at any given moment in any given case."

Hodgson v. Minnesota (497 U.S. 417: 1990) and *Ohio v. Akron Center for Reproductive Health* (497 U.S. 502: 1990) examined parental notification statutes from Minnesota and Ohio. The Minnesota statute had two key parts. First, the state required notification of both biological parents when a minor daughter sought an abortion. In a 5-4 decision, the Court struck down the requirement. The statute contained contingency language that if a court enjoined enforcement of the notification requirement the statute would be amended automatically to provide a judicial bypass as an alternative to parental notification. This alternative allowed a minor child to petition a court for permission to obtain an abortion without notifying her parents. The Court upheld this alternative, again by a 5-4 vote, with Justice O'Connor providing the decisive vote in both instances. She joined Justices Marshall, Brennan, Blackmun, and Stevens in striking down the statute without judicial bypass. She was joined by Chief Justice Rehnquist and Justices Kennedy, White, and Scalia in upholding the alternative. The Ohio statute required notification of only one parent. It also contained judicial bypass language, but the Court upheld the one-parent notification requirement on its own by a 6-3 vote—Justice Stevens joining the five justices who had upheld the Minnesota alternative. The defect with the Minnesota statute without the judicial bypass arose from the fact that only about half of Minnesota's minors resided with both biological parents. Justice Stevens spoke of the "particularly harmful effects" of the two-parent notification requirement on "both the minor and the custodial parent when parents were divorced or separated." In addition, the Court concluded the requirement "does not reasonably further any legitimate state interest." The principal justification for notification is that it "supports the authority of a parent who is presumed to act in the minor's best interest and thereby assures that the minor's decision to terminate her pregnancy is knowing, intelligent, and deliberate." To the extent "such an interest is legitimate," it could be "fully served" by the notification of one parent, who can then seek counsel from the other parent or anyone else. The state has no legitimate interest in questioning the one parent's judgment on whether to seek wider counsel. The Court concluded that the two-parent requirement actually "disserves" any state interest in protecting a minor in "dysfunctional families." Two-parent notice in such situations is "positively harmful to the minor and her family." As in cases involving judicial hearings as an alternative to securing parental consent for an abortion, the Court found the bypass alternative constitutionally sufficient for notification as well. The judicial bypass feature allows a minor to demonstrate she is fully capable of making the abortion decision. The Court decided the Ohio case without actually ruling on whether the judicial bypass provision is necessary in the one-parent notice situation. Rather, it upheld the one-parent notification requirement as a "rational way" for a state to assist a pregnant minor who is considering abortion. "It would deny all dignity to the family," Justice Kennedy said, "to say that the State cannot take this reasonable step . . . to ensure that, in most cases, a young woman will receive guidance and understanding from a parent." Both *Casey* and *Webster* underscore the broad authority states retain to regulate in this highly volatile policy area.

Habeas Corpus Review

***Coleman v. Thompson*, 504 U.S. 188, 119 L.Ed. 2d 1, 112 S.Ct. 1845 (1992)** *Coleman* examined whether a state prisoner could pursue federal *habeas corpus* review before a state appellate court had concluded its review. Under *Fay v. Noia* (372 U.S. 391: 1963), federal *habeas* petitions could be granted even in cases where state appellate review had not taken place, unless the petitioner had "deliberately bypassed" the state appellate courts. The Court overruled *Fay v. Noia* in *Coleman*. In a 6-3 decision, the Court ruled that virtually any failure to satisfy state processes would constitute procedural default and preclude the prisoner from petitioning for federal *habeas* review, including cases where failure to pursue state review was the result of "inadvertent error" by defense counsel. Coleman's petition for state review had been dismissed because it had not been filed within the prescribed time period. The missed deadline was clearly outside the "deliberate bypass" provision of *Fay v. Noia*. Justice O'Connor said the case was "about federalism" and the respect federal courts owe state court processes. It was necessary to overturn *Fay v. Noia* because that decision was "based on a conception of federal-state relations that undervalued the importance of state procedural rules." *Coleman* holds that federal courts can undertake *habeas* review only if the petitioner can show cause why state processes were not completed. Justice O'Connor said cause must be the consequence of something external to the petitioner, something that "cannot be fairly attributed to him." Justices Blackmun, Marshall, and Stevens dissented. Justice Blackmun characterized the ruling as part of a "crusade" by the majority to limit the ability of state prisoners to access federal courts. He said the Court has created a "byzantine morass of arbitrary, unnecessary, and unjustifiable impediments to the vindication of Federal rights." *See also* FEDERALISM, p. 29; *HABEAS CORPUS*, p. 616.

Significance Another significant *habeas corpus* question was considered in *McCleskey v. Zant* (499 U.S. 467: 1991). Among the evidence against McCleskey was the testimony of an informant who occupied a jail cell next to him. After his conviction was affirmed by the Georgia Supreme Court, McCleskey unsuccessfully sought *habeas* relief in the state courts. He argued that his incriminating statements to the informant in the adjoining cell were elicited in violation of his Sixth Amendment right to counsel under *Massiah v. United States* (377 U.S. 201: 1964). *Massiah* prohibits use of informants to elicit incriminating information after formal charges have been brought against a suspect. McCleskey then filed a federal *habeas* petition. This petition did not include the *Massiah* claim, however, since the evidence available to McCleskey's counsel at the time suggested such a claim could not be adequately supported. Rather, McCleskey argued that Georgia administered its death penalty law in a racially discriminatory manner. The case reached the U.S. Supreme Court, but the Court rejected McCleskey's discrimination claim (*McCleskey v. Kemp*, 481 U.S. 279: 1987). McCleskey then filed a second federal *habeas* petition, this time asserting the *Massiah* claim. The petition was granted by a federal district court but was reversed by the Court of Appeals for the Eleventh Circuit. The Supreme Court affirmed. The principal issue in this case was whether McCleskey's failure to include the *Massiah* issue in his first petition precluded his raising that claim in a second petition. Key to resolving this issue was whether McCleskey's second petition constituted an abuse of the writ. McCleskey's position was that such abuse could only occur as a result of deliberately abandoning a claim in the first petition or through inexcusable neglect. In other words, McCleskey sought a nonrestrictive interpretation of the abuse of the writ standard. Georgia, on the other hand, argued that the standard requires prisoners to include all claims that they were aware of in the first petition. Justice Kennedy said doctrines such as abuse of the writ are based on concerns about the "significant cost" of federal *habeas corpus* review. First, the writ "strikes at finality." Perpetual disrespect for the finality of state convictions, in turn, "disparages the entire criminal system." Second, *habeas* review burdens scarce federal judicial resources by threatening the "capacity of the system to resolve primary disputes." *Habeas* review may also give litigants "incentives to withhold claims for manipulative purposes." Kennedy then turned to the abuse of writ standard. The Court sought to modify the doctrine to "curtail the abusive petitions that in recent years have threatened the integrity of the *habeas corpus* process." Under the new standard, *habeas* petitions following the first one will be dismissed unless a prisoner can demonstrate cause for not asserting the claim earlier. A mere showing of good faith was seen as insufficient to establish cause.

Rather, the prisoner had to demonstrate "some external impediment preventing counsel from constructing or raising a claim." The Court said it was also necessary for the petitioner to demonstrate that he or she suffered "actual prejudice resulting from errors of which he complains." The burden of disproving abuse of the petition falls to the prisoner once the state describes the prior petition(s) and isolates claims raised for the first time. In the absence of cause, a petition could be accepted only to prevent a "fundamental miscarriage of justice," something Kennedy said would occur only in "extraordinary instances."

In *Keeney v. Tamayo-Reyes* (504 U.S. 1: 1992), the Court continued to restrict federal *habeas corpus* access from those convicted of state crimes. Under the standards that applied prior to *Keeney,* a state prisoner was entitled to *habeas corpus* review of evidence not adequately developed in state trial courts as long as the evidence was not deliberately withheld or "bypassed." In *Keeney,* the Court ruled that federal *habeas* review can take place only if "cause and prejudice" can be demonstrated. The prisoner must show cause for his failure to develop the evidence at trial and further demonstrate "actual prejudice resulting from that failure." The effect of the ruling was to make the standard for failing to develop a factual matter in a state court identical with the standard used to assert an appellate claim at the state level as required under *Coleman* and *McCleskey.* The new standard, said Justice White, "will appropriately accommodate concerns of finality, comity, judicial economy, and channeling the resolution of claims into the most appropriate forum."

Extradition

***California v. Superior Court,* 482 U.S. 400, 96 L.Ed. 2d 332, 107 S.Ct. 2433 (1987)** Richard Smolin was granted sole custody of his two minor children in a California proceeding. He secured a warrant to obtain custody of the children and went to Louisiana, where the children were living with their mother. Smolin and his father took the children and returned to California. The mother then filed kidnapping charges in Louisiana. The governor of Louisiana notified the governor of California of the charges and demanded that Smolin and his father be delivered to Louisiana authorities to stand trial. A California superior court granted the Smolins a writ of *habeas corpus* as a means of blocking the extradition warrants against them. The California Supreme Court ruled that the superior court properly considered the custody decree at the point it issued the writ of *habeas corpus.* The California Supreme Court further concluded that under the full faith and credit provisions of the Federal Parental Kidnapping Prevention Act of 1980, the custody decrees "conclusively" established that Smolin was the lawful custodian of the children when he and his father took them from the mother's home. The state court noted that Smolin had not been "substantially charged" with a crime in Louisiana because Louisiana law itself provides that the lawful custodian of minor children cannot be guilty of kidnapping them. The Supreme Court reversed. Its interpretation of the Extradition Act of 1793 was that an asylum state is "bound to deliver up" a fugitive against whom an indictment or affidavit charging a crime is lodged. The "language, history, and subsequent construction" of the Extradition Act "make clear that Congress intended extradition to be a summary procedure"; extradition proceedings are to be kept "within narrow bounds." Such proceedings are "emphatically" not the time or place for "entertaining defenses or determining the guilt or innocence of the charged party." Rather, those inquiries are left to the prosecutorial authorities and courts of the demanding state. Accordingly, the courts of asylum states "may do no more than ascertain whether the requisites of the Extradition Act have been met." A properly certified Louisiana information charged Smolin with kidnapping, and the information contains facts that "clearly satisfy each element of the crime of kidnapping" as it is defined in Louisiana law. Assuming the truth of the facts alleged, the Court concluded that the Smolins were properly charged under Louisiana law, and that "ends the inquiry into the issue of whether or not a crime is charged for purposes of the Extradition Act." Justice O'Connor said the Court was "not informed by the record" why Louisiana was "so eager to force the Smolins halfway across the continent to face criminal charges that, at least to a majority of the California Supreme Court, appear meritless." O'Connor pointed out that if the Smolins are correct, they are not only innocent of the charges against them but also "victims of a possible abuse of the criminal process." Nonetheless, under terms of the Extradition Act, it is for the Louisiana courts "to do justice" in this case, not the California courts. Surrendering the Smolins is "not to be interfered with by the summary process of *habeas corpus* upon speculation as to what ought to be the result of a trial in the place where the Constitution provides for its taking place." *See also* ARTICLE IV, p. 225; INTERSTATE RENDITION, p. 625.

Significance The purpose of the Extradition Clause of Article IV is to prevent a state from becoming a "safe haven" for fugitives from another state's criminal justice system. The Extradition Clause places a limit on the sovereign authority of states by obligating them to return fugitives to the state from which he or she fled on demand of the executive authority of that state. This obligation was immediately reinforced by the passage of the Extradition Act of 1793. Most state governors view extradition (sometimes called rendition) as an absolute obligation, and compliance is typically automatic. The recent and rapid increase of "parental kidnapping" incidents, however, clearly complicates the issue. The Court's decision in *Superior Court* suggests, however, that demands for extradition of custodians of minor children are viewed as comparable to demands for the return of persons charged with any other kind of criminal conduct.

Intergovernmental Tax Immunity

***Davis v. Michigan Department of Treasury*, 485 U.S. 505, 103 L.Ed. 2d 891, 109 S.Ct. 1500 (1989)** Paul Davis, a retired federal employee, paid state income tax on his federal retirement benefits under provisions of a Michigan law that took effect for the calendar year 1979. The same Michigan statute that required Davis to pay taxes on his federal retirement benefits exempted from taxation all retirement benefits paid by the state of Michigan or any of its subdivisions. Davis unsuccessfully sought refund on the taxes he paid, arguing that Michigan's tax policy violated section 111 of the Public Salary Tax Act that authorizes states to tax compensation of federal employees as long as the taxation "does not discriminate against the employee because of the source of the pay or compensation." The Michigan Court of Claims denied relief, a ruling upheld by the Michigan Court of Appeals. The appellate court ruled that as a retiree (an "annuitant"), Davis was not an "employee" under the federal law such that the nondiscrimination language did not apply to him. The court further concluded that Michigan's discriminatory tax did not violate the doctrine of intergovernmental tax immunity, because the state's interest in attracting and keeping qualified employees was reasonably achieved by a retirement tax exemption advantageous to the state employee. The Michigan Supreme Court refused to review the case. In an 8-1 decision, the U.S. Supreme Court struck down the Michigan exemption.

Michigan argued that the nondiscriminatory language of section 111 applied only to current federal employees and not federal retirees. The Court found that the "plain language" of section 111 dictates the opposite conclusion. Although retirement pay is not disbursed during the time an individual is actually working for the government, the amount of benefit to be received "is based and computed upon the individual's salary and years of service." The Court found Michigan's reading of section 111 as "implausible," concluding that it was unlikely that Congress "consented to discriminatory taxation of retired federal civil servants' pensions while refusing to permit such taxation to current employees." Nothing in the statutory language or legislative history of section 111 "suggest[s] such a result." To the contrary, the overall meaning of section 111 "unmistakabl[y]" waives whatever immunity past and current federal employees would otherwise enjoy from state taxation "except to the extent that such taxation discriminates on account of the source of the compensation." Michigan argued that the intergovernmental tax immunity doctrine is designed to protect governments and not private individuals. As long as a tax does not interfere with the federal government's ability to perform its functions, the constitutional doctrine has not been violated. The Court agreed that the doctrine is intended to protect sovereign governmental operations from undue interference by the other. It does not follow, however, that private individuals who are subjected to discriminatory taxation "because of their dealings with a sovereign" cannot themselves receive the protection of the doctrine. The imposition of a heavier tax on those who deal with one sovereign must be justified by "significant differences between the two classes." In determining if this justification has been established, the Court said it was "inappropriate" to use exclusively the analytic approach developed for equal protection cases. Prior decisions of this kind are "not necessarily controlling" where problems of intergovernmental tax immunity are involved because the government's interests "must be weighed in the balance." Instead, the "relevant" inquiry is whether the inconsistent tax treatment is "directly related to and justified by significant differences between the two classes." Michigan asserted two "allegedly significant differences" between the two classes of retirees. First, Michigan claimed that its interest in hiring and retaining qualified civil servants through the use of inducements such as the tax exemption was sufficient to justify the differential treatment. The Court found this argument "wholly beside the point" since it "does nothing" to demonstrate a significant difference between the two classes. The Court found the discriminatory tax "simply irrelevant to an inquiry into the nature of the two classes." Second, Michigan argued that its retirement benefits are substantially less generous than those offered by the federal government. Even assuming Michigan's representation of the relative value of retirement benefits to be correct, the Court did not find this difference adequate to justify the "type of blanket exemption" at issue in this case. A tax exemption truly intended to account for differences in retirement benefits would not "discriminate on the basis of the source of those benefits" but rather would "discriminate on the basis of the amount of benefits received by the individual retirees." *See also* FEDERALISM, p. 29; *GRAVES v. NEW YORK EX. REL. O'KEEFE* (306 U.S. 466: 1939), p. 402; INTERGOVERNMENTAL TAX IMMUNITY, p. 623; TENTH AMENDMENT, p. 229.

Significance Challenges to state taxation on federal constitutional grounds may take various forms. The doctrine of intergovernmental tax immunity is the most common form. A different application of the doctrine from that found in *Davis* can be seen in *South Carolina v. Baker* (485 U.S. 505: 1988). Section 310(b)(1) of the Tax Equity and Fiscal Responsibility Act of 1982 withdrew the federal income tax exemption for interest earned on state and local government bonds unless the bonds were issued in registered form. Registered bonds differ from unregistered, or bearer, bonds in that ownership of the former is registered on sale or transfer and recorded on a single list. Ownership of bearer, or unregistered, bonds, on the other hand, comes simply from possession. Because there are no central records for unregistered bonds, it is much easier to evade taxation. Section 310 was designed to generally address the problem of unregistered bonds and applied to bonds issued by the United States, the states, and private corporations. South Carolina invoked the Supreme Court's original jurisdiction and asserted that section 310(b)(1) violated the Tenth Amendment and the doctrine of intergovernmental tax immunity. The Court appointed a special master (a designated officer of the Court), who conducted a hearing, took evidence, and recommended that the challenged provision was constitutional. Judgment was subsequently entered for James Baker, secretary of the U.S. Treasury Department. South Carolina challenged the factual findings and conclusions of the special master. The Supreme Court agreed that section 310(b)(1) did not violate the Tenth Amendment or the principles of federalism.

The Tenth Amendment's limits on congressional authority to regulate state activities are "structural, not substantive." States must find their protection from congressional regulation through the "national political process," not by having the courts define "spheres of unregulatable state activity." In this case, South Carolina had not argued that it was deprived of any right to participate in the national political process or that it was "singled out" in a way that left it "politically isolated and powerless." Arguments that Congress made an "uninformed" decision and chose an "ineffective remedy" do not qualify as an allegation that the political process operated in some deficient manner. Section 310(b)(1) did not seek to "control or influence" the manner in which states regulate private parties. A state wishing to engage in certain activity must occasionally take legislative or administration action to comply with federal standards. The Court called this "commonplace" and concluded it presented no constitutional defect. A state cannot immunize its activities from federal regulation "simply by codifying the manner in which it engages in those activities." The nondiscriminatory tax imposed under section 310 is collected from bondholders and not states, and any increased administrative costs incurred in implementing the registration system are not taxes within the scope of the immunity doctrine.

A challenge of a different kind came in the California Proposition 13 case, *Nordlinger v. Hahn* (505 U.S. 1: 1992). In 1978, California voters approved Proposition 13, a ballot initiative that amended the state constitution by establishing an "acquisition value" system of property taxation. Under this approach, property is reassessed up to a current appraised value when new construction occurs or when the property changes ownership. The effect of this change was to produce substantial differences in taxation across owners of similar property. Owners holding property for long periods of time paid taxes based on property values at the time of acquisition, whereas newer owners paid higher taxes based on more recent and elevated values. Stephanie Nordlinger brought suit against Los Angeles County and its tax assessor in state court, arguing that the tax disparities created by the acquisition value system violated the Equal Protection Clause of the Fourteenth Amendment. Nordlinger's claims were rejected by the California Supreme Court and the U.S. Supreme Court.

The appropriate standard of review in cases such as this is whether the differential treatment of newer and older property owners "rationally furthers a legitimate state interest." The Court concluded that Proposition 13 did not discriminate with respect to either the tax rate or the annual rate of adjusting assessments. Newer and older owners similarly benefit in the long term and short term from the tax-rate ceiling and the limitation on the increase in assessed value. New and old owners are treated differently with respect to only one factor—the basis on which their property is initially assessed. The Court found two "reasonable considerations of difference" that justified denying Nordlinger the benefits enjoyed by other property owners. First, the state has a legitimate interest in "local neighborhood preservation, continuity, and stability." The state can thus structure its tax system to discourage rapid turnover of property in order to "inhibit displacement of lower income families by the forces of gentrification or of established 'mom and pop' businesses by newer chain operations." By allowing older owners to pay progressively less than new owners of comparable property, the assessment scheme of Proposition 13 "rationally furthers this interest." Second, the state can legitimately conclude that a new owner at the time of acquiring property does not have the same reliance interest warranting protection against higher taxes as does an existing owner. An existing owner rationally may be thought to have "vested expectations in his property or home that are more deserving of protection than the anticipatory expectations of a new owner at the point of purchase." The Court also found that the two exemptions "rationally further" legitimate purposes. California could have reasonably concluded that older persons in general "should not be discouraged from moving to a residence more suitable to their changing family size or income." Similarly, California could have reasonably concluded that the interests of family and neighborhood continuity and stability are furthered by and warrant an exemption for transfers between parents and children.

Immunity from Lawsuit (Eleventh Amendment)

***Dellmuth v. Muth*, 491 U.S. 223, 105 L.Ed. 2d 181, 109 S.Ct. 2397 (1989)** The Education of the Handicapped Act (EHA) was designed to make sure that handicapped children receive a free public education "appropriate for their needs." The EHA provides that parents may challenge the sufficiency of their child's "individualized education program" (IEP) through an administrative proceeding that is subject to subsequent judicial review. The Muths requested a hearing to contest the IEP developed for their son by the local school district. Before the hearing, however, the Muths enrolled their child in a private school. The school district revised the IEP, and the revised plan was later deemed appropriate by a hearing officer and Pennsylvania's secretary of education. In the interim, the Muths filed suit in U.S. district court, challenging the appropriateness of the IEP and the validity of administrative proceedings. The Muths also sought reimbursement for their child's private-school tuition and for attorney fees. The district court ruled that the EHA had abrogated Pennsylvania's Eleventh Amendment immunity from suit. Accordingly, the district court found the school district and the state liable for reimbursement of the tuition and attorney fees. The Court of Appeals for the Third Circuit affirmed. In a 5-4 decision, the U.S. Supreme Court ruled that the EHA did not abrogate Pennsylvania's immunity from suit in federal courts.

Congress has authority under the Fourteenth Amendment, Section 5, to abrogate the states' Eleventh Amendment immunity. Nonetheless, abrogation of sovereign immunity "upsets the fundamental constitutional balance" between the federal government and the states and places a "considerable strain" on the principles of federalism that inform Eleventh Amendment doctrine. The Muths asserted textual arguments from the EHA and supplemented these with nontextual arguments as well, but the Court concluded that the act's treatment of the abrogation question was "ambiguous at best." The textual provisions, in particular, failed to demonstrate with "unmistakable clarity" that Congress intended to abrogate the state's immunity from suit. The Court ruled that although the "statutory structure lends force to the inference" that the states were intended to be subject to damage actions for

EHA violations such an inference, "whatever its logical force, would remain just that: a permissible inference." It would not be the "unequivocal declaration" that is necessary to determine that Congress intended to exercise its power of abrogation. *See also CHISHOLM v. GEORGIA* (2 Dallas 419: 1793), p. 230; ELEVENTH AMENDMENT, p. 598; FEDERALISM, p. 29; *FITZPATRICK v. BITZER* (427 U.S. 445: 1976), p. 232; FOURTEENTH AMENDMENT, p. 612.

Significance The Court held in *Fitzpatrick v. Bitzer* (427 U.S. 445: 1976) that Congress has authority to require a state to pay damages to employees who have suffered discrimination at the hands of the state. *Fitzpatrick* makes clear that a state's Eleventh Amendment immunity from suit is not absolute. At the same time, it is the Court's view that abrogation ought not be undertaken easily given the potentially damaging effects on the federal system. The Court explicitly reaffirmed in *Muth* that Congress must "unequivocally" abrogate state immunity from suit.

A state may choose to waive or relinquish its immunity, as seen in *Port Authority Trans-Hudson Corp. v. Feeney* (491 U.S. 223: 1989). The Port Authority Trans-Hudson Corp. (PATH) is an entity created by New Jersey and New York to operate specified transportation facilities. Patrick Feeney and another employee claimed they were injured while they worked for PATH and brought suit in U.S. district court to recover damages under the Federal Employers' Liability Act (FELA). The court dismissed the complaints, concluding that PATH was immune from suit in federal court under terms of the Eleventh Amendment. The Court of Appeals for the Second Circuit reversed, ruling that immunity that might extend to PATH had been waived by both New York and New Jersey—that both states had consented to any suit against PATH under terms of the interstate compact entered in 1921 creating the Port Authority of New York and New Jersey. The Supreme Court affirmed the Second Circuit's ruling that the Eleventh Amendment does not preclude federal suit against a subsidiary of the Port Authority where the state had statutorily waived the Port Authority's immunity. In determining whether a state has waived its immunity, the Court uses a similarly demanding standard as with congressional abrogation. A waiver will be given effect only when stated by the "most express language or by such overwhelming implication as will leave no room for any other reasonable construction." The Court found that this standard had been met in *Trans-Hudson*. The statute establishing PATH expressly indicated the states' consent to suit in federal court through unambiguous venue provisions that clearly demonstrated an intent to allow the Port Authority to be sued in designated federal courts. In the Court's view, this constituted an explicit waiver of Eleventh Amendment immunity.

A ruling that could significantly alter Eleventh Amendment immunity doctrine came in *Seminole Tribe of Florida v. Florida* (517 U.S. 44: 1996). Congress passed the Indian Gaming Regulatory Act in 1988. The act allowed Indian tribes to conduct a range of gaming activities as long as they entered into contracts with the states in which the gambling would occur. The act required that states enter into "good-faith" negotiations in pursuit of reaching contractual agreement and further authorized tribes to bring legal action against states in federal courts if negotiations were unsuccessful. Negotiations between Florida and the Seminole Tribe of Florida reached impasse in 1991, and the Seminoles commenced legal action under the act that same year. The state of Florida sought to have the suit dismissed from federal district court on Eleventh Amendment grounds. The district court ruled against Florida, but the Court of Appeals for the Eleventh Circuit reversed, ruling that the Eleventh Amendment prohibits Congress from using the Indian Commerce Clause to abrogate a state's immunity from suit in federal court. The Supreme Court agreed in a 5-4 decision.

The Court "reconfirm[ed]" that the "background principle of state sovereign immunity embodied in the Eleventh Amendment is not so ephemeral as to dissipate" when the subject of the suit involves an area like the regulation of Indian commerce that is under the "exclusive control of the Federal Government." Even when the Constitution gives Congress complete lawmaking power over a particular area, said Chief Justice Rehnquist, the Eleventh Amendment "prevents congressional authorization of suits by private parties against unconsenting States." The Eleventh Amendment limits the power of federal courts, and Article I "cannot be used to circumvent the constitutional limitations placed on federal jurisdiction." Justices Stevens, Souter, Ginsburg, and Breyer strongly dissented in this case, just as they had in a number of very significant rulings in the mid-1990s, such as *United States v. Lopez* (514 U.S. 549: 1995), *City of Boerne v. Flores* (138 L.Ed. 2d 624: 1997), and *Printz v. United States* (138 L.Ed. 2d 914: 1997). It is plain that the Rehnquist Court is deeply divided over the issue of federal and state power. The individual justices have engaged in extremely strong rhetoric on this question, and it is unlikely that any consensus will be possible with the current group of justices. The next two or three appointments to the Court will prove particularly significant on the broad question of American federalism.

Takings Clause

***Lucas v. South Carolina Coastal Council,* 505 U.S. 1003, 120 L.Ed. 2d 798, 112 S.Ct. 2886 (1992)** David Lucas bought two oceanfront lots on one of the barrier islands off the coast of South Carolina. Lucas intended to build homes comparable to those already located on adjacent property. At the time Lucas acquired the lots there were no use restrictions on the property. Subsequently, South Carolina enacted the Beachfront Management Act, which empowered a state coastal council to protect endangered shoreline. The council determined that Lucas's property was in a "critical" zone and banned any new construction on it. Lucas brought suit in state court, seeking compensation for the property he claimed was made "worthless" by the restriction. He characterized the regulation as a "taking" of his property for a public purpose. The state trial court agreed and ordered payment in excess of $1 million as just compensation. The South Carolina Supreme Court reversed, ruling that when a regulation is designed to prevent a "harmful use" of property no compensation is required under the Takings Clause. In a 6-3 decision, the Supreme Court reversed.

Justice Scalia spoke of "two discrete categories" of regulatory action as compensable under the Takings Clause. The first involves regulations that compel the property owner to "suffer a physical invasion of his property." The second is where regulation "denies economically beneficial or productive use of land." When the owner of property "has been called upon to sacrifice all economically beneficial uses in the name of the common good, that is to leave his property economically idle, he has suffered a taking." Where a state seeks to sustain regulation that deprives land of all economically beneficial use, it may resist compensation "only if the logically antecedent inquiry into the nature of the owner's estate shows that the proscribed use interests were not part of his title to begin with." In this case, it was the Court's view that the position taken by the coastal council, that title is somehow held subject to the "implied limitation" that the state may subsequently eliminate all economically valuable use, is "inconsistent with the historical compact recorded in the Takings Clause that has become part of our constitutional culture." *See also DOLAN v. CITY OF TIGARD* (512 U.S. 374: 1994), p. 204 (Supp.); DUE PROCESS CLAUSES, p. 411; *PENN CENTRAL TRANSPORTATION COMPANY v. NEW YORK CITY* (438 U.S. 104: 1978), p. 451.

Significance The Takings Clause decisions do not directly address the intersection of federal and state authority. Rather, takings cases focus exclusively on the power of states and their political subdivisions to regulate property. The Fifth Amendment provides that government should not "take" private property for public use "without just compensation." The Takings Clause has not been a major limitation on state power historically. The Court's ruling in *Penn Central Transportation*

Company v. New York City (438 U.S.104: 1978) is a good example. In *Penn Central,* the Court allowed local authorities to prevent modifications to Grand Central Station because it was a "historic landmark." Many of the takings cases involve actual physical appropriation of property by a government. Under those circumstances, owners are clearly entitled to compensation. Regulations that fall short of full appropriation present more difficult questions. Again, from a historical perspective, the Court has generally allowed state regulation without the need to compensate under the Takings Clause. Justice Oliver Wendell Holmes suggested in *Pennsylvania Coal Company v. Mahon* (260 U.S. 393: 1922), however, that private property owners were also entitled to compensation when government "redefined the range of interests included in the ownership of property." The implications of this view were not immediately evident but have recently become the foundation of the Rehnquist Court's Takings Clause rulings, which have been more receptive to private property claims.

An early indicator of the doctrinal changes was *Nollan v. California Coastal Commission* (483 U.S. 825: 1987). A local coastal regulatory agency attempted to require property owners to set aside a portion of the property to connect two public beaches as a precondition to getting a building permit. The Court said that California was free to enact a comprehensive program of oceanfront regulations, but if it wanted to get an easement across private property, "it must pay for it." A similar ruling came in *Dolan v. City of Tigard* (512 U.S. 374: 1994). The Dolans sought to expand their business, but a municipality conditioned approval on their committing a portion of their property to a public "greenway." In this case, the Court said that there must be an "essential nexus" between a legitimate state interest and the condition placed on the property owner. In other words, the government must demonstrate a "rough proportionality" between the requirement and the proposed land use. And though "no precise mathematical calculation" is required, a city must adequately support its attempt to acquire private property. Most recently, the Court ruled in *Suitum v. Tahoe Regional Planning Agency* (137 L.Ed. 2d 980: 1997) that the landowner had received a final decision from a regulatory agency for purposes of determining whether a takings claim was ripe for judicial review. Suitum's property rendered without value by the agency environmental regulation but had only been restricted from certain uses. The Court's decision did not expand landowner eligibility for compensation as such but did allow this case to proceed to court for judicial determination of whether Suitum must be compensated. A subsequent ruling that Suitum must be compensated would further limit the extent to which a state may regulate private land use.

Termination of Medical Treatment

***Cruzan v. Director, Missouri Department of Health,* 497 U.S. 261, 111 L.Ed. 2d 224, 110 S.Ct. 2841 (1990)** Held that a person has a right to discontinue life-sustaining medical treatment. At the same time, the Court ruled 5-4 that a state can require maintenance of the treatment in the absence of "clear and convincing" evidence the person wanted the treatment stopped. Nancy Cruzan was injured in an automobile accident in 1983. From that time, she remained in a "persistent vegetative" state. She was administered food and water through a tube attached to her stomach. Cruzan's parents, acting as legal guardians, requested that the life-sustaining feedings be stopped. The hospital refused to stop the feedings, and the Cruzans initiated legal action. A state trial court found that a person has the right to refuse procedures that were "death prolonging." Cruzan, of course, was incapable of stopping the feedings herself. The issue then became whether her statements uttered prior to the accident constituted sufficient evidence of her desire to discontinue medical treatment under the postaccident circumstances. The trial court concluded that all medical treatment should be terminated. The Missouri Supreme Court reversed, however. It ruled that Missouri's "living will" statute favored "preservation of life" in the absence of "clear and convincing" evidence for withdrawal of treatment. The "clear and convincing" standard is the highest standard of evidence used in a civil proceeding. The Missouri Supreme Court decided that Cruzan's preaccident statements were "unreliable" for determining her intent. The issue before the U.S. Supreme Court was whether the U.S. Constitution precludes a state "from choosing the rule of decision which it did." The Court rested its decision on Fourteenth Amendment due process grounds rather than the right of privacy. It was the Court's view that a "competent person has a constitutionally protected liberty interest in refusing unwanted medical treatment." That, however, said Chief Justice Rehnquist, "does not end our inquiry." Whether constitutional rights have been violated requires that liberty interests be weighed against the "relevant state interests." The problem in this case was that Nancy Cruzan herself was incompetent to "make an informed and voluntary choice." Rather, the right "must be exercised for her . . . by some sort of surrogate." Missouri recognizes actions by surrogates but has "established a procedural safeguard to assure that the actions of the surrogate conforms as best it may to the wishes expressed by the patient while competent."

A five-justice majority held that Missouri's standard of proof by clear and convincing evidence in such cases was not forbidden by the Constitution. This procedural requirement was established in furtherance of the state's interest in the "protection and preservation of human life, and there can be no gainsaying this interest." Furthermore, the state has an even "more particular interest" in situations like Cruzan's. The choice between "life and death is a deeply personal decision of obvious and overwhelming finality." Accordingly, Missouri may "legitimately seek to safeguard the personal element of this choice through the imposition of heightened evidentiary requirements." Rehnquist concluded by focusing on the issue of surrogate decisionmaking. He did so by characterizing the Cruzans as "loving and caring parents." Were the Constitution to require states to "repose a right of 'substituted judgment' with anyone, the Cruzans would surely qualify." But, he said, the Court does not think the Fourteenth Amendment "requires the state to repose the judgment on these matters with anyone but the patient herself." Family members may possess a "strong feeling—a feeling not at all ignoble or unworthy, but not entirely disinterested, either"—that they do not wish to witness the continuation of the life of a loved one that they regard as "hopeless, meaningless, and even degrading." But there is no "automatic assurance" that the view of the close family members will necessarily be the "same as the patient's would have been had she been confronted with the prospect of her situation while competent." That being the case, the Court concluded that Missouri could reasonably defer to the patient's own wishes rather than those of close family members by imposing a clear and convincing standard of evidence. Justices Brennan, Marshall, Blackmun, and Stevens dissented. The decision, said Brennan, "robs a patient of the very qualities protected by the right to avoid unwanted medical treatment." Although the right "may not be absolute, no state interest could outweigh the rights of an individual in Nancy Cruzan's position." The state's "general interest" in life "must accede" to Nancy Cruzan's "particularized and intense interest in self-determination in her choice of medical treatment. There is simply nothing legitimately within the state's purview to be gained by superseding her decision." *See also* FEDERALISM, p. 29.

Significance *Cruzan* was the Court's first "on the merits" response to the so-called right-to-die issue. In 1976, the Burger Court had declined to review the New Jersey case involving Karane Ann Quinlan. Unlike *Cruzan, Quinlan* involved discontinuation of life-support machinery as opposed to discontinuing administration of food and fluids. It may prove to be of consequence that the Court in *Cruzan* did not distinguish between feeding and other kinds of medical treatment. What is clear from *Cruzan* is that persons who provide a desire for the discontinuation of any form of treatment in "living wills" can effectively protect their wishes. Currently most states have living will laws, although they vary substantially. *Cruzan* prompted virtually every state to enact such a law. Living wills convey a person's instructions on how physicians and family are to handle life-sustaining treatment decisions in the event the person becomes incapable of making that decision. Had Nancy Cruzan documented her wishes in a living will, her treatment could have been terminated by her parents, because the will would have provided a "clear and convincing" expression of her preference under such circumstances.

The Supreme Court consolidated two cases during the 1996 term, *Vacco v. Quill* (138 L.Ed. 2d 834: 1997) and *Washington v. Glucksberg* (138 L.Ed. 2d 772: 1997), to review state prohibitions on physician-assisted suicide. Under New York law, it is a felony to assist someone to commit suicide. Several physicians, including Timothy Quill, and terminally ill patients unsuccessfully challenged the law in federal district court. The Court of Appeals for the Second Circuit reversed, however, finding an equal protection violation in New York's policy criminalizing physician-assisted suicide, at the same time allowing withdrawal of life-sustaining treatment. Like New York, Washington makes assisting in a suicide a felony. A combination of physicians (including Harold Glucksberg) and terminally ill patients brought suit in federal court, claiming violation of a right of competent, terminally ill patients to choose suicide. The district court agreed, finding the same equal protection defect as that found in the New York case. Drawing on the reasoning from abortion precedents, the district court also concluded in *Glucksberg* that the criminal sanction on assisted suicide places an "undue burden" on the right of the terminally ill to voluntarily choose suicide. Sitting *en banc,* the Court of Appeals for the Ninth Circuit affirmed, finding an interest protected by the Due Process Clause. The Supreme Court unanimously upheld the criminal prohibitions on assisted suicide in these two cases. Chief Justice Rehnquist started with the observation that it is a crime to assist a suicide in "almost every state, indeed, in also most every Western democracy." The state bans on assisted suicide "are not innovations." Rather, they are "long-standing expressions of the states' commitment to the protection and preservation of all human life." Opposing suicide and suicide assistance are "consistent and enduring themes of our philosophical, legal, and cultural heritages." Rehnquist then turned to the due process considerations focused in *Glucksberg.* The Due Process Clause guarantees more than "fair process," and the liberty it protects includes more than the "absence of physical restraint." The Clause also provides "heightened protection against government interference with certain fundamental rights and liberty interests." In addition to the specific Bill of Rights protections, the "libert[ies]" protected by the Due Process Clause include, among others, the rights to marry, have children, marital privacy, and abortion. The Court has also assumed the clause protects the "traditional right to refuse unwanted lifesaving medical treatment." At the same time, the Court has "always been reluctant to expand the concept of substantive due process because the guideposts for responsible decision making in this uncharted area are scarce and open-ended."

The Court's method of substantive due process analysis, said Rehnquist, "has two primary features." First, the clause protects those fundamental rights that are objectively "deeply rooted in the nation's history and tradition" and "implicit in the concept of ordered liberty, such that neither liberty nor justice would exist if they were sacrificed." Second, the Court has required a "careful description of the asserted fundamental liberty interest." Inquiry into the place of assisted suicide in our nation's traditions shows a "consistent and almost universal tradition that has long rejected the asserted right, and continues explicitly to reject it today, even for terminally ill, mentally competent adults." To allow assisted suicide, Rehnquist said, "we would have to reverse centuries of legal doctrine and practice and strike down the considered policy choice of almost every state." The Court thus concluded that the asserted right to assistance in committing suicide is "not a fundamental liberty interest protected by the due process clause." The Constitution also requires that Washington's ban on assisted suicide must be "rationally related to legitimate government interests." This requirement "unquestionably" implicates a number of state interests. First, Washington has an "unqualified interest in the preservation of human life." Second, "all admit that suicide is a serious public health problem, especially among persons in otherwise vulnerable groups." The state thus has an interest in "preventing suicide and in studying, identifying, and treating its causes." Legalizing physician-assisted suicide could make it more difficult for the state to protect "depressed or mentally ill persons, or those who are suffering from untreated pain, from suicidal impulses." Third, the Court also noted a state interest in protecting the "integrity and ethics of the medical profession." Rehnquist pointed to the American Medical Association's position that physician-assisted suicide is "fundamentally incompatible with the physician's role as healer." Further, physician-assisted suicide could "undermine the trust that is essential to the doctor-patient relationship by blurring the time-honored line between healing and harming." Fourth, the state has an interest in protecting vulnerable groups, "including the poor, the elderly, and disabled persons from abuse, neglect and mistakes." The state's interest goes beyond protecting the vulnerable from the "real risk of subtle coercion and undue influence in end-of-life situations." It extends to protecting disabled and terminally ill people from "prejudice, negative and inaccurate stereotypes and social indifference." Washington's ban on assisted suicide reflects and reinforces its policy that "the lives of terminally ill, disabled and elderly people must be no less valued than the lives of the young and healthy and that a seriously disabled person's suicidal impulses should be interpreted and treated the same way as anyone else's." Finally, said Rehnquist, the state "may fear that permitting assisted suicide will start it down the path to voluntary and perhaps even involuntary euthanasia." If suicide becomes a protected constitutional right, then "every man and woman in the United States must enjoy it." This "expansive reasoning" provides "ample support" for the state's concerns that the Ninth Circuit's decisions cannot be limited to "competent, terminally ill adults who wish to hasten their deaths by obtaining medication prescribed by their doctors."

Several justices, including the chief justice, suggested that these rulings did not end the continued discussion of the issue. To the contrary, Rehnquist said the decision "does not absolutely foreclose" subsequent claims by terminally ill people that they have a right to physician assistance in expediting their deaths. Rehnquist noted the "earnest and profound debate" in which Americans are engaged about the "morality, legality, and practicality" of physician-assisted suicide. Our holding "permits this debate to continue, as it should in a democratic society." Justice O'Connor concurred, saying that there is "no generalized right to commit suicide." At the same time, she saw no need to reach the narrower question about whether a "mentally competent person who is experiencing great suffering has a constitutionally cognizable interest in controlling the circumstances of his or her imminent death." Justice Souter urged great caution in recognizing unenumerated rights. If recognized, they would differ in "no essential way" from enumerated rights or those derived from some "more definite textual source" than due process. Recognition of a right of "lesser promise" would create a "constitutional regime too uncertain to bring with it the expectation of finality that is one of this Court's central obligations in making constitutional decisions." The Court should, accordingly, "stay its hand to allow reasonable legislative consideration." And though Souter did not "decide for all time" that assisted suicide claims should not be recognized, he acknowledged the "legislative institutional competence as the better one to deal with that claim at this time." The Court was similarly unpersuaded by the equal protection arguments advanced in the New York case (*Vacco v. Quill*). Generally, said Rehnquist, "laws that apply evenhandedly to all unquestionably comply with the equal protection clause." Neither the state's ban on assisting suicide and its laws permitting patients to refuse medical treatment "treat anyone differently . . . or draw distinctions between persons." "Everyone, regardless of physical condition, is entitled, if competent, to refuse unwanted lifesaving medical treatment; no one is permitted to assist a suicide." Unlike the Second Circuit, the Court thought the distinction between assisting suicide and withdrawing life-sustaining treatment is "widely recognized and endorsed in the medical profession and in our legal traditions [and] is both important and logical; it is certainly rational." These decisions clearly reaffirm the state's broad authority in this sensitive area of public policy.

5. Federal Commerce Power

Guns and Schools

***United States v. Lopez*, 514 U.S. 549, 131 L.Ed. 2d 626, 115 S.Ct. 1624 (1995)** The Gun-Free School Zones Act of 1990 made it a crime to possess a firearm within 1,000 feet of a public or private elementary or secondary school. Alfonso Lopez was indicted under the act for bringing a handgun into his high school in San Antonio, Texas. He unsuccessfully sought to have the indictment dismissed on the grounds that the act exceeded federal authority to regulate interstate commerce. Lopez was tried, convicted, and sentenced to six months in prison. His conviction was overturned by the Court of Appeals for the Fifth Circuit. It was the Fifth Circuit's conclusion that Congress had not established a close enough connection between firearms in local schools and interstate commerce. The Supreme Court agreed in a 5-4 ruling.

Chief Justice Rehnquist spoke for the majority and began by pointing to some general principles of separation of power and federalism. Just as the "separation and independence of the coordinate branches . . . serves to prevent the accumulation of excessive power in any one branch," said Rehnquist, "a healthy balance of power between the States and the Federal Government will reduce the risk of tyranny and abuse from either front." The power to regulate interstate commerce resides with the Congress and may be applied to three broad categories of activity—regulation of the "channels of interstate commerce," protection of the "instrumentalities of interstate commerce," and regulation of those activities that "substantially affect interstate commerce." Neither the first nor second category applied to this case, thus if the act were to be sustained, suggested Rehnquist, it must be under the third category (as a regulation of activity that substantially affects interstate commerce). Yet the Court concluded that the act did not fit within the third category. The act is a "criminal statute that by its terms has nothing to do with 'commerce' or any sort of economic enterprise, however broadly one might define those terms." The government contended that possession of a firearm in a local school zone substantially affects interstate commerce because violent crime affects the functioning of the national economy—the costs are substantial and spread nationally through the "mechanism of insurance, and violent crime impacts interstate travel to areas of the country perceived to be unsafe." The government further contended that guns in schools impair the educational process by threatening the learning environment. That, in turn, could have adverse effects on the well-being of the national economy. The Court focused on the implications of the "cost of crime" rationale advanced by the government. Under this approach, suggested Rehnquist, Congress could regulate not only all violent crime but "all activities that might lead to violent crime, regardless of how tenuously they relate to interstate commerce. . . ." It is difficult, he continued, to "perceive any limitation on federal power, even in areas such as criminal law enforcement or education where States historically have been sovereign." Indeed, if the Court accepted the arguments offered by the government here, it would be "hard-pressed to posit any activity by an individual that Congress is without power to regulate." Rehnquist concluded by focusing on education. If the interstate commerce power allows Congress to regulate those activities that adversely affect the learning environment, it could then regulate the educational process directly. The Court acknowledged that Congress has authority under the Commerce Clause to regulate "numerous commercial activities that substantially affect interstate commerce and also affect the educational process." That authority, "though broad, does not include the authority to regulate each and every aspect of local schools." Justice Kennedy said in a concurring opinion that were the federal government to "take over regulation of entire areas of traditional state concern"—areas unrelated to commercial activities—the boundaries between the spheres of federal and state authority "would blur and political responsibility would become illusory." Without a stronger "connection or identification" with commercial activities that are "central to the Commerce Clause," such federal intrusion into the domain of the states "contradicts the federal balance the Framers designed and that this Court is obliged to enforce." Justice Thomas concurred and suggested more generally that Commerce Clause jurisprudence has "drifted far from the original understanding of the Commerce Clause." Justice Breyer, joined by Justices Stevens, Souter, and Ginsburg, dissented. They saw the act as falling "well within the scope of the commerce power as this Court has understood this power over the last half-century." Courts, said Breyer, must give Congress "a degree of leeway in determining the existence of a significant factual connection between the regulated activity and interstate commerce." The question before the Court, in the view of the dissenters, was whether Congress could have had a "rational basis for finding a significant (or substantial) connection between gun-related school violence and interstate commerce." The dissenters answered that question affirmatively. To find the act constitutional is not to "obliterate" the distinction between what is national and what is local, nor is it to hold that the Commerce Clause permits the federal government to regulate "any activity that it found was related to the economic productivity of individual citizens, to regulate marriage, divorce, and child custody, or to regulate any and all aspects of education." Upholding the act would not expand the scope of the commerce power, said Breyer. Rather, it "simply would apply pre-existing law to changing economic circumstances." *See also* COMMERCE CLAUSE, p. 291; FEDERALISM, p. 29; *HEART OF ATLANTA MOTEL v. UNITED STATES* (379 U.S. 241: 1964), p. 343; *NEW YORK v. UNITED STATES* (505 U.S. 144: 1992), p. 118 (Supp.).

Significance Since the late 1930s, the Court has used the commerce power to expand the role of the federal government. The commerce power provided the constitutional basis for the Civil Rights Act of 1964, for example. Title II of the act prohibited racial discrimination in "public accommodations." The Warren Court had an expansive view of the Commerce Clause, and it upheld the act in *Heart of Atlanta Motel v. United States* (379 U.S. 241: 1964). The "determinative test" for the exercise of the commerce power is "simply whether the activity sought to be regulated is commerce which concerns more states than one" and that such activity has a "real and substantial relation to the national interest." The Warren Court saw the contemporary commerce power as "broad and sweeping."

The Burger and Rehnquist Courts have not fully shared that view. Both assigned a higher value to state authority that, in some respects, is incompatible with an expansive view of the federal commerce power. As a result, considerations of federalism have influenced the decisions in some cases and led to the devolving of power to the states. *Lopez* is a clear reflection of this tendency. It was explicitly noted by Chief Justice Rehnquist that, were the Court to allow Congress to regulate gun control and violent crime at the local level, it is "difficult to perceive any limitation on federal power, even in such areas as criminal law enforcement or education where States historically have been sovereign." Indeed, Rehnquist concluded, the Court would be "hard-pressed to posit any activity by an individual that Congress is without the power to regulate." This view also governed the Court's ruling in *Printz v. United States* (138 L.Ed. 2d 914: 1997), in which the background-check provisions of the Handgun Violence Prevention Act (also known as the Brady Act) were ruled unconstitutional. The Court reaffirmed in *Printz* the principle that the federal government cannot "compel the States to enact or administer a Federal regulatory program." The Court's position was that the commerce power simply does not extend to the regulation of wholly intrastate transactions. The four dissenters in *Printz* were of the view that Congress had a "rational basis" for finding a connection between school violence and interstate commerce, and they would have deferred to that legislative judgment. Cases containing questions about the scope of the commerce power will continue to divide the current Court, in large part because these questions hinge on the broader issue of federal-state sovereignty.

Sherman Act

***Business Electronics Corp. v. Sharp Electronics Corp.*, 485 U.S. 717, 99 L.Ed. 2d 808, 108 S.Ct. 1515 (1988)** Business Electronics and another retailer, Gilbert Hartwell, were authorized by Sharp to sell electronic calculators in Houston, Texas. Sharp withdrew Business Electronics's dealership when Hartwell complained about its price-cutting practices. Business Electronics brought suit in U.S. district court, alleging that Sharp and Hartwell had conspired to terminate Business Electronics's dealership in violation of the Sherman Act. A jury found for Business Electronics, and the district court entered judgment for treble damages. The U.S. Court of Appeals for the Fifth Circuit reversed, however, concluding that for an illegal "vertical agreement" to exist between a manufacturer and a dealer to terminate a second dealer the agreement must also establish pricing levels for the first dealer. The Supreme Court agreed.

The Court ruled that vertical agreements are not necessarily prohibited by the Sherman Act. The act categorically bans vertical agreements on resale prices, but extension of that prohibition to other vertical restraints must be based on a "demonstrable economic effect." Such determinations are made through a case-by-case application of the "rule of reason" rather than "formalistic line drawing," because some vertical nonprice restraints have the potential to "stimulate interbrand competition." In this case, there was no showing that "different characteristics" attach to an agreement between a manufacturer and a dealer to terminate another dealer who cuts prices without an explicit agreement on the prices to be charged by the remaining dealer. The Court found it "plausible" that the purpose of the agreement in question was simply to enable Hartwell to "provide better services" under its sales agreement with Sharp. Business Electronics had also argued that a categorical or per se rule was required in order to prevent a price agreement occurring after a dealer had been terminated. The Court was unconvinced that a prophylactic rule was necessary. Justice Scalia suggested that the Sherman Act reference to "restraint of trade" was not targeting a "particular list of agreements" but particular "economic consequences which may be produced by quite different sorts of agreements" occurring at different times and under varying circumstances. Finally, the Court rejected the assertion that a categorical rule of illegality was required for vertical agreements even when no pricing agreements were in place because such a rule existed for horizontal agreements. Prior Sherman Act rulings of the Court, however, had explicitly rejected any notion of equivalence between the scope of horizontal per se illegality and vertical per se illegality. *See also* ANTITRUST LAWS, p. 579; COMMERCE CLAUSE, p. 291; *PARKER v. BROWN* (317 U.S. 341: 1943), p. 332.

Significance The Commerce Clause provides the basis for the federal government's attempts to regulate activities and practices that restrain trade. The various antitrust laws, such as the Sherman Act, are designed to facilitate market competition. Vertical restraints of trade, such as the one examined in *Business Electronics,* are agreements between entities operating at different levels in the market that might have anticompetitive consequences. Manufacturers and distributors occupy two distinct levels in the market structure, and a price-fixing agreement between the two would constitute a vertical restraint of trade or vertical agreement. A horizontal restraint of trade, by contrast, would involve businesses at the same market level. Either kind of trade restraint may constitute a violation of the Sherman Act. Three examples help clarify the underlying constitutional questions.

The first case is *Eastman Kodak Co. v. Image Technical Services, Inc.* (504 U.S. 451: 1992). Suit was brought against Eastman Kodak by a number of independent service organizations (ISOs), such as Image Technical Services, after Kodak limited the availability of replacement parts for its equipment to the ISOs. The ISOs alleged that Kodak had unlawfully attempted to monopolize the sale of service and parts for its machines. The district court granted summary judgment for Kodak, but the U.S. Court of Appeals for the Ninth Circuit reversed. The Ninth Circuit found that the ISOs provided sufficient evidence of Kodak's market influence in the service and parts markets. The Supreme Court found that Kodak had created "tying agreements" that violate the Sherman Act. Kodak "tied" the sale of two distinct products, services, and parts, by indicating that it would sell parts to third parties only if they did not use ISOs for service. A seller of a product is deemed as having "appreciable market power" if it can force a purchaser to "do something that he would not do in a competitive market." When such a situation is examined, the Court said it ordinarily infers the existence of such power "from the seller's possession of a predominate share of the market."

The second case is *Federal Trade Commission v. Ticor Title Insurance Co.* (504 U.S. 451: 1992). The Federal Trade Commission (FTC) filed a complaint against six large title insurance companies, including Ticor, for horizontal price-fixing in setting fees for title searches. The states in which these title insurance companies operated had uniform rates established by an agency licensed by the state. An administrative law judge ruled that the anticompetitive activities of the companies were covered under the "state-action immunity" doctrine from *Parker v. Brown* (317 U.S. 341: 1943). Under this doctrine, a state regulatory scheme can create antitrust immunity if the state has a "clear and affirmative" policy allowing anticompetitive practices and sufficiently supervises any such anticompetitive conduct by private entities. The FTC concluded that none of the states involved in this case provided sufficient supervision to warrant state-action immunity. The Court of Appeals for the Third Circuit reversed, ruling that the existence of a regulatory program, "if staffed, funded, and empowered by law," satisfied the supervision requirement of *Parker* and thus entitled the companies to state-action antitrust immunity. The Supreme Court ruled that such immunity was not available for the regulatory programs involved in this case. The party claiming immunity must demonstrate that state officials have taken the necessary steps to determine the specifics of the price-setting or rate-setting scheme. The "mere potential" for state supervision is an inadequate substitute for the state's decision. Without "active" supervision there can be no state-action immunity for private price-fixing arrangements. Review by the state courts does not constitute active supervision. The Court concluded that actions in *Ticor* involved horizontal price-fixing under a "vague imprimatur in form and agency inaction in fact," and it should be read in light of the "gravity" of the antitrust offense, the involvement of private actors throughout, and the "clear absence" of state supervision.

The question of collecting damages for antitrust violations was addressed in *Kansas & Missouri v. Utilicorp United, Inc.* (497 U.S. 199: 1990). Utilicorp United is a public utility operating in Kansas and Missouri. Utilicorp and several other utilities and natural gas purchasers brought suit in federal district court against a pipeline company and five gas producers under section 4 of the Clayton Act. Section 4 provides that any person injured as a result of an antitrust law violation is entitled to triple damages. The utilities claimed that the defendants had unlawfully conspired to elevate gas prices to purchasers; they sought damages for overcharges and for sales lost because of the overcharges. Kansas and Missouri filed separate section 4 actions against the same defendants, asserting parens patriae claims on behalf of all persons residing in the states who had purchased gas at the inflated price levels. The district court ruled that because the purchasing utilities had passed on the alleged overcharges to their customers they lacked standing to bring the section 4 damages suit because they had suffered no direct injury themselves. Under the Supreme Court's decision in *Illinois Brick Co. v. Illinois* (431 U.S. 720: 1977), only direct purchasers are eligible for damages through section 4. Similarly, the district court dismissed the parens patriae claims, a ruling affirmed by the U.S. Court of Appeals for the Tenth Circuit. The Supreme Court ruled that the utilities had standing to bring an antitrust violation action under section 4, but the states were precluded from actions brought on behalf of utility customers. The Court based its ruling on the three reasons underlying the indirect-purchaser rule from *Illinois Brick*. First, determination of the amount of an overcharge passed on to indirect purchasers would normally prove "insurmountable" given the many factors influencing a pricing decision. Second, a "pass-on" defense would reduce the effectiveness of section 4 claims by reducing the recovery available to any potential claimant. Third, allowing suits by indirect purchasers would risk "multiple liability" because the alleged antitrust violators could not use a pass-on defense in an action by the direct purchasers.

Title VII: Workplace Regulation

***Equal Employment Opportunity Commission v. Arabian American Oil Co.*, 499 U.S. 244, 113 L.Ed. 274, 111 S.Ct. 1227 (1991)** Ali Boureslan, a naturalized U.S. citizen born in Lebanon and working in Saudi Arabia, was discharged from his job by Arabian American Oil Company. Boureslan filed a charge with the Equal Employment Opportunity Commission (EEOC) and commenced a suit in U.S. district court, seeking relief under Title VII of the Civil Rights Act of 1964. He alleged that Arabian American terminated his employment on the basis of his race, national origin, and religion (Muslim). The district court dismissed his claim, ruling that Title VII did not extend to U.S. citizens employed overseas by American employers. As a result, the district court concluded it had no jurisdiction over Boureslan's Title VII claim, and the U.S. Court of Appeals for the Fifth Circuit affirmed. The Supreme Court also ruled that Title VII did not apply extraterritorially.

The Court suggested that there is a presumption against extraterritoriality unless the "affirmative intention of Congress is clearly expressed." The presumption in this case elevated the burden Boureslan and the EEOC needed to meet. The statutory interpretations they offered were "plausible, but no more persuasive than that." Rather than making an "affirmative showing," the language depended upon by Boureslan was found "ambiguous" and did not definitively support extraterritoriality in this case. Without clearer evidence, the Court was unwilling to ascribe to Congress a policy that would "raise difficult issues of international law by imposing this country's employment discrimination regime upon foreign corporations operating in foreign commerce." The Court's conclusion was "fortified" by other elements in the statute suggesting a "purely domestic focus." The statute in its entirety indicated a concern that it not "unduly interfere with the sovereignty and laws of the States." Although Title VII "consistently speaks" in terms of the states and state proceedings, it "fails to even mention foreign nations or foreign proceedings." Similarly, Congress failed to provide "any mechanisms for overseas enforcement of Title VII." On those bases, the Court concluded that Boureslan and the EEOC failed to present "sufficient affirmative evidence" that Congress intended Title VII to apply abroad. The dissenters—Justices Marshall, Blackmun, and Stevens—thought it sufficiently clear from the language, legislative history, and administrative interpretations of Title VII that Congress intended, the absence of express language notwithstanding, to protect American citizens from discrimination by American employers operating abroad. *See also* COMMERCE CLAUSE, p. 291; *HARRIS v. FORKLIFT SYSTEMS* (510 U.S. 17: 1993), p. 90 (Supp.); *HEART OF ATLANTA MOTEL v. UNITED STATES* (379 U.S. 241: 1964), p. 343; JURISDICTION, p. 629.

Significance The Civil Rights Act of 1964 is the most comprehensive legislative initiative of its kind since Reconstruction. The act was grounded on the federal government's authority to regulate interstate commerce and all that affects it. The act contains several policy mandates. Title II, for example, prohibits discrimination in public accommodations, and Titles III and IV are aimed at desegregating public schools and noneducational facilities. Title VII was the first federal law prohibiting discrimination in the workplace. Title VII prohibits employers of more than 25 workers from discriminating on the basis of race, color, religion, gender, or national origin when making hiring, classifying, training, or promotion decisions. Title VII also created the Equal Employment Opportunity Commission and authorized it to hear complaints of discrimination and to enforce Title VII provisions. The scope of Title VII was expanded by amendment in 1972 and now applies to employers with 15 or more employees, state and local governments, and educational institutions. The 1972 statute also expands the enforcement powers of the EEOC to include, among other things, authority to seek enforcement of Title VII in federal courts.

The first constitutional challenges to the act came in *Heart of Atlanta Motel v. United States* (379 U.S. 241: 1964) and *Katzenbach v. McClung*

(379 U.S. 294: 1964). These cases focused on the public-accommodations section of the act, but the Warren Court found that the commerce power could be used to combat discrimination in a wide range of contexts. The "determinative" consideration for the exercise of the commerce power, said Justice Clark, is "simply whether the activity sought to be regulated is commerce which concerns more states than one" and that the activity has a "real and substantial relation to the national interest." The Warren Court, when reviewing a congressional action of this type, thought only two questions were appropriate: whether Congress had a "rational basis" for its finding that discrimination affected commerce and whether the means chosen to address the problem were "reasonable."

Discrimination in the workplace has the most direct connection to commerce of all the areas covered by the 1964 act. As a result, the Court has generally found that various discriminatory practices fall within the scope of the law, and it has supported a range of remedies for the victims of employment discrimination. The Court's recent rulings in the area of sexual harassment provide a good example. The Court held in *Meritor Savings Bank, FSB v. Vinson* (477 U.S. 57: 1986) that harassment claims can be brought under Title VII. In *Harris v. Forklift Systems* (510 U.S. 17: 1993), the Court refined *Meritor* by saying that an abusive work environment, even one that "does not seriously affect employees' psychological well-being," can "detract from employees' job performance, discourage employees from remaining on the job, or keep them from advancing in their careers." Justice O'Connor concluded in *Harris* that conduct that is so severe as to create an abusive workplace environment "offends Title VII's broad rule of workplace equality."

The Court has not automatically supported such an expansive view of Title VII as seen in *Harris,* however. The Court's reluctance to apply the statute to employees working overseas in *Arabian American Oil* reflects some apprehension about broadening the bounds of Title VII without a clear and explicit congressional mandate. *Arabian American Oil* was not the only Rehnquist Court ruling that defined tighter limits for Title VII. In *Wards Cove Packing Co. v. Atonio* (490 U.S. 642: 1989) and *Lorance v. AT&T Technologies, Inc.* (490 U.S. 900: 1989), the Court made it more difficult for employees alleging employment discrimination to demonstrate that an employer's conduct was actually illegal. The Court termed "nonsensical" the mere comparison of proportions of minorities in a workforce as the basis for determining statutory violations. Critics of decisions like *Wards Cove* and *Lorance* were concerned that the balance in Title VII cases had been tipped too greatly in favor of employers. Congress apparently agreed: It reduced the burden of proof required of workers claiming job discrimination in the

Civil Rights Act of 1991, thereby essentially overruling *Wards Cove* and *Lorance.*

Commerce and State Taxation

***American Trucking Associations, Inc. v. Scheiner,* 483 U.S. 266, 97 L.Ed. 2d 226: 107 S.Ct. 2829 (1987)** Two separate Pennsylvania laws required trucks operating on the state's highways to display an identification marker obtained by the payment of an annual flat fee and to pay an annual axle tax. Trucks registered in the state had the cost of obtaining the identification marker included in the registration fee and had the registration fee reduced by the amount of the axle tax. Legal action was brought in Pennsylvania court by American Trucking Associations, Inc., which includes organizations that represent interstate carriers whose vehicles were registered outside Pennsylvania and subject to the marker fee and axle tax. They contended that the marker fee and axle tax discriminated against interstate commerce since the entire fee or tax burden fell on out-of-state vehicles. The commonwealth court ruled that the taxes were unconstitutional, but the Pennsylvania Supreme Court reversed. The U.S. Supreme Court agreed with the trial court and found the annual taxes to be in violation of the Commerce Clause.

The Commerce Clause created an area of trade free from interference by the states. One consequence of this restriction is that a state may not tax a "transaction or incident more heavily when it crosses state lines than when it occurs entirely within the State." The Commerce Clause guarantee of free trade among the states, however, has a "deeper meaning" that may be implicated even though state provisions, such as the ones in this case, "do not allocate tax burdens between insiders and outsiders in a manner that is facially discriminatory." Tax initiatives of states must pass an "internal consistency" test. Under this test, a state tax must result in no "impermissible interference with free trade" if applied by every jurisdiction. In this case, the Pennsylvania fees failed the test because the "inevitable effect" was to threaten the free movement of commerce by "placing a financial barrier around Pennsylvania." The Court also concluded that Pennsylvania's axle fee was different from a "flat user fee," which may be allowed. Examination of the "practical consequences" of the tax is determinative. A flat tax is not permissible simply because the formula by which it is calculated "extends the same nominal privilege to interstate commerce that it extends to in-state activities." Although out-of-state carriers may access Pennsylvania highways to essentially the same extent as local carriers, the fees make that access "several times more valuable to a local business than to its out-of-state competitors" in a way that is "unquestionably discriminatory." *See also* COMMERCE CLAUSE, p. 291.

Significance A number of constitutional disputes have arisen over state taxation of interstate commerce. The four-pronged test the Court currently uses in these cases was set forth in *Complete Auto Transit, Inc. v. Brady* (430 U.S. 274: 1977). The four components of the test are: (1) the state tax must apply to a commercial activity with a "substantial nexus" to the taxing state; (2) the tax must be "fairly apportioned"—the tax must target intrastate commercial activity or income not subject to taxation by another state; (3) the tax may not "unduly burden" or discriminate against interstate commerce; and (4) the tax must be "fairly related" to the services provided by the state. Two state taxes recently reviewed by the Rehnquist Court passed muster under the *Complete Auto* test.

Kent County, Michigan, owns and operates the Kent County International Airport. The county collects rents and fees from three categories of airport users: commercial airlines, general aviation, and concessionaires. The county apportions its air operations costs to the commercial airlines and general aviation users in proportion to their airport use and its terminal maintenance costs to the airlines and concessionaires in proportion to their square footage in the terminal. The airlines are charged the full amount of their allocated costs, but the general aviation users pay only 20 percent of their apportioned costs. Similarly, the rate charged concessionaires "substantially exceeds" their allocated costs; the surplus is used to offset the general aviation shortfall. Northwest Airlines challenged the apportionment of the fees as violating the Anti-Head Tax Act (AHTA), which prohibits states and their subdivisions from collecting "unreasonable" rents, user fees, and other charges from aircraft operators for using local airport facilities. Northwest also argued that Kent County's preferential treatment of general aviation users discriminated against interstate carriers in violation of the Commerce Clause. A U.S. district court ruled Northwest had an implied right of action under AHTA but found that the challenged fees were not unreasonable; the Court of Appeals for the Sixth Circuit affirmed. In *Northwest Airlines v. Kent County* (510 U.S. 355: 1994), the Supreme Court ruled that the Kent County user fees were neither unreasonable nor discriminatory in violation of the Commerce Clause or AHTA. A levy such as the one here is reasonable if it is based on some "fair approximation of the facilities" use, is not "excessive" in relation to conferred benefits, and does not discriminate against interstate commerce. The Court concluded Kent County's decision to exclude concessionaires from the air operation cost assessment reflected a "fair, if imperfect approximation of the use of facilities for whose benefit they are imposed." Similarly, the

Court concluded Kent County's rate practices for concessionaires was not illegal simply because it produced a surplus. Finally, the Court did not find that the lower rate for general aviation fees discriminated against interstate commerce and travel. The Court saw no evidence that the "large and diverse" group of general aviation operators "seldom ventures beyond Michigan's borders."

Jefferson Lines, Inc., a bus line that provided interstate and intrastate services, collected and remitted to the state of Oklahoma a sales tax for intrastate travel but did not collect the state sales tax on bus tickets sold in Oklahoma for interstate travel beginning in the state. Jefferson Lines filed for bankruptcy, and the Oklahoma Tax Commission filed claims for the uncollected taxes. The bankruptcy court, however, found the tax unconstitutional in that it imposed an undue burden on interstate commerce; a U.S. district court agreed. The Court of Appeals for the Eighth Circuit affirmed, also finding that the state sales tax was unfairly apportioned. The U.S. Supreme Court, however, ruled in *Oklahoma Tax Commission v. Jefferson Lines, Inc.* (514 U.S. 175: 1995) that Oklahoma could tax the sale of both interstate and intrastate transportation services. The principal inquiry focused on the second prong of the *Complete Auto* test: whether the tax was fairly apportioned. A properly apportioned tax must be both "internally and externally consistent." The former looks to whether application of the same tax by every other state would disadvantage interstate over intrastate commerce. Oklahoma's tax met the test, because if every state imposed an identical tax on ticket sales for travel originating in that state, no sale would be subject to more than one state's tax. External consistency, on the other hand, considers the "economic justification for the state's claim upon the value taxed" to determine whether the tax "reaches beyond the portion of value that is fairly attributable to economic activity within the taxing State." The Court found Oklahoma's tax externally consistent as well. Finally, the Court held that a sale of services can be typically treated as a "local state event" just as readily as a sale of tangible goods can be located within the state of delivery. In this case, although the service is performed only in part within the taxing state, the ticket buyer is "no more subject to double taxation on the sale of services than the buyer of goods would be." The subject of taxation in this case "comprises agreement, payment, and delivery of some of the services in the taxing State." No other state can claim to be the "site of the same combination and these combined events are commonly understood to suffice for a sale."

***Quill Corp. v. North Dakota*, 504 U.S. 298, 119 L.Ed. 2d 91, 112 S.Ct. 1904 (1992)** Quill Corp. is a mail-order vendor of office equipment and supplies. Quill is incorporated in Delaware and has offices and warehouses in several states. It has no offices or personnel in North Dakota, although it has customers who reside in the state. North Dakota sought to collect a use tax from Quill for merchandise purchased for use in the state. Quill challenged the tax and prevailed in a state trial court, but the North Dakota Supreme Court upheld the tax. The U.S. Supreme Court ruled that the Due Process Clause does not prohibit enforcement of the use tax against Quill. Nonetheless, the Court found the tax unconstitutional because it placed an undue burden on interstate commerce.

The Court said that although Due Process and Commerce Clause claims are "closely related" they pose "distinct limits" on the taxing powers of the states and "differ fundamentally in several ways." The Due Process Clause requires some "definite link, some minimum connection, between a state and the person, property or transaction it seeks to tax." If a foreign corporation "purposely fully avails itself of the benefits of an economic market in the forum State, it may subject itself to the State's . . . jurisdiction even if it has no physical presence in the State." The Court had no question in this case that Quill Corp. had "purposefully directed its activities" at North Dakota residents, that the magnitude of those contacts is "more than sufficient" for due process purposes, and that the use tax was "related to the benefits Quill receives from access to the State." As a result, the Court concluded that the Due Process Clause did not prohibit enforcement of North Dakota's use tax against Quill.

Due process "centrally concerns the fundamental fairness of governmental activity." At the most general level, due process "nexus" analysis requires that the Court inquire whether an individual's connections with a state are "substantial enough to legitimate the State's exercise of power over him." The Court, said Justice Stevens, has often identified "notice or fair warning as the analytic touchstone of due process nexus analysis." In contrast, the Commerce Clause, and its nexus requirement, "are informed not so much by concerns about fairness for the individual defendant as by structural concerns about the effects of state regulation on the national economy." The four-pronged test from *Complete Auto Transit, Inc. v. Brady* (430 U.S. 274: 1977) "reflects these concerns about the national economy." A state tax will be sustained against a Commerce Clause challenge if the tax: (1) is applied to an activity with a "substantial nexus" with the taxing state; (2) is "fairly apportioned"; (3) does not discriminate against interstate commerce; and (4) is "fairly related" to the services provided by the state. The second and third prongs of the *Complete Auto* analysis prohibit taxes that pass an "unfair share of the tax burden onto interstate commerce." The first and fourth prongs are intended to "limit the reach of State taxing authority so as to ensure that State taxation does not unduly burden interstate commerce." The "substantial nexus" requirement is not, like the due process "minimum contacts" requirement, a "proxy for notice, but rather a means for limiting state burdens on interstate commerce." A corporation may thus have the "minimum contacts" with a taxing state as required by the Due Process Clause yet lack the "substantial nexus" with that state as required by the Commerce Clause. Here, because Quill's only connection to North Dakota was by mail, the state could collect sales or use taxes because it lacked "substantial nexus" as required by the Commerce Clause. *See also ASSOCIATED INDUSTRIES OF MISSOURI v. LOHMAN* (511 U.S. 641: 1994), p. 198 (Supp.); COMMERCE CLAUSE, p. 291; DUE PROCESS CLAUSES, p. 594.

Significance The *Complete Auto* standard remains the basis for assessing the constitutionality of state taxes. The test often has produced different results from that in *Quill,* as seen in two cases decided several years before *Quill.* D.H. Holmes Co. operates department stores in Louisiana. Holmes contracted with several out-of-state companies to produce merchandise catalogs. The catalogs were shipped by the producers to lists of addresses provided by Holmes. Eighty-two percent of the addresses were Louisiana residents. The company did not pay any sales taxes where the catalogs were produced. The Louisiana Department of Revenue and Taxation, headed by Shirley McNamera, imposed a 3 percent use tax on the value of the catalogs. Holmes refused to pay, and the state won a tax-collection suit in Louisiana district court. The Louisiana Court of Appeals affirmed, finding that the catalogs were no longer part of interstate commerce at the point they were placed in the mailboxes of Louisiana residents and that the distribution of catalogs constituted a "use" properly subject to the state tax. Likewise, the U.S. Supreme Court ruled in *D.H. Holmes Company, Ltd. v. McNamera* (486 U.S. 24: 1988) that Louisiana's taxation of the catalogs did not violate the Commerce Clause. The Court found it "largely irrelevant" whether the catalogs "came to rest" in the mailboxes of Louisiana residents or whether the catalogs were considered as remaining in the "stream of interstate commerce." Under the *Complete Auto* test, interstate commerce may be required to pay its "fair share" of state taxes, and the Louisiana tax satisfies each of the elements of *Complete Auto*'s four-pronged test. The Louisiana tax was fairly apportioned because it provided a credit for taxes paid in other states and because it was imposed only on those catalogs distributed in the state. Furthermore, the tax did not discriminate against interstate commerce, since the use tax compensated for revenue lost on out-of-state purchases in an amount equal to that collected on instate sales.

In another case, Illinois adopted an excise tax on telecommunications that imposed a 5 percent tax on the gross charges of interstate telecommunications originating or ending in Illinois and charged to an Illinois service address. A credit was provided upon proof that another state had taxed the same call. Telecommunications retailers such as GTE Sprint, a party in a companion suit, were required under the law to collect the tax from consumers. An Illinois circuit court ruled that the tax violated the Commerce Clause. The Illinois Supreme Court reversed, concluding that the tax satisfied the *Complete Auto* test. The U.S. Supreme Court agreed in *Goldberg v. Sweet* (488 U.S. 252: 1989). The tax was found "internally consistent"; it was structured such that if every state imposed an identical tax on interstate phone calls charged to an in-state service address, only one state would tax each call—and no multiple taxation would occur. In addition, the tax was not found to be discriminatory against interstate commerce, since its burden fell on instate consumers rather than out-of-state consumers.

***Kraft General Foods v. Iowa Department of Revenue*, 505 U.S. 71, 120 L.Ed. 2d 59, 112 S.Ct. 2365 (1992)** Iowa's tax on corporations allows a deduction for dividends from domestic but not foreign subsidiaries. Iowa does not allow credit paid to foreign countries. Kraft General Foods, Inc., which operates in the United States and in several foreign countries, deducted its foreign subsidiary dividends from its taxable income when it filed its 1981 Iowa tax return. The Iowa Department of Revenue and Finance assessed Kraft a deficiency, and Kraft challenged in administrative proceedings and the Iowa courts. The Iowa Supreme Court rejected Kraft's contention that the state's different treatment of domestic and foreign subsidiaries violated the Commerce Clause, concluding instead that Kraft failed to show that the Iowa tax policy advantaged Iowa businesses over foreign commerce. The U.S. Supreme Court reversed.

The Court said it was "indisputable" that the Iowa law treated dividends from foreign subsidiaries "less favorably" than dividends from domestic subsidiaries. Although admitting that the two kinds of dividends were treated differently, Iowa (and the United States as an amicus participant) offered several arguments in support of the proposition that such differential treatment does not constitute prohibited discrimination against foreign commerce. The Court rejected all of these arguments. First, it was asserted that the disparate treatment of dividends "does not translate into discrimination based on the location or nature of business activity" and thus is not prohibited by the Commerce Clause. The Court agreed that the domicile of a corporation "does not necessarily establish that it is engaged in either foreign or domestic commerce."

In this case, however, it was stipulated that the foreign subsidiaries did operate in foreign commerce, and the "flow of value" between Kraft and its foreign subsidiaries "clearly constitutes foreign commerce." Second, the applicability of the Iowa tax "necessarily depends" not only on the domicile of the subsidiary but also on the location of the subsidiary's business activities. When the federal government taxes the income a foreign corporation earns in the United States, it allows a deduction for foreign subsidiary dividends that reflects such domestic earnings. In attempting to parallel this approach, Iowa also allows a deduction for dividends received from a foreign subsidiary "if the dividends reflect business activity in the United States." Although the dividends of all domestic subsidiaries are excluded from the Iowa tax base, the dividends of foreign subsidiaries are excluded "only to the extent they reflect domestic earnings." As a result, the only subsidiary dividend payments taxed by Iowa are those "reflecting the foreign business activity of foreign subsidiaries." It was the Court's view that this "discriminatory treatment" could not be justified on the ground that "some of the (untaxed) dividend payments from domestic subsidiaries also reflect foreign earnings." The Court agreed that the Iowa law did not treat Iowa subsidiaries more favorably than subsidiaries located elsewhere, but it was not convinced that such favoritism is an "essential element of a violation of the Foreign Commerce Clause." Nonetheless, a state's "preference for domestic commerce over foreign commerce is inconsistent with the Commerce Clause even if the State's own economy is not a direct beneficiary of the discrimination." Just as the absence of local benefit does not "eliminate the international implications of the discrimination, it cannot exempt such discrimination from Commerce Clause prohibitions." *See also* COMMERCE CLAUSE, p. 291.

Significance As we have seen in cases involving state taxation of domestic interstate commerce, the operative standards come from *Complete Auto Transit, Inc. v. Brady* (430 U.S. 274: 1977). Two years after *Complete Auto,* the Court modified the requirements for foreign transactions, in *Japan Line, Ltd. v. County of Los Angeles* (441 U.S. 434: 1979). A state tax on international business activities cannot create an "enhanced risk of multiple taxation," and it cannot prevent the federal government from "speaking with one voice" when regulating foreign commerce. These criteria were applied in the case of *Itel Containers International Corp. v. Huddleston* (507 U.S. 60: 1993). Itel Containers is a domestic company that leases cargo containers for use exclusively in international shipping. Tennessee collected its sales tax, under protest from Itel, on proceeds from the lease of containers delivered in Tennessee. Itel challenged the constitutionality of the tax under the Commerce, Import-Export, and Supremacy Clauses. A Tennessee chancery court modified the assessment on the basis of state law but rejected the constitutional claims, a ruling affirmed by the Tennessee Supreme Court. The U.S. Supreme Court ruled that the Tennessee sales tax did not violate the federal Commerce Clause.

The language contained in federal regulations and two international container conventions signed by the United States "makes it clear" that only taxes imposed "based on the act of importation itself" are disallowed. The fact that other signatory nations to the conventions place only indirect taxes on container leases "does not demonstrate that Tennessee's direct tax on container leases is prohibited." More importantly, the Court concluded that the Tennessee tax, which applied to both domestic and foreign goods "without differentiation, does not impede" the federal objectives expressed in the conventions and related federal statutes and regulations. Nowhere in the federal regulatory scheme for containers used in foreign commerce was there evidence of congressional intent to "exempt these containers from all or most domestic taxation." In short, the Court found that the Tennessee tax neither created a substantial risk of multiple taxation nor prevented the federal government from speaking with "one voice"; the tax was compatible with all federal conventions, statutes, and regulations, and it did not "conflict with international custom."

A final case returns to the issue of state taxation of wholly domestic interstate commerce. Massachusetts imposed an assessment (called a "premium payment") on all milk sold to retailers in the state. Although two-thirds of the milk sold in Massachusetts was produced outside the state, the revenues from the assessment were distributed exclusively to Massachusetts dairy farmers. Two licensed dealers who sold milk produced outside the state refused to pay their assessments, and Massachusetts commenced license revocation procedures against them. The dealers unsuccessfully attempted to enjoin enforcement of the pricing order under the Commerce Clause. A Massachusetts superior court denied relief, and the licenses were revoked. The Supreme Judicial Court of Massachusetts ruled that the benefits to the state's dairy industry outweighed any burden on interstate commerce. The U.S. Supreme Court disagreed in *West Lynn Creamery, Inc. v. Healy* (512 U.S. 186: 1994).

Previous Court rulings on this issue consistently invalidated state laws intended to benefit local producers by creating "tariff-like barriers that neutralize the competitive and economic advantages possessed by lower-cost out-of-state producers." The "premium payments are effectively a tax making milk produced out of State more expensive." Although the payments also applied to milk produced in Massachusetts, the effects on Massachusetts producers was "entirely (indeed more than) offset by the subsidy provided exclusively to Massachusetts dairy farmers." Even granting that both components of the Massachusetts Department of Food and Agriculture's pricing order (the premium and the subsidy) would be constitutional "standing alone," the Court concluded that the order was defective because it is "funded principally from taxes on the sale of milk produced in other States," thereby burdening interstate commerce. In addition, the Court held that the contention that the lawfulness of the individual components of the scheme establishes the legality of their combination was "logically flawed." In fact, by joining a tax and a subsidy, the state, in the Court's view, "created a program more dangerous to interstate commerce" than either part alone because the State's political processes could not be relied upon to "prevent legislative abuse" where dairy farmers, a "powerful in-state interest" that would ordinarily oppose the premium payments as a tax, would have been "mollified by the subsidy." The Court also rejected the argument that the order was not discriminatory because the dealers who pay the premiums were not competitors of the farmers who received the subsidies. The imposition of a "differential burden on any part of the stream of commerce . . . is invalid because a burden placed at any point will result in a disadvantage to the out-of-state producer." The Court reiterated a view present in Commerce Clause cases since the 1930s that the American economy is highly integrated. The Massachusetts tax and subsidy program "ignores the fact that Massachusetts dairy farmers are part of an integrated interstate market." The "obvious impact" of the assessment on out-of-state production "demonstrates that it is simply wrong to assume that it burdens only in-state dealers and consumers."

Environmental Regulation

***Pennsylvania v. Union Gas Co.*, 491 U.S. 1, 105 L.Ed. 2d 1, 109 S.Ct. 2273 (1989)** Sections 104 and 106 of the Comprehensive Environmental Response, Compensation, and Liability Act of 1980 and the Superfund Amendments of 1986 permit suits in federal court for monetary damages against a state resulting from environmental contamination. The predecessors of Union Gas Co. operated a coal gasification plant along a creek in Pennsylvania. A by-product of the gasification process was coal tar. Pennsylvania was proceeding with a flood control project on the creek, and workers struck a deposit of coal tar that then entered the creek. The Environmental Protection Agency (EPA) deemed the coal tar to be a hazardous substance and designated the area the nation's first Superfund cleanup site. The federal and state governments jointly cleaned up the area, and Pennsylvania was reimbursed for its costs in the project. The federal government brought suit against Union Gas in an attempt to recover the cleanup costs. Union Gas filed a third-party complaint against Pennsylvania, claiming that the state was liable as the "owner and operator" of the site since it had acquired easements in the property along the creek prior to commencing the flood control project. A U.S. district court dismissed the complaint on Eleventh Amendment sovereign immunity grounds. The U.S. Court of Appeals for the Third Circuit affirmed, finding nothing in the act indicating federal intent to hold states liable in damage cases brought under the act. The Supreme Court remanded the case to the Third Circuit in light of the Superfund amendments. The Third Circuit then ruled that the amended language "clearly rendered the States liable" for money damages and that the Commerce Clause empowered Congress to do so notwithstanding the Eleventh Amendment. The Supreme Court agreed with both conclusions.

The Court was fragmented on the underlying rationale for its decision in *Union Gas,* which diminishes the holding's value as precedent. Nonetheless, the Court concluded that Congress has the authority when legislating pursuant to the Commerce Clause to override state immunity and make states liable for damages in actions brought in federal courts. The plenary power conferred on Congress by the Commerce Clause allows displacement of state regulation. Similarly, Congress may render states liable when exercising the commerce power notwithstanding the sovereign immunity of the states recognized in the Eleventh Amendment. It was the Court's judgment that in many situations it is "only money damages that will effectuate Congress' legitimate Commerce Clause objectives." The fact situation of *Union Gas* provides a useful example. After failing to solve the hazardous waste problem through "preventive measures," Congress chose to "extend liability to *everyone* potentially responsible for contamination." Finding the cost of cleanup efforts to be "enormous" and governmental resources "finite," Congress sought to "encourage private parties to help out by allowing them to recover for their own cleanup efforts." Accordingly, the Court rejected Pennsylvania's argument that allowing damages suits by private citizens against unconsenting states "impermissibly expands the jurisdiction of federal courts beyond the bounds of Article III." *See also* COMMERCE CLAUSE, p. 291; ELEVENTH AMENDMENT, p. 598; FEDERALISM, p. 29; *PHILADELPHIA v. NEW JERSEY* (437 U.S. 617: 1978), p. 353.

Significance *Union Gas* directly addresses the convergence of two constitutional provisions that may conflict under certain conditions: the federal power to regulate interstate commerce and the sovereign powers of the states to regulate health and safety at the local level. Protection of the environment is one policy area that has been particularly problematic. One of the leading cases on this matter is *Philadelphia v. New Jersey* (437 U.S. 617: 1978). New Jersey had attempted to limit dumping at landfill sites in the state to waste produced within the state. In addition to claiming that the law promoted essential health and environmental interests, New Jersey also argued that waste was not commerce. The Court disagreed. "All objects of interstate trade merit Commerce Clause protection," with none "excluded by definition at the outset." The banning of "valueless" items like out-of-state waste "implicates" the clause. It was the Court's view that state actions that pursue "economic isolationism and protectionism" are virtually always unconstitutional. In this case, New Jersey had attempted to "isolate itself" from a "problem common to many by erecting a barrier against the movement of interstate trade." The primary rule of impermissible state action is that a state may not "block the flow of commerce at its borders." A similar ruling came in *C & A Carbone, Inc. v. Clarkstown* (511 U.S. 383: 1994).

Clarkstown, New York, entered into an agreement with a private contractor to build and operate for five years a solid waste transfer station. Among other things, the contractor was to separate recyclable from nonrecyclable items at the transfer station. Clarkstown guaranteed a minimum waste flow to the facility and allowed the contractor to charge a fee for its use as a means of underwriting the costs of the station. The town adopted an ordinance requiring that all nonhazardous solid waste within the town be deposited at the transfer station. Other recyclers in the area, such as C & A Carbone, were allowed to receive and sort solid waste at their own facilities, but they were required to bring all nonrecyclable waste to the transfer station rather than dispose of it themselves. Carbone and the other recyclers were, of course, required to pay the tipping fees on the waste deposited at the transfer station. After finding that Carbone was shipping nonrecyclable waste out of state, Clarkstown brought suit, seeking to obtain an injunction requiring that Carbone's residue be taken to the transfer station. A state court issued the injunction, and Carbone went to federal court in an effort to prevent implementation of Clarkstown's flow-control ordinance. The federal court found for Carbone and issued an injunction. The New York Supreme Court, which exercised appellate jurisdiction over the original state case, subsequently granted summary judgment for the town and ordered Carbone to comply with the ordinance (after which the federal court vacated its injunction). The U.S. Supreme Court reviewed the decision of the New York courts and concluded that the local ordinance violated the Commerce Clause.

The immediate effect of the ordinance was seen as local, but "its economic effects are interstate in reach." The ordinance increases the cost for out-of-state interests to dispose of their solid waste, but it also "deprives out-of-state businesses of access to the local market by preventing everyone except the favored local operator from performing the initial processing step." Unlike the law at issue in *Philadelphia v. New Jersey* (437 U.S. 617: 1978), the Clarkstown ordinance did not create a barrier to the movement of solid waste as such. The "article of commerce," however, was not the waste itself but the service of processing and disposing of the waste. The ordinance thus discriminated within the "stream of commerce" because it allowed only the franchised operator to process waste that was within Clarkstown's limits. Conferring favor to a single local operator "makes the ordinance's protectionist effect even more acute, for it squelches competition in the waste-processing service altogether, leaving no room for outside investment." It was the Court's view that Clarkstown had alternative means to advance its local health and safety interests. Justifying the ordinance as a way to direct solid waste away from disposal sites that Clarkstown deemed "harmful" to the environment would extend its "police power beyond its jurisdictional boundaries." Furthermore, the Court concluded that the revenue-raising aspect of the ordinance by itself was not a local interest that could justify discriminating against interstate commerce. If some form of "special financing" was required to ensure the "long-term survival" of the transfer station, Clarkstown could subsidize the facility through general taxes or by issuing bonds, but the town may not use a discriminatory regulation to "give the project an advantage over rival out-of-state businesses."

***Chemical Waste Management, Inc. v. Hunt*, 504 U.S. 334, 119 L.Ed. 2d 121, 112 S.Ct. 2009 (1992)** An Alabama law imposed a fee on hazardous wastes generated within the state. An additional fee was charged for hazardous wastes brought into Alabama from other states for disposal. Chemical Waste Management, Inc., operated a hazardous waste landfill in Alabama that received both instate and out-of-state wastes. Chemical Waste obtained an injunction against enforcement of the act in an Alabama trial court, but the Alabama Supreme Court reversed, finding that the additional fee advanced legitimate state interests that could not be achieved by nondiscriminatory alternatives. The U.S. Supreme Court ruled that the higher disposal fee imposed exclusively on out-of-state waste violated the Commerce Clause.

The Court began with the central proposition from *Philadelphia v. New Jersey* (437 U.S. 617: 1978) that no state may "isolate itself from a problem common to the several States by raising barriers to the free flow of interstate commerce." The Alabama act "facially discriminate[d]" against hazardous waste generated outside the state with the additional fee, and the law "plainly discouraged the full operation of Chemical Waste's facility." Alabama argued the additional fee served "legitimate local purposes," but the Court was not satisfied that Alabama had demonstrated the "unavailability of nondiscriminatory alternatives adequate to preserve the local interests at stake." In the Court's view, Alabama's concern about the volume of waste entering the disposal facility could be addressed by less discriminatory means, such as imposing an additional fee on all hazardous waste disposed of in the state. Any concerns about protecting citizens' health and safety as well as the environment "do not vary with the waste's point of origin," and Alabama has the authority to "monitor and regulate the transportation and disposal of all hazardous waste within its borders." Alabama's potential financial and environmental risks "do not vary with the waste's State of origin in a way allowing foreign, but not local, waste to be burdened." The Court also rejected Alabama's assertion that its regulation was a form of quarantine law. Alabama's law permitted hazardous waste to be generated and disposed of within the state. The law also allowed the importation of additional hazardous waste from out of state. Even quarantine laws designed to isolate items that endanger public health or safety cannot discriminate against interstate commerce as such. Rather, quarantine laws "simply prevent traffic in noxious articles, whatever their origin." Since the hazardous waste at issue here is the same regardless of its point of origin and since "adequate means other than overt discrimination" meet Alabama's concerns, the Court concluded that the differential fee violates the Commerce Clause. *See also* COMMERCE CLAUSE, p. 291; *PHILADELPHIA v. NEW JERSEY* (437 U.S. 617: 1978), p. 353.

Significance Disposal of hazardous and nonhazardous wastes creates a number of problems. Waste is generated everywhere, but no community wants the waste disposed in its backyard. State and local governments have adopted a number of regulations designed to minimize the amount of waste that can be disposed in a particular state or locality. The discriminatory-fee approach seen in *Chemical Waste* is an example of one such regulation. A similar outcome came in *Oregon Waste Systems v. Department of Environmental Quality* (511 U.S. 93: 1994). As in *Chemical Waste,* a state (Oregon) imposed a higher fee for the instate disposal of solid waste generated in other states. Oregon Waste Systems, which operated a solid waste landfill in Oregon, and a company that transported waste into Oregon challenged the differential fee on Commerce Clause grounds. The Oregon courts upheld the fee schedule, finding a close enough connection of the higher fees to actual costs incurred to make the extra charge on out-of-state waste "compensatory" rather than discriminatory. The U.S. Supreme Court, relying heavily on its decision in

Chemical Waste, ruled that the extra surcharge on out-of-state waste violated the Commerce Clause.

The Commerce Clause has been read to contain a "negative" dimension that denies states the power to unjustifiably discriminate against or burden the interstate flow of articles of commerce. The first consideration in reviewing a state law under the negative Commerce Clause is the determination of whether the law regulates "even-handedly with only incidental effects on interstate commerce." If a state regulation is discriminatory—that is, if it favors state economic interests over out-of-state counterparts—it is "virtually per se invalid." Nondiscriminatory regulations are typically permissible unless the burden imposed on interstate commerce is "clearly excessive in relation to the putative local benefits." The Court found Oregon's surcharge "obviously discriminatory on its face." It subjected waste from other states to a charge almost three times greater than the charges on waste generated instate, and the statutory trigger for imposition of the charge was whether the waste came from out of state. Since the charge was found discriminatory (and thus presumed invalid), Oregon was required to show that the surcharge "advanced a legitimate local purpose that cannot be adequately served by reasonable nondiscriminatory alternatives." For the charge to be justified as a "compensatory" tax necessary to make shippers of out-of-state waste to pay their "fair share" of disposal costs, the fee must be the "rough equivalent of an identifiable and substantially similar surcharge on intrastate commerce." Even assuming that other means of taxation, such as the state income tax, could serve as a rough equivalent, the Court rejected Oregon's argument, because any such taxes are "not imposed on substantially equivalent events"; taxes on income and utilizing Oregon landfills are "entirely different kinds of taxes." Oregon's surcharge was seen by the Court as having an "illegitimate protectionist objective." Even Oregon's recharacterization of the surcharge as "resource protectionism"—discouraging the importation of out-of-state waste to conserve more landfill space for instate waste—did not change the Court's conclusion. A state simply may not "accord its own inhabitants a preferred right of access over consumers in other States to its natural resources."

A different kind of regulation came before the Court in *Fort Gratiot Landfill v. Michigan Department of Natural Resources* (504 U.S. 353: 1992). A Michigan law provides that solid waste generated in "another county, state, or country" cannot be accepted for disposal unless the county receiving such waste is expressly authorized to do so by its own solid waste management plan. Fort Gratiot Landfill filed an application to receive out-of-state waste. The Michigan Department of Natural Resources denied authorization, since disposal of such waste was not included in St.

Clair County's plan. Fort Gratiot Landfill attempted to have the Michigan law set aside on Commerce Clause grounds, but a U.S. district court dismissed the complaint, a ruling affirmed by the U.S. Court of Appeals for the Sixth Circuit. The Supreme Court, however, ruled that the law prohibiting a private landfill from accepting out-of-county waste violated the Commerce Clause.

As in a number of other environmental regulation cases, the Court used its ruling in *Philadelphia v. New Jersey* (437 U.S. 617: 1978) as the "proper analytic framework" for *Fort Gratiot.* Under that approach, Michigan's waste-import restrictions discriminate against interstate commerce, since they "authorize each county to isolate itself from the national economy and, indeed, afford local waste producers complete protection from competition from out-of-state producers seeking to use local disposal areas" without prior county approval. States may not avoid "strictures of the Commerce Clause" by limiting the movement of commerce through subdivisions of the state any more than it can by imposing statewide restrictions. Furthermore, the Michigan law retains its discriminatory character even though it permits individual counties to accept solid waste from outside the state. Finally, the Court rejected Michigan's contention that the law targets public health and safety regulation rather than "economic protectionism." The law's waste-import restrictions "unambiguously discriminate against interstate commerce." As a result, Michigan carries the burden of showing that its concerns for public health and safety cannot be adequately furthered by nondiscriminatory alternatives. The Court concluded Michigan had not met this burden, as it provided no persuasive health and safety reason for limiting the amount of waste that a landfill operator may accept from out of state with no comparable restriction on waste generated instate.

State Instate Preferences

***Wyoming v. Oklahoma*, 502 U.S. 437, 117 L.Ed. 2d 1, 112 S.Ct. 789 (1992)** Until 1986, virtually all the coal purchased by four Oklahoma electric utilities came from Wyoming. Although the state itself did not sell the coal, it collected a severance tax from those who extracted the coal. In 1985, Oklahoma passed a law requiring coal-fired electric utilities to burn a mixture of coal, at least 10 percent of which came from Oklahoma. Each of the utilities reduced their purchases of Wyoming coal in order to buy Oklahoma coal. As a result, Wyoming's revenues from the severance tax on coal declined. Wyoming brought a complaint under the U.S. Supreme Court's original jurisdiction, seeking to enjoin enforcement of the Oklahoma law on Commerce Clause grounds. The

Court found this case appropriate for its original jurisdiction. Wyoming's Commerce Clause action "implicates serious and important concerns of federalism in accord with the purpose and reach of original jurisdiction." After resolving questions relating to standing and original jurisdiction, the Court struck down the Oklahoma law as discriminatory against interstate commerce.

The Court found that Wyoming satisfied standing requirements because its loss of "severance tax revenue fairly can be traced" to Oklahoma's action. The Court further concluded that the type of direct injury suffered by Wyoming was "cognizable in a Commerce Clause action," since its severance tax revenues were directly tied to the extraction and sale of its coal and since both the extraction and sale of Wyoming coal were affected by Oklahoma's law.

Oklahoma argued that Wyoming suffered only minimal injury since the revenue loss directly attributable to Oklahoma was less than 1 percent of the total severance tax collected. The Court disagreed. Wyoming coal is a "natural resource of great value" primarily carried into other states for use, and Wyoming derives "significant revenue from this interstate movement." The practical effect of Oklahoma's act must be calculated by considering the "consequences of the act itself" and by considering "what effect would arise if many States or every State adopted similar legislation." In addition, the Court concluded that the Oklahoma law was unconstitutional because it discriminated against interstate commerce in the absence of any substantial purpose justifying such discrimination. The "small volume" of commerce affected by the Oklahoma law "measures only the extent of the discrimination, but is not relevant in determining whether there has been discrimination against interstate commerce." Oklahoma contended that sustaining the state's coal-mining industry meant lessening reliance on a single source of coal. The Court did not find these local benefits sufficient to justify the discrimination against interstate commerce. *See also* COMMERCE CLAUSE, p. 291; ORIGINAL JURISDICTION, p. 640; STANDING, p. 655.

Significance The Court's ruling in *Wyoming v. Oklahoma* paralleled its ruling four years earlier in *New Energy Company of Indiana v. Limbach* (486 U.S. 269: 1988). Ohio awarded a tax credit against the sales tax on vehicle fuel for each gallon of Ohio-produced ethanol sold. A credit was also extended to sales of ethanol produced in another state but only to the extent that state conferred a similar tax advantage to Ohio ethanol. New Energy Company manufactured ethanol in Indiana, a state that had no sales tax exemption for ethanol. This, of course, made New Energy's ethanol sold in Ohio ineligible for any tax credit. New Energy sought declaratory and injunctive relief in an Ohio court of common pleas but was unsuccessful. The Ohio appellate courts, including the Ohio Supreme Court, affirmed the trial court. The U.S. Supreme Court held that the Ohio statute violated the Commerce Clause by discriminating against interstate commerce.

The Court's ruling was based on the "negative" aspect of the Commerce Clause. This negative dimension limits a state's power to adopt regulatory measures intended to "benefit in-state economic interests by burdening out-of-state competitors." State laws that discriminate are unconstitutional unless the discrimination is justified by a "valid factor unrelated to economic protectionism." The Court found no merit in Ohio's argument that the availability of the tax credit to some out-of-state producers actually promoted interstate commerce by "encouraging other States to enact similar tax advantages that would spur the interstate sale of ethanol." Discriminatory tax treatment for out-of-state goods is "no more validated by the promise to remove it if reciprocity is accepted than would be the categorical exclusion of out-of-state goods." Where discrimination is "patent," as in this case, neither a "widespread advantage to in-state interests nor a widespread disadvantage to out-of-state competitors need be shown." Furthermore, the "market participant" doctrine under which the "negative Commerce Clause's limitations apply only to a State's acting in its governmental capacity, not to its acting in the capacity of a market participant, has no application here." Ohio's action under review in this case was not its purchase or sale of ethanol but its "assessment and computation of taxes." Although Ohio's tax-credit scheme had the purpose and effect of subsidizing a particular industry, "that does not transform it into a form of state participation in the free market." Finally, the Court rejected Ohio's contention that the law was designed to reduce harmful exhaust emissions, a purpose that in its view justified the discrimination against interstate commerce. Health was not seen as the principal interest of the Ohio law but was merely an "occasional and accidental effect" of achieving favorable tax treatment for Ohio-produced ethanol, the principal purpose of the law.

6. Taxing, Spending, and State Economic Regulation

Federal Taxation

Commissioner of Internal Revenue v. Soliman, **506 U.S. 168, 121 L.Ed. 2d 634, 113 S.Ct. 701 (1993)** Section 280A of the Internal Revenue Code generally prohibits a business use deduction for a place a residence. An exception is permitted if the dwelling is also the "principal place of business" for the taxpayer. Nader E. Soliman, an anesthesiologist, practiced his specialty in three hospitals in Bethesda, Maryland. None of the three hospitals provided him with an office. Nader spent a portion of each day in a room in his McLean, Virginia, residence working on tasks directly related to his medical practice. This room was used for no other purpose. He claimed a deduction for household expenses attributable to the home office, but the deduction was disallowed by the Internal Revenue Service (IRS), which determined that the office was not his "principal place of business." The U.S. Tax Court disagreed with the IRS and allowed the deduction. The Court of Appeals for the Fourth Circuit affirmed, using the standard applied by the tax court. The Fourth Circuit allowed the "principal place of business" exception if: the office is "essential" to the taxpayer's business, the taxpayer spends a "substantial" amount of time in the location, and there is no alternative location available for these business functions. The Supreme Court reversed the Fourth Circuit decision. Justice Kennedy suggested there was no "objective formula that yields a clear answer" in every situation. Rather, the inquiry is "more subtle," with the particular facts of each case providing the basis for determining the "principal" place of business. Two "primary considerations," however, must be given in each case. The first is the relative importance of the activities performed at each business location. The place where client or patient contact occurs is "often an important indicator" of a principal place of business. Indeed, the location where goods and services are actually delivered must be given "great weight" in determining where the most important functions are performed. Second, the amount of time spent at home must be compared with the time spent at other places where business activities occur. The comparative analysis of business locations may not always result in the specification of which location is the principal place of business. The only question that must be answered, said

Kennedy, is "whether the home so qualifies." In some cases, no principal place of business may be identified. In such instances, the courts and the commissioner of the IRS "should not strain to conclude that a home qualifies for a deduction simply because no other location seems to be the principal place." The taxpayer's house does not become the principal place of business "by default." When these principles were applied to Dr. Soliman's claim, the Court concluded he was not entitled to a deduction for home office expense. *See also* GENERAL WELFARE CLAUSE, p. 377.

Significance *Soliman* focused on the difficulty in distinguishing personal and business expenses for federal income tax purposes. The Age Discrimination in Employment Act of 1967 (ADEA) prohibits the discharge of an employee on the basis of the person's age. If an employee is unlawfully terminated under terms of the ADEA, a number of remedies, such as reinstatement and back pay, are possible. The ADEA also provides for damages up to the amount of a back-pay award if intentional violation of ADEA can be shown. Erich Schleier was discharged by United Airlines when he reached the mandatory retirement age of 60 in 1979. Schleier filed suit, claiming violation of the ADEA. In 1986, United settled with Schleier. He was paid almost $75,000 in back pay and given an equal amount in liquidated damages. Schleier and his wife filed a 1986 federal income tax return reflecting the back pay but not the liquidated damages. Following an audit, the IRS notified the Schleiers that they needed to pay taxes on the liquidated damages. The Schleiers contested the notice of tax deficiency in tax court. The tax court ruled that the liquidated damages as well as the back pay were exempt from taxation. The Court of Appeals for the Fifth Circuit affirmed the tax court. The Supreme Court ruled in *Commissioner of Internal Revenue v. Schleier* (515 U.S. 323: 1995) that the funds recovered under the ADEA must be included as part of gross income. The Court, drawing from the "plain language" of the IRS code and the rationale contained in *United States v. Burke* (504 U.S. 229: 1992), held that a taxpayer must meet two independent requirements before a recovery may be excluded from gross income for tax purposes. First, the taxpayer must show that the underlying cause of action producing the recovery is based on "tort or tort-type rights." Recovery under ADEA does not include awards for compensatory or punitive damages, only liquidated damages. Because ADEA addresses legal injuries of an exclusively "economic character," remedies available under ADEA are not tort-like. Second, the taxpayer must show that the damages were received "on account of personal injuries or sickness." In an ADEA action, the discrimination may cause some personal injury of a psychological but largely intangible kind.

Whatever the "injury," however, "no part of the recovery is attributable to that injury"; the amount of back wages recovered is "completely independent of the existence or extent of any personal injury." Justices O'Connor, Thomas, and Souter dissented. They suggested that the injuries from discrimination that can be redressed under ADEA "may not always manifest themselves in physical symptoms, but they are no less personal, and thus no less worthy of excludability" under the IRS code.

State Taxation on Foreign Commerce

***Barclays Bank v. Franchise Tax Board of California*, 512 U.S. 298, 129 L.Ed. 2d 244, 114 S.Ct. 2268 (1994)** The issue in *Barclays Bank* (and the consolidated case of *Colgate-Palmolive Co. v. Franchise Tax Board of California*) involved the method California used to determine corporate income of a unitary multinational business. The method, known as the "worldwide combined reporting" method, begins with the worldwide income of the business and then levies a tax on a percentage of that income equal to the average of the proportions of worldwide payroll, property, and sales located within the state. This method for determining income tax differs from the transactional method used by the federal government. The Court had earlier upheld the method used in California as applied to American-based multinational corporations in *Container Corp. of America v. Franchise Tax Board of California* (463 U.S. 159: 1983). The Court did not consider the constitutionality of applying this to domestic corporations with foreign parents or to foreign corporations with foreign parents or subsidiaries. Barclays Bank (a foreign multinational) and Colgate-Palmolive (a domestic multinational) operate in California. The state Franchise Tax Board challenged the manner in which Barclays and Colgate calculated their corporate income and required that both corporations use the worldwide combined reporting method. Application of this method increased the amount of tax owed for both corporations. Barclays and Colgate paid the additional tax and unsuccessfully sought refund of the additional tax in the California courts. The Supreme Court ruled that the California tax was constitutional. The Court concluded that the tax computation method survived Commerce Clause scrutiny, that is, California's use of the worldwide combining reporting method applied to an activity having a sufficiently close relationship to California, was fairly apportioned, did not discriminate against interstate commerce, and was fairly related to the services provided these corporations by the state.

The method also affected foreign commerce, however, thus raising two additional considerations. The first is the "enhanced risk of multiple taxation." Multiple taxation was not seen as the "inevitable result" of California's computational method, nor was the Court convinced that use of such an alternative method as the "unitary business" approach does not lessen the risk of double taxation. The second consideration relates to the federal government's capacity to "speak with one voice" when regulating commercial relations with foreign governments. The Court "discern[ed] no specific indications of congressional intent to bar the state action here challenged." Congress is the branch responsible for the regulation of foreign commerce. Congress had been "aware that foreign governments were displeased with the worldwide combined reporting method" for the past three decades. Had Congress considered "nationally uniform use of separate accounting 'essential,'" it could have enacted legislation barring the states from taxing corporate income based on the method. Given the "indicia" of Congress's willingness to accept state use of the worldwide combined reporting method, the Court concluded that the foreign policy of the United States—"whose nuances . . . are much more the province of the Executive Branch and Congress than of this Court—is [so] seriously threatened by California's practice as to warrant our intervention." Having determined that the California policy met due process and Commerce Clause criteria, the Court left it to Congress to "evaluate whether the national interest is best served by tax uniformity, or state autonomy." *See also BROWN v. MARYLAND* (12 Wheaton 419: 1827), p. 296; COMMERCE CLAUSE, p. 291; FEDERALISM, p. 29; JUDICIAL REVIEW, p. 627.

Significance Taxation of foreign commerce has prompted troublesome questions from the outset of our constitutional history. The problem usually involves the extent to which states may exercise their police power to regulate international commercial activity. The Marshall Court addressed the question in *Brown v. Maryland* (12 Wheaton 419: 1827) and concluded that goods coming into the United States were not subject to state taxation until they were outside their "original package." *Barclays Bank* does not involve imported goods as such but rather the taxation of income of multinational businesses. The concern these two cases have in common is that the actions of individual states should not discriminate against or otherwise impair international commerce. The worldwide combined reporting method is generally perceived as counterproductive to international business. One of the problems associated with the method is that different states may use it differently. A state may, for example, disproportionately factor measures of gross sales if a multinational has large sales in that state. States with lower sales may weight other factors more heavily. The federal government calculates federal income tax liability for multinationals on the basis of transactions and where those transactions occur. This approach is generally favored by most nations active in international commerce. The issue of the worldwide combined reporting method was before the Court in *Container Corp. of America v. Franchise Tax Board of California* (463 U.S. 159: 1983). In *Container Corp.,* the Court was not persuaded that the method interfered with national objectives pursued in international business policy. *Container Corp.* did not examine the case of the domestically owned multinational business, however. The Court chose not to use the distinction between foreign- and domestically owned businesses to provide the basis for a different outcome. *Barclays Bank* reflects an ongoing preference of the Court to defer to the judgments of the other two branches in cases implicating international relations. The Court explicitly places this matter in the hands of Congress.

State Taxation and Retroactivity of Refunds

***Harper v. Virginia Department of Taxation,* 509 U.S. 86, 125 L.Ed. 2d 74, 113 S.Ct. 2510 (1993)** The Court decided in *Davis v. Michigan* (489 U.S. 803: 1989) that a state may not tax the retirement benefits paid by the federal government while exempting such benefits paid by the state or local units of government within the state from similar taxation. Virginia changed its policy to bring it into compliance with *Davis.* Henry Harper and others sought refunds on taxes paid prior to the *Davis* ruling. The state courts ruled that *Davis* should not be applied retroactively and denied the refunds. The Supreme Court held that *Davis* must be applied retroactively but allowed Virginia some discretion in how to do so. Mindful of the "basic norms of constitutional adjudication that animated our view of retroactivity in the criminal context," said Justice Thomas, we now "prohibit the erection of selective temporal barriers to the application of federal law in noncriminal cases." When a rule of federal law is applied in a civil case, that rule is the "controlling interpretation of federal law and must be given full retroactive effect in all cases still open and on direct review." Further, the Supremacy Clause does not allow federal retroactivity doctrine to be "supplanted by the invocation of a contrary approach to retroactivity under state law." Whatever freedom state courts may enjoy to limit the retroactive operation of their own interpretations of state law "cannot extend to their interpretations of federal law." And though *Davis* must apply retroactively, the Court concluded federal law does not "necessarily entitle [Harper et al.] to a refund." Rather, Virginia is required to provide "relief consistent with federal due process principles." The "constitutional sufficiency," the Court went on, of any remedy "turns (at least initially) on whether Virginia law provides an adequate form of 'predeprivation process,'" for example, allowing taxpayers to bring suit to stop imposition of a tax before it is paid or allowing taxpayers to withhold payment and then present objections as defenses in a tax enforcement proceeding. *See also DAVIS v. MICHIGAN DEPARTMENT OF TREASURY* (489 U.S. 803: 1989), p. 144 (Supp.); FEDERALISM, p. 29; SUPREMACY CLAUSE, p. 227.

Significance A state's obligation to refund taxes collected under terms of laws subsequently held to be unconstitutional seems self-evident. The question has been before the Supreme Court several times in recent years, yet the Court's decisions have reflected an absence of consensus. The general approach to retroactivity in civil cases was set out in *Chevron Oil Co. v. Huson* (404 U.S. 97: 1971). *Chevron* offered three criteria to be used in retroactivity cases: (1) whether the basis for finding a tax statute unconstitutional was new; (2) whether Commerce Clause objectives were advanced by retroactive relief; and (3) whether any inequities would result from the requiring tax refunds. The *Chevron* guidelines notwithstanding, the Court has often been deeply divided in cases involving retroactive tax refunds. A leading example is *James B. Beam Distilling Co. v. Georgia* (501 U.S. 529: 1991). The issue in *Beam* was whether Georgia needed to refund taxes imposed in a discriminatory manner on imported liquor in violation of the Commerce Clause. The Court required retroactive refund, but four separate opinions were issued from the six-justice majority. *Harper* provides some greater clarity, as seven justices shared the view that "*Beam* controls this case, and we accordingly adopt a rule that reflects the majority of Justices in *Beam.*"

Concrete Pipe and Products of California, Inc. v. Construction Laborers' Pension Trust Fund for Southern California (508 U.S. 602: 1993) did not involve the issue of retroactive tax refunds but touched on several matters of contemporary consequence, including due process, property-taking, and impairment of contracts. The Multiemployer Pension Plan Amendments Act of 1980 (MPPAA) modified provisions of the Employee Retirement Income Security Act of 1974 (ERISA) by requiring an employer withdrawing from a multiemployer pension fund to pay into the plan an amount representing the employer's proportionate share of the plan's unfunded vested benefits. Liability for withdrawal is determined by the plan's sponsor. If the employer objects and the parties cannot resolve the dispute, the dispute goes to arbitration. Two presumptions apply to the arbitration process: (1) the plan sponsor's determinations made under MPPAA are presumed correct unless the challenging party can show them to be either "unreasonable or clearly erroneous"; and (2) the sponsor's calculation of unfunded vested benefits is presumed correct unless the methods used in making the determination is, "in the aggregate, unreasonable." Construction Laborers' Pension Trust notified Concrete Pipe and Products, a withdrawn employer, of liability in excess of $250,000. The trust filed an action in federal district court, seeking the assessed liability. Concrete Pipe and Products countersued, claiming that their complete withdrawal from the plan had occurred prior to the effective date of MPPAA and that MPPAA was unconstitutional. An arbitrator concluded that the employer had not fully withdrawn before MPPAA became effective and that the employer had not demonstrated that the methods used to assess liability were unreasonable. The district court affirmed the arbitrator's judgment, and that decision was affirmed by the Court of Appeals for the Ninth Circuit. The Supreme Court also affirmed. The Court ruled that the MPPAA did not deprive the employer of an "impartial adjudicator," even though determination of withdrawal liability was located with the sponsor of the retirement plan under the statute. The Due Process Clause is not violated here because the first adjudication took place during the arbitration proceeding, not during the plan trustees' liability review. Second, although the MPPAA is ambiguous with respect to the "degree of certainty required to overturn a plan sponsor's determination," the approach taken by the arbitrator and lower courts applied the statute in a way that avoided serious constitutional problems. Moreover, the presumptions that operate under the MPPAA "raise no procedural due process problems." The "technical nature" of the presumptions and methods limits an actuary's "opportunity to act unfairly toward a withdrawing employer." Finally, the Court concluded that application of the MPPAA in this case did not take Concrete Pipe and Products's property without just compensation. The application of a regulatory statute that is otherwise within Congress's power may not be avoided by private contractual provisions. More important, the Court concluded that the government had not "permanently appropriated" Concrete Pipe and Products's assets for its own use. The conditions on its contractual obligations did not give Concrete Pipe and Products a "reasonable expectation" that it would not be faced with liability for promised benefits under MPPAA given that substantial federal regulation of pension plans had been in place under ERISA prior to the effective date of the MPPAA.

Regulatory Taxation

***Department of Revenue of Montana v. Kurth Ranch*, 511 U.S. 767, 128 L.Ed. 2d 767, 114 S.Ct. 1937 (1994)** The Supreme Court ruled in *Department of Revenue of Montana v. Kurth Ranch* that states could not levy a drug tax upon persons who have been subjected to criminal penalties for the same conduct. The Montana Dangerous Drug Tax Act provided that a person who stored or possessed marijuana (or other specified controlled substances) could be taxed at 10 percent of the drug's market value or $100 per ounce of marijuana, whichever is greater. The act also provided that the tax could be "collected only after any state or federal fines or forfeitures have been satisfied." Six members of the Richard Kurth family were charged with various drug offenses following a raid on the family farm, during which federal officers seized a variety of contraband, including 2,155 live marijuana plants. The local prosecutor also filed a civil action, seeking forfeiture of cash and equipment confiscated from the Kurth ranch. An officer participating in the raid completed a tax assessment form totaling $865,000 (at $100 per ounce of seized marijuana). The Kurths filed for bankruptcy and challenged the constitutionality of the tax on double jeopardy grounds. The federal bankruptcy court ruled for the Kurths. The district court and court of appeals affirmed. The Supreme Court also affirmed in a 5-4 ruling. Justice Stevens wrote for the five-justice majority.

As a general proposition, said Stevens, the "unlawfulness of an activity does not prevent its taxation." The Court had no doubt that Montana could collect its marijuana possession tax had it not previously punished the taxpayer for the same offense. The issue in this case was whether the tax has punitive characteristics that place it under the constraints of the Double Jeopardy Clause. Previous decisions, Stevens said, suggest that a tax should not be invalidated simply because "its enforcement might be oppressive or because the legislature's motive is suspect." Nonetheless, the penalizing features of a tax can cause it to lose its character of a tax and become a "mere penalty with the characteristics of regulation and punishment." Legislative labeling does not control whether a tax is immune from double jeopardy scrutiny. At some point, an exaction labeled as a tax approaches punishment, and the Court's task is to determine whether the tax under review crosses that line. Neither a high rate of taxation nor an obvious deterrent purpose automatically make a tax a form of punishment. Here, however, these factors are "consistent with a punitive character." Stevens pointed to an assessment against marijuana that was more than eight times the market value. That Montana intended the tax to deter people from possessing marijuana is "beyond question." Even these features of the Montana law were not wholly dispositive. Other unusual features, however, "set the Montana statute apart from most taxes." First, the tax is conditioned on the commission of a crime. This condition, said Stevens, is "significant of penal and prohibitory intent" rather than the raising of revenue. Second, the tax is also exacted only after the taxpayer has been arrested for the "precise conduct that gives rise to tax obligation in the first place." People arrested for possession of marijuana in Montana "constitute the entire class of taxpayers subject to the Montana tax." Stevens distinguished taxes imposed on illegal activities from "mixed motive" taxes, such as those imposed on cigarettes. The justifications for so-called mixed motive taxes do not apply when the taxed activity is completely prohibited, however. In such instances, the need to raise revenue would be "equally well served" by simply increasing the fine imposed on conviction. Third, the Montana tax is purportedly a form of property tax—a tax on the possession and storage of controlled substances. At the time the tax is imposed, the property is likely to have been confiscated by the state and destroyed. A tax on possession of goods that no longer exist or that could have been lawfully possessed also reflects the punitive character of the Montana tax. Taken as a whole, Stevens concluded, the Montana drug tax is a "concoction of anomalies, too far removed in crucial respects from a standard tax assessment to escape characterization as punishment for the purpose of Double Jeopardy analysis." Chief Justice Rehnquist, joined by Justices O'Connor and Scalia, dissented. He saw the Court's ruling as substantially departing from existing double jeopardy doctrine. It was also the view of the dissenters that the Montana tax had a nonpenal purpose of raising revenue as well as a legitimate deterrence purpose. Because the tax did not have a punitive purpose, it could not be regarded as a second punishment. Justice Scalia, joined by Justice Thomas, authored a dissent separate from Rehnquist's. He suggested that to be "'put in jeopardy'" does not remotely mean "'to be punished.'" The Double Jeopardy Clause prohibits "not multiple punishments, but only multiple prosecutions." *See also BAILEY v. DREXEL FURNITURE COMPANY* (259 U.S. 20: 1922), p. 396; *McCRAY v. UNITED STATES* (195 U.S. 27: 1904), p. 394; REGULATORY TAX, p. 648; *UNITED STATES v. KAHRIGER* (345 U.S. 22: 1953), p. 398.

Significance The taxing power may be used for purposes other than raising revenue. The constitutional question that arises with regulatory taxes focuses on legislative motive and the extent to which any regulatory intent might violate some explicit limit on the taxing power. The matter of motive controlled the Court's ruling in *Kurth Ranch.* The punitive character of the Montana drug tax made it subject to double jeopardy limitations. The Court arrived at a similar conclusion in *Bailey v. Drexel Furniture Company* (259 U.S. 20: 1922), wherein the federal government attempted to tax profits of businesses who used child labor. In this instance, the tax provisions were so "obviously" intended as penalties that the regulatory objective overrode all tax characteristics in the law. Generally, however, the Court has concluded that federal or state taxing power need not be confined exclusively to generating revenue. The Court historically has been reluctant to examine legislative intent as closely as it did in *Kurth Ranch.* In *McCray v. United States* (195 U.S. 27: 1904), the Court found a tax on oleomargarine to be a legitimate exercise of the taxing power despite the tax's obvious protective objective. Since the tax was obviously an excise, and because it did yield some revenue, the Court concluded it was a tax levied through the lawful exercise of the federal taxing authority. The Court said in *J.W. Hampton, Jr. and Company v. United States* (276 U.S. 394: 1928) that the existence of nonrevenue or "mixed" objectives does not necessarily invalidate a tax; taxes that augment the exercise of others' express powers are constitutional. Finally, the Court has allowed the taxation of illegal activities, as in *United States v. Kahriger* (345 U.S. 22: 1953). The Revenue Act of 1951 levied a 10 percent tax on wagering. A tax "does not cease to be valid merely because it discourages or deters the activities taxed." Furthermore, a tax is not invalid because the revenue it generates is "negligible." As long as a tax raises some revenue, as the wagering tax did in *Kahriger,* it remains a valid tax "regardless of its regulatory effect."

State Taxation

***Associated Industries of Missouri v. Lohman*, 511 U.S. 641, 128 L.Ed. 2d 639, 114 S.Ct. 1815 (1994)** Missouri has a statewide use tax on goods purchased out of state but "stored, used, or consumed" instate. One of the objectives of the state in levying the use tax is to offset or compensate for the locally imposed sales taxes on all instate goods. These local sales tax rates are not uniform in Missouri, and in some jurisdictions the use tax is greater than the sales tax. Action was brought in a state court by a trade association on behalf of member businesses that must collect the use tax and a manufacturer (Alumax Foils, Inc.). Associated Industries contended that the use tax discriminated against interstate commerce. Summary judgment was granted by the state trial court to the state, and the Supreme Court of Missouri affirmed. The state appellate court concluded that because the tax was intended to equalize tax liability on intrastate and interstate commerce the tax ought to be evaluated under the "compensatory tax" doctrine. Although the use tax exceeded the sales tax in some localities, the overall effect was to lighten the aggregate tax burden on interstate commerce when the local sales tax rates were averaged statewide. The U.S. Supreme Court ruled that Missouri's tax scheme impermissibly discriminated against interstate commerce in those parts of the state where the use tax exceeded the sales tax. The Commerce Clause "prohibits economic protectionism—that is, 'regulatory measures designed to benefit in-state economic interests by burdening out-of-state competitors.'" The "fundamental command" of the Commerce Clause is that a state may not "tax a transaction or incident more heavily when it crosses state lines than when it occurs entirely within the State." A tax may withstand Commerce Clause scrutiny if it is a "valid compensatory tax" designed to make interstate commerce "bear a burden already borne by intrastate commerce." Under the compensatory tax doctrine, a facially discriminatory tax that imposes on interstate commerce the "equivalent of an identifiable and substantially similar tax" on intrastate commerce is constitutional. In this case, Missouri's use tax scheme "runs afoul" of the basic compensatory tax requirement that burdens imposed on interstate and intrastate commerce "must be equal." Missouri argued that review of the use tax ought not focus on each political subdivision within the state in which a "disparity between the two taxes may result in discrimination against interstate commerce." Rather, Missouri proposed that the overall impact of the use tax and the various sales taxes on interstate commerce should be measured "across the State as a whole," and that discrimination in some parts of a state tax system may be permissible if it is of a "sufficiently limited magnitude to be offset by preferential treatment for interstate trade in other portions of the tax scheme." The Court rejected these arguments, saying that actual discrimination, wherever it is found, is "impermissible, and the magnitude and scope of the discrimination have no bearing on the determinative question whether discrimination has occurred." Under the Missouri view, the Commerce Clause "would interpose no bar to the systematic subdivision of the national market through discriminatory taxes as long as the taxes were imposed by counties, rather than by States." *See also* COMMERCE CLAUSE, p. 291; FEDERALISM, p. 29; *QUILL CORP. v. NORTH DAKOTA* (504 U.S. 298: 1992), p. 172 (Supp.).

Significance State taxes on interstate commerce raise constitutional questions that have become more complex over time. A state tax may not excessively "burden" interstate commerce, but early in our constitutional history, when most commerce activity was local, problems of this kind were infrequent. As the American economy has become more integrated, very little commercial activity is confined within a state's boundaries. As a result, virtually any tax on business imposes a burden to some extent on interstate commerce. The Court has developed doctrine intended to balance the competing federal and state interests. Maintaining state sovereignty requires that states be able to generate revenue by taxing various business activities, and interstate commercial activity is not per se immune from state taxation. At the same time, state taxes that discriminate against interstate commerce or excessively burden such activity are prohibited. Most current doctrine in this area of constitutional law stems from the Court's ruling in *Complete Auto Transit v. Brady* (430 U.S. 274: 1977). The case involved a Mississippi tax on the privilege of doing business in the state. The tax was levied against businesses engaged in both inter- and intrastate commerce. The Court unanimously upheld the tax, and the opinion set out four requirements that state taxes on interstate commerce must meet. First, the tax must apply to a commercial activity with a "substantial nexus" with the taxing state. Second, the tax must be "fairly apportioned"; the tax must target intrastate commercial activity or commercial income not subject to taxation by other states. Third, the state tax may not "unduly burden" or discriminate against interstate commerce. Finally, the tax must be "fairly related" to the services provided by the state. The inter- and intrastate activities were separated in *Complete Auto,* with the tax applied only to the intrastate portion. The state tax under review in *Quill Corp. v. North Dakota* (504 U.S. 298: 1992) was levied against a mail-order company with no employees, offices, or warehouses in North Dakota. The Court struck down the tax on lack of "substantial nexus" grounds. Unlike the nexus considerations that apply to the due process concerns of fundamental fairness, the nexus requirement of the Commerce Clause is informed by "structural concerns about the effects of state regulations on the national economy." The first and fourth prongs of the *Complete Auto* test require a "substantial nexus and a relationship between the tax and State-provided services." These two criteria limit the reach of state taxing authority "so as to ensure that State taxation does not unduly burden interstate commerce." The "substantial nexus" requirement is not a "minimum contacts" requirement, a "proxy for notice," but rather is a means for "limiting state burdens on interstate commerce." As a result of this distinction, the Court concluded that although Quill Corp. may have had the minimum contacts with North Dakota to meet Due Process Clause requirements it lacked the "substantial nexus" with the state as required by the Commerce Clause.

Delegation of Taxing Power

***Skinner v. Mid-America Pipeline Co.*, 490 U.S. 212, 104 L.Ed. 2d 250, 109 S.Ct. 1726 (1989)** The Consolidated Omnibus Budget Reconciliation Act of 1985 (COBRA) authorized the secretary of transportation to establish pipeline safety user fees and collect the tax from anyone operating pipelines subject to the Hazardous Liquid Pipeline Safety Act and the Natural Gas Pipeline Safety Act. Mid-America Pipeline Co. owned and operated a pipeline transporting hazardous liquid. Mid-America paid the user fee mandated by COBRA under protest and filed suit against the secretary of transportation (Samuel K. Skinner) in U.S. district court. The district court struck down the pipeline user fees provision as an unconstitutional delegation of the taxing power. The secretary took direct appeal to the Supreme Court, which upheld the user fees. The core of the nondelegation doctrine is that as long as Congress "provides an administrative agency with standards guiding its actions"—such that a court could determine whether the "will of Congress has been obeyed"—no delegation of legislative authority "trenching on the principle of separation of powers has occurred." The Court concluded in this case that Mid-America "[did] not seriously contend" that the guidelines provided by Congress to the secretary do not meet the normal requirements of the nondelegation doctrine. The provisions of COBRA "delimited the scope of the Secretary's discretion with much greater specificity" than in delegations upheld in previous cases. Mid-America argued that although COBRA delegation provisions may be sound under "ordinary nondelegation analysis," the assessment of the pipeline user fees must be "scrutinized under a more exacting nondelegation lens." Mid-America contended that the user fees were actually tax assessments levied by the secretary and that, unlike any other enumerated power, Congress's taxing power must be delegated with "much stricter guidelines" than those that apply to other congressional delegations. Even if the user fees were considered a form of taxation, the Court concluded that the delegation of discretionary authority under Congress's taxing power is "subject to no constitutional scrutiny greater than that we have applied to other nondelegation challenges." Congress may choose to be "more circumspect" in delegating authority under the taxing power than under other enumerated powers, but this is "not a heightened degree of prudence required by the Constitution." *See also* DELEGATION OF LEGISLATIVE POWER, p. 591; *J.W. HAMPTON, JR. AND COMPANY v. UNITED STATES* (276 U.S. 394: 1928), p. 388; SEPARATION OF POWERS, p. 56.

Significance The nondelegation doctrine has been in existence for much of our constitutional history. Congress has been given the legislative power in Article I, and the nondelegation doctrine would suggest that when power is delegated it cannot be redelegated. Some delegation may be needed, however, to allow the executive branch to effectively administer laws. Thus, a balance is necessary between the prohibition on reassigning fundamental legislative prerogatives and the practical needs that arise in the administration of statutory mandates. The rationale for permitting the delegation of some legislative power begins with the premise that any legislative branch, including the U.S. Congress, is unable to enact more than general laws. Administrative experts involved with actual implementation "fill the gaps" of general policy set out in legislation. This is particularly the case as legislation addresses increasingly complex policy issues. The line between permissible and impermissible delegation hinges on the extent to which the legislature establishes objectives and standards prior to turning implementation over to the executive. Chief Justice Taft observed in *J.W. Hampton, Jr. and Company v. United States* (276 U.S. 394: 1928) that the limits of legislative delegation "must be fixed according to common sense and the inherent necessities of the governmental coordination." Legislative action is not a forbidden delegation if an act of Congress contains an "intelligible principle" to which the administrative agent is "directed to conform." The nondelegation doctrine provided the basis for a number of Court rulings during the 1930s. Since that time, the Court has had infrequent occasion to reconsider the question. When delegation challenges to legislative enactments have occurred in recent years, the Court has been generally unreceptive. A representative decision is *Mistretta v. United States* (488 U.S. 361: 1989), wherein the Court upheld Congress's decision to direct a specially created commission to develop criminal sentencing guidelines. The Court's unwillingness in *Skinner* to create more stringent nondelegation standards when the taxing power is involved reflects the same view.

Federal Highway Funds and Drinking Age

***South Dakota v. Dole*, 483 U.S. 203, 97 L.Ed. 2d 171, 107 S.Ct. 2793 (1987)** Congress passed a law in 1984 directing the secretary of commerce to withhold up to 10 percent of federal highway funds from any state that did not set its minimum drinking age at 21. South Dakota, which had a minimum drinking age of 19 for 3.2 percent beer, filed suit in district court, claiming that Congress had exceeded its Article I spending authority and had violated the Twenty-First Amendment, which repealed Prohibition. The district court upheld the law, and the Court of Appeals for the Eighth Circuit affirmed. The U.S. Supreme Court affirmed in a 7-2 decision. Although the Twenty-First Amendment would bar Congress from setting the minimum drinking age itself, the Court found no constitutional ground for allowing Congress to address the issue indirectly through the spending power. Congress has offered "relatively mild encouragement" to the states, said Chief Justice Rehnquist, to set a higher minimum drinking age than they might have otherwise. The enactment of such laws, however, "remains the prerogative of the states, not merely in theory but in fact." The "incentive" offered to the states to raise their minimum drinking ages was seen as a valid use of the spending power as well. Congress may "attach conditions" on the receipt of federal funds and "has repeatedly" used the spending power to further policy objectives by conditioning receipt of federal funds on recipient compliance with federal directives. The congressional interest in reducing drinking and driving by younger drivers was seen by the Court as "directly related" to one of the main objectives of federal highway expenditures—"safe interstate travel." The congressional power to authorize expenditure of federal funds is "not limited by the direct grants of legislative power" found in the Constitution. Thus, Rehnquist continued, "objectives not thought to be within Article I's enumerated legislative fields, may nevertheless be attained through the use of the spending power and the conditional grant of federal funds." *See also* GENERAL WELFARE CLAUSE, p. 377; *STEWARD MACHINE COMPANY v. DAVIS* (301 U.S. 548: 1937), p. 391.

Significance The Court acknowledged in *Dole* that the spending power is not "unlimited" and is subject to several general restrictions. The first is that the spending power must be used "in pursuit of the general welfare." Second, if Congress wishes to condition state receipt of federal funds, it must do so "unambiguously," thereby enabling the states to "exercise their choice knowingly, cognizant of the consequences of their participation." Finally, conditions on federal grants might be unconstitutional if they are unrelated to the "federal interest in particular national projects or programs." In *Dole,* South Dakota did not "seriously claim" that the challenged section of the federal statute was incompatible with any of these limitations. The approach taken in *Dole* was much like that seen in the 1930s when the Court upheld the Social Security Act. In *Steward Machine v. Davis* (301 U.S. 548: 1937), the Court upheld a taxation initiative that collected a tax on employers but credited employers who contributed to comparable state unemployment compensation programs. The Court characterized the unemployment problem as "national in area and dimensions," a problem to which the states were "unable to give the requisite relief." Persuaded of the existence of an "urgent" national need, the Court then concluded that the mean chosen by Congress to address the problem was not a "weapon of coercion" that impaired state autonomy. In the companion case to *Steward Machine, Helvering v. Davis* (301 U.S. 619: 1937), the Court focused on the concept of general welfare. The concept is "not static," and the needs that may have been "narrow or parochial" in the past may become "interwoven" later with the nation's well-being. *Steward Machine* and *Helvering* recognized substantial congressional discretion to determine what constitutes the general welfare. More recently, in *Fullilove v.*

Klutznick (448 U.S. 448: 1980), the Court allowed Congress to designate a portion of federal construction grant funds for award to minority-owned or -operated businesses. The Court was satisfied that Congress had sufficient evidence to conclude that minority businesses had impaired access historically to public contracting opportunities and that the problem was national in scope. So long as Congress uses racial or ethnic criteria in fashioning a narrowly tailored remedial program, it has the authority to do so.

Takings Clause

***Dolan v. City of Tigard*, 512 U.S. 374, 129 L.Ed. 2d 304, 114 S.Ct. 2309 (1994)** John and Florence Dolan, residents of Tigard, Oregon, wished to expand their electrical and plumbing supply business and pave the adjacent parking lot. Under state law, they needed the approval of the city planning commission. The commission conditioned its approval on the applicants' committing a portion of their property to a public "greenway" running along a creek. The greenway was intended to minimize flooding of the creek. The commission also wanted to use some of the Dolan property as part of a pedestrian and bicycle system designed to reduce traffic congestion in downtown Tigard. The Dolans objected to the commission's ruling and unsuccessfully appealed to a land use appeal board. A state appeals court and the Oregon Supreme Court affirmed. The U.S. Supreme Court reversed in a 5-4 decision. Chief Justice Rehnquist pointed to previous rulings on zoning or land use regulations in acknowledging that state and local governments have the authority to "engage in land use planning." These kinds of regulations differed in "two relevant particulars" from this case. First, they involved "essentially legislative determinations" classifying entire areas of a city, whereas here Tigard had made an "adjudicative decision" to condition the Dolan application for a building permit on an individual parcel of land. Second, the conditions imposed were not just a limitation on the use to which the Dolans might put the property but a requirement that they actually "deed portions of the property to the city." The government may not "require a person to give up a constitutional right—here the right to receive just compensation when property is taken for a public use—in exchange for a discretionary benefit conferred by the government where the property sought has little or no relationship to the benefit." In evaluating claims such as that brought by the Dolans, the Court must first determine whether the "'essential nexus' exists between the 'legitimate state interest' and the permit condition exacted by the city." If such a nexus exists, the Court must then determine the "required degree of connection between the exactions and the projected impact of the proposed development." The prevention of flooding and the reduction of traffic congestion, said Rehnquist, qualify as the type of legitimate public purposes upheld in previous cases. The Court must also examine whether the degree of the exactions demanded through the permit conditions "bear[s] the required relationship to the projected impact of [any] proposed development." In other words, the city must make "some sort of individualized determination" that the property taken from the Dolans is related "both in nature and extent" to the impact of the proposed development and that the government show a "rough proportionality" between the requirement and the proposed land use. It was the Court's judgment that the findings on which the city relied did not show the required relationship between the "flood plain easement and the proposed new building." The Court did agree that the larger sales facility proposed by the Dolans would increase downtown traffic. The city did not, however, sufficiently demonstrate that the additional traffic generated by the proposed expansion "related to the city's requirement for a dedication of the pedestrian/bicycle pathway easement." Although "no precise mathematical calculation" is required, the city must "make some effort to quantify its findings" in support of its attempt to acquire part of the Dolan property for the pathway. Although the city's goals of reducing flood hazards and traffic congestion and providing for public greenways are "laudable," there are "outer limits" on how this may be done. In dissent, Justice Stevens suggested the Court had applied standards that "run contrary to the traditional treatment of these cases and break considerable and unpropitious new ground." The Court recognized that Tigard had satisfied the "essential nexus" requirement established in previous decisions but then "erect[ed] a new constitutional hurdle in the path of these conditions." The dissenters saw the "rough proportionality" test imposed by the Court as a "novel burden of proof," one that "resurrect[s] . . . a species of substantive due process analysis that it firmly rejected decades ago." *See also* DUE PROCESS CLAUSES, p. 411; *PENN CENTRAL TRANSPORTATION COMPANY v. NEW YORK CITY* (438 U.S. 104: 1978), p. 451; *VILLAGE OF EUCLID v. AMBLER REALTY COMPANY* (272 U.S. 365: 1926), p. 439.

Significance The Fifth Amendment provision that government should not "take" private property for "public use without just compensation" historically has not been a substantial constitutional obstacle to broad local authority to regulate land use. Extensive land use regulation through zoning ordinances was upheld by the Court in *Village of Euclid v. Ambler Realty Company* (272 U.S. 365: 1926). More recently, the Court upheld a local historic preservation ordinance in *Penn Central Transporta-*

tion Company v. New York City (438 U.S. 104: 1978). A commission had designated Grand Central Terminal a historic "landmark." The owner of the terminal, Penn Central, sought approval from the commission to construct a multistory office building above the terminal. Penn Central submitted building modification proposals to the commissions, but both were rejected because they either involved destruction of portions of the terminal or were architecturally incompatible with the existing building. The Court's position on the Takings Clause became decidedly more receptive to private property claims when William Rehnquist was elevated to chief justice. Several cases reflect this changing view, but the best early indicator was *Nollan v. California Coastal Commission* (483 U.S. 825: 1987). California wished to improve public access to ocean beaches. The Nollans wished to construct a structure on their beachfront property and sought a permit from the California Coastal Commission. The permit was conditioned on their setting aside a small portion of their property to connect two public beaches, thereby enabling the public to move more easily between them. The Nollans eventually filed an action, claiming that the condition attached to the building permit's approval constituted a taking for which they were entitled to compensation. In a 5-4 decision, the Court concluded that California was "free to advance its comprehensive program" by using its power of eminent domain for this purpose, but "if it wants an easement across the Nollans' property, it must pay for it." A similar ruling came in *Lucas v. South Carolina Coastal Council* (505 U.S. 1003: 1992). Lucas bought two oceanfront lots in South Carolina, intending to build a home. Shortly after Lucas's purchase, South Carolina passed an environmental law that gave the South Carolina Coastal Council authority to protect sensitive shoreline areas from erosion. Lucas's property was designated as "critical," meaning no new building could occur. The Court ruled for Lucas, however, concluding that government cannot undertake "permanent physical occupation" of land without compensation "no matter how weighty the asserted 'public interests' involved." Similar treatment must be accorded, said Justice Scalia, for "confiscatory regulations . . . that prohibit all economically beneficial use of land." In dissent, Justice Blackmun saw the decision as making "sweeping and . . . misguided and unsupported changes" in Takings Clause jurisprudence. The Court's ruling in *Dolan* maintains the course.

Punitive Damages

***BMW of North America, Inc. v. Gore*, 517 U.S. 559 (1996)** Dr. Ira Gore purchased a new BMW sports car from an authorized dealer. Several months after buying the car, Gore attempted to enhance the finish and discovered that the car had been repainted prior to its sale to him. He brought suit against BMW of North America for failure to disclose that the vehicle had been repainted. BMW admitted at trial that it had a policy not to disclose any repairs if the repair cost did not exceed 3 percent of the retail price. The repainting of Gore's car prior to its sale as new was less than 2 percent of the retail cost, and the dealership from whom Gore purchased the car was not informed of the repair. Gore introduced evidence at trial that refinished cars had diminished value of about 10 percent, or $4,000. Gore asked for punitive damages of $4 million, an amount subsequently awarded by the jury. The Alabama Supreme Court ruled that the jury miscalculated the punitive damages by including the number of sales of repaired vehicles nationally, and it reduced the punitive damages to $2 million. In a 5-4 decision, the Supreme Court ruled that the reduced award was excessive. States pursue legitimate interests by using punitive damages for "punishing unlawful conduct and deterring its repetition." Our federal system requires that states must have "considerable flexibility," said Justice Stevens, in determining the level of punitive damages that they will allow across a wide range of differing cases. The deference to be accorded states in imposing punitive damages is substantial, and only when an award can be "fairly categorized as 'grossly excessive' in relation to [its legitimate] interests does it enter the zone of arbitrariness that violates the Due Process Clause of the Fourteenth Amendment." Federal inquiry into the excessiveness of a punitive damages award must begin with an "identification of state interests a punitive award is designed to serve." Dr. Gore had argued that a large award was necessary to "induce BMW to change the nationwide policy" of not disclosing that "minor" repairs had taken place. The principles of state sovereignty and comity, however, preclude a state from "imposing economic sanctions on violators of its laws with the intent of changing the [wrongdoers'] lawful conduct in other states." Thus, the jury in this case should not have been presented evidence of BMW's out-of-state conduct, an error properly identified by the Alabama Supreme Court as it reduced the award. When the "scope of the interest in punishment and deterrence" that the state court may appropriately consider is "properly limited, it is apparent . . . that this award is grossly excessive." The Court identified three "guideposts" that prompt a conclusion of excessiveness: the "degree of reprehensibility" of not disclosing the repairs; the "disparity" between the harm or potential harm suffered by the plaintiff and the punitive award; and the "difference between this remedy and the civil penalties authorized or imposed in comparable cases." Prior cases suggested that the "relevant ratio" between compensatory and punitive damages was "not more than

10 to 1." The award in Gore's case was more than 500 times the amount of "actual harm." The Court also found that award excessive when compared to civil penalties that could be imposed for comparable conduct in Alabama. The maximum civil penalty for violation of the state's deceptive trade practices law is $2,000. Finally, Stevens concluded that the sanction imposed in this case could not be justified on the grounds that it was necessary to "deter future misconduct" without considering whether "less drastic remedies" could be expected to achieve that goal. Since there was no history of BMW's noncompliance with any statutory requirements in the state, the Court found no basis for assuming that a "more modest sanction would not have been sufficient to motivate full compliance with the disclosure requirement imposed by the Alabama Supreme Court in this case." Justices Scalia and Thomas, in dissent, were critical of the "latest manifestation of this Court's recent and increasing insistent 'concern about punitive damages that run wild.'" Since the Constitution "does not make that concern any of our business," said Scalia, the Court's decisions in this area are an "unjustified incursion into the province of state governments." *See also* DUE PROCESS CLAUSES, p. 415; FEDERALISM, p. 29.

Significance Assessment of punitive damages is something a state has the power to pursue. It is not a tax as such but rather is a penalty imposed on a defendant for civil (as distinct from criminal) misconduct. An award of punitive damages typically requires more than a showing of wrongdoing; it requires some form of aggravated or particularly malicious misconduct. Punitive damages may also be used by a state to deter future misconduct by others. The size of punitive damage awards in recent years has generated wide media coverage that, in turn, has prompted legislative initiatives aimed at capping awards. The issue of punitive damages has been before the Supreme Court several times since 1990. Like *Gore,* these cases have challenged punitive damage awards on a number of constitutional grounds (primarily substantive and procedural due process grounds). The Court, however, has been unable as yet to fashion clear guidelines for punitive damage cases. In *Pacific Mutual Life Insurance Co. v. Haslip* (499 U.S. 1: 1991), for example, the Court upheld a $1 million award, concluding that even where the punitive damages award was more than four times the amount of compensatory damages the award did not "cross the line into the area of constitutional impropriety." The Court refused in *Haslip* to draw a "mathematical bright line" by which to review punitive damages awards that would "fit every case." Two years after *Haslip,* a highly divided court upheld a $10 million award in *TXO Products Corp. v. Alliance Resources Corp.* (509 U.S. 443: 1993) that was more than 500 times the compensatory damages. The award was not seen as "grossly excessive" despite the "dramatic disparity" between actual damages and the punitive award. Under the circumstances of this particular case, the Court did not see the ratio between actual and punitive damages as controlling. The Court's ruling in *Gore* that the punitive damages award was excessive is more compatible with the widespread sentiment in support of legislative reforms in this area.

7. Justices of the U.S. Supreme Court

Harry A. Blackmun (1971–1994) Justice Harry A. Blackmun was nominated to the Supreme Court by President Richard Nixon in April 1970. He replaced Justice Abe Fortas, who resigned in May 1969. Blackmun was the third Nixon nominee for the Fortas seat, as the Senate failed to confirm two earlier nominations—Clement F. Haynsworth Jr. of South Carolina and G. Harrold Carswell of Florida. Blackmun was confirmed by the Senate without a dissenting vote. Blackmun was born in Nashville, Illinois, in 1908, but spent most of his young life in St. Paul, Minnesota. It was in grade school that Blackmun first met Warren Burger, and the two became close friends. Blackmun did his undergraduate work as a scholarship student at Harvard University. He graduated Phi Beta Kappa, majoring in mathematics. Choosing law over medicine, Blackmun went on to Harvard Law School and graduated in 1932. While at Harvard, he took a course from Felix Frankfurter and was influenced by the Frankfurter self-restraint viewpoint of constitutional adjudication.

Following law school, Blackmun returned to Minnesota, where he served 18 months as clerk to U.S. Circuit Judge John B. Sanborn. After a year on the faculty of the Mitchell College of Law in St. Paul, he entered private practice, joining a large and prestigious firm in Minneapolis. Blackmun's practice specialized in estates, taxation, and civil litigation. He continued to teach on a part-time basis during this period. In 1950 Blackmun took the position of resident legal counsel for the Mayo Clinic in Rochester, Minnesota, a post he held for nine years immediately preceding his first judgeship.

A seat became vacant on the U.S. Court of Appeals for the Eighth Circuit in 1959 upon the retirement of Judge Sanborn, for whom Blackmun had clerked a quarter-century earlier. Possessing the appropriate Republican credentials for the seat, Blackmun was appointed by President Dwight Eisenhower. Blackmun's record as a circuit judge was generally conservative and reflected commitment to self-restraint. He was also highly regarded as a legal scholar and was known for thorough and tightly crafted opinions. Blackmun retired from the Supreme Court in 1994 and was replaced by Stephen G. Breyer. *See also* WARREN E. BURGER, p. 503; JUDICIAL SELF-RESTRAINT, p. 627.

Significance It was expected that Justice Blackmun would become a second Warren Burger on the Court. Indeed, the two were often termed the "Minnesota Twins" after Blackmun joined his longtime friend on the Court in 1971. Blackmun generally took a conservative course, but he was flexible and independent. He showed an inclination to separate himself from the conservative majority on certain issues and join the most liberal members of the Burger and Rehnquist Courts—Justices Brennan and Marshall. The dominant value for Blackmun in most instances was judicial self-restraint. Blackmun was fundamentally committed to legislative resolution of major policy issues, even if those judgments were incompatible with his own preferences. His view of limited judicial intervention is well reflected in his dissent in *Furman v. Georgia* (408 U.S. 238: 1972), where the Court struck down the sentencing procedures of a state capital punishment law. Blackmun said, "I yield to no one in the depth of my distaste, antipathy, and, indeed, abhorrence, for the death penalty. Were I a legislator, I would vote against the death penalty." "But," he went on, "I do not sit on these cases . . . as a legislator." The judiciary "cannot allow our personal preferences as to the wisdom of legislation and congressional action to guide our judicial decision in cases such as these."

His record on rights of the accused was generally conservative. He was not willing to extend the exclusionary rule beyond the trial stage in criminal cases and subscribed to some of the Burger Court's highly critical comments on the rule itself. He did not favor extending the *Miranda* rationale, and he usually sustained convictions from which come Fourth or Fifth Amendment challenges. Blackmun's pragmatism and exacting focus on factual underpinnings of cases generally led him to affirm most criminal convictions. This approach, however, may explain his change of view about the constitutionality of capital punishment.

Blackmun was certainly not an ideological liberal. He was not averse, however, to taking positions that expanded federal legislative or judicial power. In *Equal Employment Opportunity Commission v. Arabian American Oil Co.* (499 U.S. 244: 1991), Blackmun read Title VII of the Civil Rights Act of 1964 as protecting employees from workplace discrimination even when working for employers operating abroad. He also found that the Commerce Clause prevented states from enacting laws that discriminated against the free flow of interstate commerce. Blackmun was among the majority in *Chemical Waste Management, Inc. v. Hunt* (504 U.S. 334: 1992), in which the Court struck down an Alabama law that imposed higher fees on hazardous wastes brought into Alabama from other states. It was the Court's view that any legitimate concerns about protecting citizens' health and safety "do not vary with the waste's point of origin." The Commerce Clause simply does not permit states to isolate themselves from problems common to all the states by "raising barriers" to the free flow of interstate commerce. Similarly, Blackmun was in the majority in *Wyoming v. Oklahoma* (502 U.S. 437: 1992), in which the Court struck down an Oklahoma law that required coal-burning utilities within the state to use at least a minimum proportion of coal mined within the state. As a result of the law, the Oklahoma utilities required less coal from Wyoming, which diminished Wyoming's revenues from its severance tax on coal. The Court ruled that the constitutionality of laws such as Oklahoma's must be calculated by considering the potential effect if every state adopted similar legislation. This approach led the Court to conclude that the Oklahoma law impermissibly discriminated against interstate commerce.

On some issues Blackmun distanced himself from conservative positions. Three stand out in particular: religious establishment, equal protection, and abortion. Blackmun could typically be found among those opposing aid to nonpublic schools. In one of his first establishment cases, *Lemon v. Kurtzman* (403 U.S. 602: 1971), Blackmun voted to strike down a state program that supplemented salaries paid to teachers of secular subjects in nonpublic schools. He also opposed the state tax deduction for public and private school expenses in *Mueller v. Allen* (463 U.S. 388: 1983). Blackmun dissented from the Court's ruling in *Lynch v. Donnelly* (465 U.S. 668: 1984), which allowed the display of a nativity scene on public property.

Blackmun's strong establishment position carried over to other First Amendment issues. Blackmun consistently opposed content-based regulation of expression. For that reason, he voted to strike down laws that prohibited flag desecration (*Texas v. Johnson,* 491 U.S. 397: 1989; *United States v. Eichman,* 496 U.S. 310: 1990) and a local ordinance that criminalized "hate speech" (*R.A.V. v. St. Paul,* 505 U.S. 377: 1992). Blackmun was also at the forefront of extending First Amendment coverage for commercial speech, a category of expression that advertises a product or service and that was previously subject to governmental regulation (see *Bigelow v. Virginia,* 421 U.S. 809: 1975; *Virginia State Board of Pharmacy v. Virginia Citizens Consumer Council, Inc.,* 425 U.S. 748: 1976).

Blackmun departed from the conservative bloc on a number of equal protection issues. He generally supported the transition to the "new" equal protection, that is, a widening of the scope of the Fourteenth Amendment to other than race-based classification schemes. He frequently voted to invalidate classifications that discriminate against women, the poor, and illegitimate children (see, for example, *Frontiero v. Richardson,* 411 U.S. 667: 1973; *James v. Valtierra,* 402 U.S. 137: 1971; *Weber v. Aetna Casualty and Surety Company,* 406 U.S. 164: 1972). Indeed, Blackmun was quite protective of those he viewed as disadvantaged. For example, he concluded in *Plyler v. Doe* (457 U.S. 202: 1982) that education was a fundamental right that could not be denied to children of illegal aliens.

Blackmun's greatest impact, however, came in the policy area of abortion rights. He authored the majority opinion in the landmark decision *Roe v. Wade* (410 U.S. 113: 1973), which established the right to abortion. Thereafter, he was an outspoken opponent of attempts to regulate access to abortions (see, for example, *City of Akron v. Akron Center for Reproductive Health, Inc.,* 462 U.S. 416: 1983) and restrictions on public funding of abortion costs (see, for example, Blackmun's dissents in *Beal v. Doe,* 432 U.S. 438: 1977, and *Harris v. McRae,* 448 U.S. 297: 1980). In *Harris,* Blackmun forcefully argued that the poor are discriminated against in their pursuit of a protected right merely because of their poverty. His strongest statements in support of reproductive rights can be found in his dissent in *Webster v. Reproductive Health Services* (492 U.S. 490: 1989) and in his concurring opinion in *Planned Parenthood of Southeastern Pennsylvania v. Casey* (505 U.S. 833: 1992), where the Court upheld various regulatory initiatives on abortion and made inroads into the trimester framework of *Roe v. Wade.* He feared for the future of *Roe,* noting that the Court was but a single vote short of fully overturning *Roe.* He recognized that he could not carry on the defense of *Roe* indefinitely, saying he could not "remain on this Court forever." Though on balance Blackmun remained a conservative, he was not an ideological captive. He clearly demonstrated an independence of thought that resulted in his taking strong liberal positions on important constitutional questions.

William J. Brennan (1956–1991) Justice William J. Brennan Jr. was born in Newark, New Jersey, in 1906. He received his B.S. from the Wharton School of Finance at the University of Pennsylvania in 1928. Three years later, he obtained his law degree from Harvard Law School. He joined a leading Newark law firm following graduation and cultivated an expertise in labor law. Brennan was one of a number of attorneys who worked on comprehensive reform of the New Jersey state court system. He left his successful private practice to serve on the newly established New Jersey Superior Court in 1949. His performance was distinguished enough to earn him elevation to the appellate division of the Superior Court the following year. Two years later, Brennan was named to the New Jersey Supreme Court. In 1956, Justice Sherman Minton left the U.S. Supreme Court. President Dwight Eisenhower gave Brennan a recess appointment in October 1956 despite Brennan's nominal Democratic Party affiliation. Brennan was confirmed by the Senate the following year and served until his retirement in 1991. He was replaced by David H. Souter. Justice Brennan died in July 1997. *See also* *BAKER v. CARR* (369 U.S. 186: 1962), p. 123; THURGOOD MARSHALL, p. 533.

Significance Justice William J. Brennan was one of three Warren Court holdovers who served on both the Burger and Rehnquist Courts. At the outset of his tenure on the Court, Brennan tended toward moderate positions on most issues. Through the early 1960s, Brennan could not have been characterized as a liberal or as a judicial activist. Reflective of his more cautious approach is *Roth v. United States* (354 U.S. 476: 1957), a decision that established new definitional standards for obscenity. Brennan spoke for the majority in saying that the First Amendment was not intended to protect every utterance and that obscenity was not protected speech. As the Warren Court moved into the 1960s, Brennan took more liberal positions and utilized judicial intervention as a means of safeguarding individual rights. It was Brennan who wrote for the Court in the landmark case *Baker v. Carr* (369 U.S. 186: 1962). *Baker* held that legislative apportionment was an appropriate matter for judicial consideration. *Baker* opened the door for extensive federal court activity on the matter and resulted in comprehensive redistricting based on the "one person–one vote" standard. Brennan consistently endorsed ongoing monitoring of legislative district populations thereafter.

Brennan was not a constitutional literalist. To the contrary, he was often willing to expand the scope of constitutional protections based on constitutional inference. For example, Brennan joined the Warren Court majority in *Griswold v. Connecticut* (381 U.S. 479: 1965), the birth-control case in which the Court established a constitutional right of privacy. Similarly, in *Plyler v. Doe* (457 U.S. 202: 1982), Brennan wrote for the Court as it brought education within the "framework of equality embodied in the Equal Protection Clause." Brennan also supported expanding equal protection coverage to such classifications as gender and wealth. With Justice Marshall, he consistently supported claims of unconstitutional discrimination based not only on race but other classifications as well.

Brennan was the prototypical liberal judicial activist over the last 25 years of his tenure on the Court. He consistently supported an expansionist view of federal legislative power and judicial interventionism. In Brennan's view, the federal government was the principal protector of civil liberties and the facilitator of sociopolitical equality. His last significant affirmative action case, *Metro Broadcasting, Inc. v. FCC* (497 U.S. 547: 1990), is illustrative. The issue involved the FCC practice of giving preference to minorities in making broadcaster license decisions. The overriding factor in this case, said Brennan, was that this minority preference program was "specifically approved—indeed mandated—by Congress." When reviewing affirmative action initiatives of the federal government, Brennan felt a relaxed level of review was appropriate. Such programs need only serve "important" governmental interests; the preferential means need only be "substantially related" to achievement of those interests. Enhancing diversity in the broadcasting industry was a sufficiently important governmental objective to support the affirmative action initiative in this case. While serving on the Burger and Rehnquist Courts, Brennan was the strongest advocate for the kind of federal authority represented by the *Metro Broadcasting* decision. It is not surprising that a more conservative Court overruled *Metro Broadcasting* soon after Brennan's departure.

Brennan became the Court's most demanding justice on First Amendment issues—the Free Press and Establishment Clauses being illustrative. Brennan's opinion in *New York Times v. Sullivan* (376 U.S. 254: 1964) established some insulation for the press from libel actions. The Court held that a public official could not recover damages for defamation relating to conduct in office without proof that statements were made with "actual malice." Brennan also joined the Court majority in voting to dissolve the injunction against the *New York Times* restraining publication of the Pentagon Papers (*New York Times v. United States,* 403 U.S. 713: 1971). In addition, Brennan supported the concept of reporter's privilege in *Branzburg v. Hayes* (408 U.S. 665: 1972). On establishment issues, Brennan was strongly separationist. He was part of the Warren Court majority striking down both the prayer and Bible-reading exercises in public schools in the 1960s (see *Engel v. Vitale,* 370 U.S. 421: 1962; *School District of Abington Township v. Schempp,* 374 U.S. 203: 1963). He took essentially the same position more than 20 years later when the Court invalidated Alabama's "moment of silence" policy (*Wallace v. Jaffree,* 472 U.S. 38: 1985). Brennan consistently opposed all forms of aid to nonpublic educational institutions, including state income tax deductions for all educational costs for both public and private schools (*Mueller v. Allen,* 463 U.S. 388: 1983). Brennan also wrote the Court's opinion in *Sherbert v. Verner* (374 U.S. 398: 1963), which required states to demonstrate an overriding interest in regulations that affected free exercise rights. The highly protective standard in *Sherbert* carried into the 1990s and the Court's ruling in *Employment Division v. Smith* (494 U.S. 872: 1990), with Brennan in the minority.

Finally, Brennan typically took liberal positions when analyzing rights of the accused. Brennan fully supported the Warren Court in its extension of federal constitutional guarantees to the states and was part of the majority in such cases as *Mapp v. Ohio* (367 U.S. 643: 1961), which applied the exclusionary rule to state criminal trials. As a member of the Burger and Rehnquist Courts, Brennan more often was on the dissenting side of cases involving criminal rights. Reflective are his dissents in those decisions modifying *Miranda v. Arizona* (384 U.S. 436: 1966), such as *Harris v. New York* (401 U.S. 222: 1971) and *North Carolina v. Butler* (441 U.S. 369: 1979). Similarly, Brennan categorically rejected use of the death penalty, a position that usually placed him in the minority on the Burger and Rehnquist Courts. As the composition of the Court changed beginning with the appointment of Chief Justice Warren Burger, Brennan moved from being among the majority to virtually always being in the minority. From that time, he and Justice Marshall functioned as the spokesmen for liberal activism.

Stephen G. Breyer (1994–) Stephen Breyer was born in San Francisco, California, in 1938. He graduated Phi Beta Kappa from Stanford University in 1959. He attended Oxford University on the Marshall Scholarship for the next two years. He returned to the United States in 1961 and began at Harvard Law School, graduating three years later with high honors. Following graduation, he clerked for Supreme Court Justice Arthur J. Goldberg. Breyer spent the next two years working on antitrust enforcement in the U.S. Justice Department. He returned to Harvard in 1967 as a member of the law school faculty, where he taught courses on antitrust and administrative law. Professor Archibald Cox, a colleague, was appointed Watergate special prosecutor in 1973, and Breyer returned to Washington as part of Cox's staff. The following year, Breyer became special counsel for the Senate Judiciary Committee, where he remained for almost two years before rejoining the faculty at Harvard. Breyer became special counsel to the Senate Judiciary Committee for a second time, in 1979, and chief counsel to the committee the following year. In late 1980, President Jimmy Carter nominated Breyer to the U.S. Court of Appeals for the First Circuit. Although Carter's pending nominations were withdrawn following his loss to Ronald Reagan in the 1980 election, Breyer's nomination went through to confirmation, largely on the recommendation of Republican members of the Senate Judiciary Committee. Justice Byron White left the Supreme Court in 1993, and Breyer was considered a front-runner for the nomination. President Bill Clinton chose Ruth Bader Ginsburg, however. The following year, Justice Harry Blackmun retired, and Breyer was once again considered. This time, Clinton chose Breyer, and his nomination was subsequently confirmed by the Senate on an 87-9 vote. *See also* RUTH BADER GINSBURG, p. 224 (Supp.).

Significance Stephen G. Breyer came to the Supreme Court with a reputation for moderation. Such moderation led to his circuit court confirmation when all other Carter nominations were withdrawn. Over and above his clear record of competent performance, his moderate views led President Clinton to nominate him in 1994; his candidacy was unlikely to prompt any serious confirmation problems with the Senate. His brief tenure on the Supreme Court has reflected this moderation.

Breyer and the other Clinton nominee, Ruth Bader Ginsburg, tend to reflect moderate to liberal views on such issues as equal protection and the extent to which the federal government can exercise authority over interstate commerce. With Justice Breyer, it is possible to detect some of the liberal activism of Justice Goldberg on some issues—but certainly not across the board. Although he has not fully embraced affirmative action initiatives, it is his view that congressional districting plans containing majority-minority districts satisfy a compelling interest in complying with federal voting rights laws. Breyer was also among the dissenters in *Missouri v. Jenkins* (515 U.S. 70: 1995), in which he supported the broad use of judicial remedial power in pursuit of public school desegregation. Breyer authored the dissent in *United States v. Lopez* (514 U.S. 549: 1995), in which the Court struck down the federal Gun-Free School Zones Act, holding that the federal government had no authority under the commerce power to criminalize possession of a firearm on elementary school or secondary school grounds. Breyer saw the act as falling "well within the scope of the commerce power" and suggested that Congress be allowed substantial latitude in "determining the existence of a significant factual connection between the regulated activity and interstate commerce." Similarly, Breyer dissented in *Printz v. United States* (138 L.Ed. 2d 914: 1997), in which the Court struck down the provisions of the Brady Act (the Handgun Violence Prevention Act), which required local law enforcement authorities to conduct background checks on those attempting to purchase handguns. Breyer was of the view that Congress could impose such "affirmative obligations" on state and local government officials.

Breyer's willingness to defer to federal legislative power is reflected in the recent rulings on congressional redistricting, the issue being whether race can influence the establishment of district boundaries. The Rehnquist Court position generally has been that traditional districting criteria may not be subordinated to race; hence the Court must employ strict scrutiny when reviewing redistricting plans for equal protection violations. Justice Breyer is less inclined to use strict scrutiny in such situations. Instead, he prefers to see race as one of a number of legitimate and interrelated factors that are appropriate in redistricting. As a result, Breyer has allowed states and the federal government to pursue districting plans that enhance the electoral prospects of minority candidates.

Breyer had not been particularly receptive to claims asserted by those accused of crimes. He tends to uphold criminal convictions more often than not. Nonetheless, Breyer disagreed with the Court's expansion of the good-faith exception in *Arizona v. Evans* (514 U.S. 1: 1995). He also recognizes reasonably broad federal *habeas corpus* authority. He wrote the majority opinion in *O'Neal v. McAninch* (513 U.S. 432: 1995), in which the Court held that a federal *habeas* petitioner must prevail when a judge is uncertain as to whether or not procedural error in a criminal case is harmless. More representative is Breyer's position in *Vernonia School District 47J v. Acton* (515 U.S. 646: 1995), in which he joined the Court in allowing the drug testing of students as a precondition to participating in athletics, even in the absence of individualized suspicion.

Justice Breyer frequently joins Justices Ginsburg and Stevens on cases involving First Amendment claims. He was among the majority in *McIntyre v. Ohio Elections Commission* (514 U.S. 334: 1995), in which the Court struck down a statute requiring the identification of anyone distributing materials designed to influence elections. He dissented in the establishment of religion case *Rosenberger v. University of Virginia* (515 U.S. 819: 1995), being of the view that making student activity funds available to religious groups on a public university campus constituted a direct subsidy of religion. Yet Breyer did not think that the private religious display in a public forum in *Capitol Square Review and Advisory Board v. Pinette* (515 U.S. 753: 1995) conveyed official endorsement of religion by the state. Finally, he was among the five-justice majority upholding a regulation on direct-mail advertising by lawyers in *Florida Bar v. Went For It, Inc.* (515 U.S. 618: 1995). It was the Court's view in this ruling that lawyer advertising was commercial speech, a form of expression entitled to limited First Amendment protection.

Warren E. Burger (1969–1986) Warren Earl Burger was born in St. Paul, Minnesota, in 1907. Unable to afford full-time schooling, Burger worked his way through the University of Minnesota and St. Paul College of Law on a part-time basis. He graduated magna cum laude from law school in 1931. He joined a firm in St. Paul and maintained a general private practice until 1953. He also retained a part-time faculty position at St. Paul College of Law during this period. Burger also became involved in Republican politics in Minnesota and worked extensively on the 1938 gubernatorial campaign of Harold Stassen. Burger continued his association with Stassen and was convention floor manager of Stassen's presidential bids in 1948 and 1952. It was at the 1948 Republican nominating convention that Burger met Herbert Brownell, then campaign manager for New York's governor, Thomas Dewey.

In 1952, Burger shifted his support from Stassen to Eisenhower at a critical point, thus assisting Eisenhower in securing the nomination from Senator Robert Taft. Following Eisenhower's election, Brownell became the U.S. attorney general. He proceeded to name Burger assistant attorney general and head of the civil division of the Justice Department. In 1955, Eisenhower nominated Burger to a seat on the U.S. Court of Appeals for the District of Columbia Circuit, a position he held until his elevation to the Supreme Court in 1969. As a circuit judge, Burger demonstrated a clearly conservative orientation, particularly on cases involving rights of the accused. Indeed, Burger was openly critical of the direction taken by the Warren Court. In 1969, Chief Justice Earl Warren retired from the Court. President Richard Nixon, who had emphasized the need to change the course of the Court during his presidential campaign, nominated Burger for the chief justiceship. The Senate confirmed his nomination on a 74-3 vote. Burger retired from the Court at the end of the 1985 term. Burger died in 1995. *See also* JUDICIAL SELF-RESTRAINT, p. 627; STANDING, p. 655; *UNITED STATES v. NIXON* (418 U.S. 683: 1974), p. 153.

Significance Warren Burger was chosen chief justice in order to lead the Court to different policy decisions than those of the Warren Court. An articulated priority of Richard Nixon's presidential campaign of 1968 was to neutralize the Warren Court's expansion of rights afforded those accused of crimes. Burger performed as expected on these issues. More generally, Nixon sought a "strict constructionist," someone whose judicial philosophy would fundamentally differ from Warren's activism. To a substantial degree, Burger satisfied this priority as well—but not entirely. Instead, the Court and Burger engaged in selective activism, although Burger typically defined the Court's authority in the limited terms of a judicial conservative. In *Plyler v. Doe* (457 U.S. 702: 1982), the Court struck down a state law that denied public education to children who were in the country illegally. The decision was based on equal protection considerations. Burger dissented, saying that the U.S. Constitution "does not provide a cure for every social ill, nor does it vest judges with a mandate to remedy every social problem." This outlook was also manifest in cases involving access to federal courts. Burger was very comfortable limiting access to federal courts on standing grounds. In *Warth v. Seldin* (422 U.S. 490: 1975), for example, he was of the view that a group must show more than generalized injury to establish standing to sue. Similarly, he wrote the opinion in *Laird v. Tatum* (408 U.S. 1: 1972), saying that claims of a "subjective chill" cannot replace demonstration of a specific present injury to establish standing.

In the area of criminal rights, Burger was the outspoken hard-liner Nixon was seeking. He supported use of capital punishment by states not only where sentencer discretion was guided but also where the death sentence was mandatory. Furthermore, Burger would not have limited use of the death penalty to the crime of murder. He was also a consistent and vocal critic of the exclusionary rule, referring to it as a "Draconian, discredited device" in *Stone v. Powell* (428 U.S. 465: 1976). In *United States v. Leon* (468 U.S. 897: 1984), Burger supported a good-faith exception to the exclusionary rule when police seize evidence in reliance on a search warrant that later is found defective. Burger also sought to limit the scope of the *Miranda* doctrine (see, for example, *Harris v. New York,* 401 U.S. 222: 1971; *North Carolina v. Butler,* 441 U.S. 369: 1979). When his Court reversed criminal convictions, Burger usually dissented. He was known on those occasions to offer broadly critical comment, such as that in *Brewer v. Williams* (430 U.S. 387: 1977), where he said the majority's holding "ought to be intolerable in any society which purports to call itself an organized society." Burger generally deferred to the power of the states to aggressively protect its citizens, a view that necessarily required a more limited application of constitutional protection for the accused.

Burger had substantial impact on First Amendment issues. His Court took a decidedly more accommodating position than the Warren Court in the religion cases, and Burger led the way. He said in *Walz v. New York City Tax Commission* (397 U.S. 664: 1970) that the Court ought to take a position of "benevolent neutrality" when reviewing establishment of religion claims, a position that favored religion over nonreligion in establishment cases. Burger fashioned the three-pronged establishment test, known as the *Lemon* test, in *Lemon v. Kurtzman* (403 U.S. 602: 1971), which remains in effect. He also wrote the Court's opinion in the case that permitted the Amish exemption from a state compulsory education law (*Wisconsin v. Yoder,* 406 U.S. 205: 1972). It was Burger who crafted new definitional standards for obscenity in *Miller v. California* (413 U.S. 15: 1973), a decision that encouraged more aggressive state and local regulation of obscenity. He was strongly in favor of state regulation of child pornography (see, for example, *New York v. Ferber,* 458 U.S. 747: 1982). His free press record was somewhat mixed. He dissented in the Pentagon Papers case (*New York Times v. United States,* 403 U.S. 713: 1971) but struck down a court order restricting coverage of a criminal trial in *Nebraska Press Association v. Stuart* (427 U.S. 539: 1976). He supported press access to criminal trials in *Richmond Newspapers, Inc. v. Virginia* (448 U.S. 555: 1980), yet he rejected a claimed privilege of source confidentiality in *Branzburg v. Hayes* (408 U.S. 665: 1972).

Likewise, Burger's record on equal protection was conservative, but here the label can be misleading. In his first case, he joined a unanimous Court, which ordered immediate desegregation of a number of Mississippi school districts, thereby closing the open-ended "all deliberate speed" language of *Brown* (see *Alexander v. Holmes County Board of Education,* 396 U.S. 19: 1969). He authored the first important busing opinion in *Swann v. Charlotte-Mecklenburg Board of Education* (402 U.S. 1: 1971), upholding the remedial authority of lower federal courts where constitutional violations are found in public education. Yet he invalidated a busing order in *Milliken v. Bradley* (418 U.S. 717: 1974), saying that interdistrict remedies could only be ordered when preceded by a finding of interdistrict violations. This seriously limited the remedial authority of lower court judges.

Burger joined the Court's decision in *Washington v. Davis* (426 U.S. 229: 1976), which required a showing of discriminatory intent in employment discrimination cases. He also rejected the use of quotas as a means of affirmative action in *Regents of the University of California v. Bakke* (438 U.S. 265: 1978). Although generally opposed to affirmative action programs in the educational arena or workplace, Burger acknowledged broad congressional authority to remediate discrimination in his majority opinion in *Fullilove v. Klutznick* (448 U.S. 448: 1980), a decision that was eventually overruled after Burger left the Court. Burger resisted extension of the Equal Protection Clause to classifications other than race. Although he occasionally supported claims of impermissible gender discrimination, as in *Reed v. Reed* (404 U.S. 71: 1971), he generally rejected the view that gender is a "suspect" classification entitled to more demanding review standards than other legislative enactments.

Burger was a highly visible chief justice. He tended to assign the majority opinion–writing task to himself in major cases. Certainly his executive privilege opinion in *United States v. Nixon* (418 U.S. 683: 1974) is illustrative. He also distinguished himself by his efforts on behalf of better judicial management and general reform of the judicial process. He was, however, unable to forge a lasting coalition of justices, despite the turnover from the Warren Court, to establish a clear ideological direction for the Court.

Ruth Bader Ginsburg (1993–) Ruth Bader was born in Brooklyn, New York, in 1933. She graduated from Cornell in 1954 and married Martin Ginsburg shortly thereafter. Ginsburg began Harvard Law School in 1956 following the birth of a daughter. Her husband took a job with a New York City law firm, and Ginsburg moved to New York with him. Once settled in New York, Ginsburg transferred to Columbia Law School, where she graduated first in her class. Unable to find a job in New York, she spent the next two years clerking for Edmund L. Palmieri, a U.S. district court judge. She then returned to Columbia, where she served as associate director of an international procedure project for the law school. In 1963, Ginsburg began teaching at Rutgers University School of Law, where she remained on the faculty until 1980. While at Rutgers, Ginsburg was an active litigator, focusing primarily on cases that involved gender discrimination. She organized the American Civil Liberties Union (ACLU) Women's Rights Project in 1971, directing the project from 1972 until 1980. She also served as general counsel for the ACLU for seven years. During this period, she argued six cases before the U.S. Supreme Court, including a challenge to gender differences in military health and housing benefits (*Frontiero v. Richardson,* 411 U.S. 677: 1973), gender-specific provisions of the Social Security Act (*Califano v. Goldfarb,* 430 U.S. 199: 1977), and underrepresentation of women on criminal juries (*Duren v. Missouri,* 439 U.S. 357: 1979). President Jimmy Carter nominated Ginsburg to the U.S. Court of Appeals for the District of Columbia Circuit; she served on that court for 13 years. In 1993, Justice Byron R. White retired from the Court, and President Bill Clinton nominated Ginsburg. *See also* STEPHEN G. BREYER, p. 219 (Supp.); STARE DECISIS, p. 656.

Significance Ruth Bader Ginsburg begs easy ideological classification. Indeed, what is most apparent is her independence, and her general deference to both legislative judgments and previous judicial decisions—stare decisis. Her prejudicial experiences, however, are apparent in her positions on several issues. She believes constitutional protections must be applied to the fullest extent, and it is evident that she elevates procedural due process and equal protection under the laws.

Justice Ginsburg's highest priority seems to be equal protection. This is not surprising given her lengthy involvement contesting gender discrimination. Her position on equal protection is represented in many cases, but the most revealing may be several recent rulings *not* involving gender-based classification schemes. The Court ruled in *Missouri v. Jenkins* (515 U.S. 70: 1995) that a federal district court had exceeded its remedial authority in its broad order attempting to relieve discrimination in the Kansas City, Missouri, schools. Ginsburg dissented, saying that given the "deep, inglorious history of segregation in Missouri, to curtail desegregation at this time and in this manner is an action at once too swift and too soon." She was also critical of the Court's decision in

Adarand Constructors, Inc. v. Pena (515 U.S. 200: 1995), which held that the federal government must demonstrate a "compelling interest" in justifying any affirmative action program. Ginsburg would have given the federal government more latitude in designing remedial affirmative action plans. She also would have upheld the Georgia redistricting plan in *Miller v. Johnson* (515 U.S. 900: 1995), which created a new majority-minority congressional district in Georgia. It was her view that the Court's decision to subject race-conscious districting plans to strict judicial scrutiny was insensitive to whether a plan "dilutes or enhances minority voting strength." Ginsburg believes that voting-rights policies deserve much greater deference in the latter instance. Ginsburg was among the majority in *Romer v. Evans* (134 L.Ed. 2d 855: 1996), in which the Court struck down a Colorado constitutional amendment that repealed legal protections for homosexuals and prohibited the adoption of any new laws designed to protect homosexual rights. Since joining the Court, Ginsburg has had no opportunity to participate in an abortion rights case. She was also part of the majority in *Madsen v. Women's Health Center* (512 U.S. 753: 1994), upholding a lower court injunction designed to keep antiabortion protesters from blocking access to abortion clinics.

One of Justice Ginsburg's most significant opinions to date is *United States v. Commonwealth of Virginia* (135 L.Ed. 2d 735: 1996). Virginia operated a male-only state college, Virginia Military Institute (VMI). Ginsburg spoke for the Court as it ruled the single-sex institution was unconstitutional. Neither the "goal of producing citizen-soldiers nor VMI's implementing methodology is inherently unsuitable to women." Virginia had argued that single-sex education promoted "diversity" in educational approaches. Ginsburg agreed but concluded that Virginia had not demonstrated that VMI was either established or maintained "with a view to diversifying, by its categorical exclusion of women" from educational opportunities within the state. Indeed, providing diversity of educational options is not served by VMI's plan to afford a "unique educational benefit only to males."

Justice Ginsburg typically has been receptive to claims of First Amendment violations. She joined the Court in upholding the free speech rights of private associations in *Hurley v. Irish-American Gay, Lesbian, and Bisexual Group* (515 U.S. 557: 1995). Although the ruling went against a homosexual group seeking to march in a privately sponsored local parade, it was the Court's view that the parade was an expressive act on the part of its organizers and that the organizers could not be compelled by the state to include expressive content with which they did not agree. She has also strongly supported fully extending First Amendment protections to commercial speech. She dissented in *Florida Bar v.*

Went For It, Inc. (515 U.S. 618: 1995), in which the Court upheld a state prohibition on direct-mail advertising by attorneys. Similarly, Ginsburg was among the majority that struck down an Ohio law that required the name and address of persons or organizations distributing materials designed to influence voters (*McIntyre v. Ohio Elections Commission,* 514 U.S. 334: 1995).

In contrast to her predecessor, Justice Byron White, Ginsburg has been much less of an accommodationist on establishment of religion issues. In *Capitol Square Review & Advisory Board v. Pinette* (515 U.S. 753: 1995), the Court permitted a private organization (the Ku Klux Klan) to display an unattended cross in Capitol Square in Columbus, Ohio. The Ohio capitol building and other government buildings are located on the square, which is clearly a public forum for First Amendment purposes. Justice Ginsburg dissented, concluding that the state endorsed the display's message, given its location so near the seat of government. She also dissented from the Court's ruling in *Rosenberger v. University of Virginia* (515 U.S. 819: 1995), in which the Court allowed funds from a student activities fund to be given to a campus religious organization to underwrite the costs of publishing a magazine containing clearly sectarian content.

Ginsburg is more inclined than many of her colleagues to support the exercise of federal power. Two examples: She was among the minority in *United States v. Lopez* (514 U.S. 549: 1995), in which the Court struck down the Gun-Free School Zones Act that made it a federal crime to possess a firearm within 1,000 feet of a public or private elementary or secondary school. It was the Court's view that the act encroached on a policy area where the states "historically have been sovereign." Ginsburg was satisfied that Congress had a rational basis for finding a significant connection between gun-related school violence and interstate commerce. Similarly, Ginsburg supported the provisions of the Brady Act in *Printz v. United States* (138 L.Ed. 2d 914: 1997), which required local law enforcement officers to conduct background checks on prospective gun purchasers. Yet Ginsburg has demonstrated that she does not support judicial intervention when traditional threshold conditions, such as standing or mootness, are not met. In *Arizonans for Official English v. Arizona* (137 L.Ed. 2d 473: 1997), Ginsburg expressed "grave doubts" that private groups such as Arizonans for Official English had not suffered "concrete injury" necessary to establish standing. She also concluded that the plaintiff's challenge of the English-only provision in the Arizona Constitution was moot, since the plaintiff had left state employment and, during the time she had been a state employee, had never been threatened with enforcement of the English-only requirement.

Anthony M. Kennedy (1988–) Anthony M. Kennedy was born in Sacramento, California, in 1936. Following high school, he attended Stanford University, where he earned his B.A. in 1958 and was elected to Phi Beta Kappa. He spent a year abroad studying at the London School of Economics before entering Harvard Law School, where he graduated cum laude. Kennedy spent two years in San Francisco as an associate at a highly regarded law firm before returning to Sacramento to assume his father's law practice. There he maintained a general practice for the next 12 years. During this time, Kennedy joined the faculty of the McGeorge School of Law at the University of the Pacific on a part-time basis. During Ronald Reagan's tenure as governor of California, Kennedy provided legal counsel to several people on Reagan's staff. Kennedy subsequently worked closely with Reagan on fashioning a constitutional amendment imposing limits on the state's power to tax and spend. Reagan recommended Kennedy for a vacancy on the U.S. Court of Appeals for the Ninth Circuit in 1974, and President Gerald Ford nominated him. He was confirmed by the Senate in early 1975.

Justice Lewis F. Powell Jr. retired from the Court in 1987. President Ronald Reagan nominated Circuit Judge Robert Bork to fill the vacancy, but after a bitter confirmation battle in the Senate the nomination failed. Kennedy was considered by many to be the next choice. Instead, Reagan nominated another circuit judge, Douglas Ginsburg. That nomination was withdrawn several days later in the wake of disclosures about Ginsburg's use of marijuana while in college. Thus, Kennedy was the third nominee to be submitted to the Senate. The confirmation hearings were uneventful, and the Senate confirmed Kennedy on a 97-0 vote. *See also ADARAND CONSTUCTORS, INC. v. PENA* (515 U.S. 200: 1995), p. 95 (Supp.).

Significance Anthony M. Kennedy is part of the conservative majority on the Rehnquist Court. He is not, however, a conservative ideologue in the fashion of his colleague, Justice Antonin Scalia. Kennedy is generally less outspoken and more cautious than Scalia. He is also reluctant to draw bright doctrinal lines in his judicial opinions. He clearly subscribes to the judicial philosophy of self-restraint, and he generally defers to judicial precedent. These orientations are reflected in several substantive areas.

Where possible, Kennedy opts to limit the exercise of federal judicial authority. In *Missouri v. Jenkins* (515 U.S. 70: 1995), for example, Kennedy was part of the five-justice majority that substantially reduced the scope of a remedial order issued by a federal trial judge in the Kansas City, Missouri, school desegregation case. Kennedy has also objected to race-conscious congressional redistricting plans. He was among the majority in *Shaw v. Reno* (509 U.S. 630: 1993) that voted to subject racial gerrymandering cases to strict judicial scrutiny. He subsequently used *Shaw* as the basis of his majority opinion in the Georgia redistricting case, *Miller v. Johnson* (515 U.S. 900: 1995). It was the *Miller* ruling that determined that compliance with federal voting rights laws was an insufficient justification for intentionally creating minority-majority districts. Kennedy was the author of the Court's opinion in *Holder v. Hall* (512 U.S. 874: 1994), in which the Court ruled that the vote "dilution" protections contained in section 2 of the Voting Rights Act could not be applied to the size of a governing body. A court must find, said Kennedy, a "reasonable alternative practice as a benchmark against which to measure the existing voting practice." Kennedy concluded that no such standard existed in cases where the size of a governing authority is challenged, since there is no reason why "one size should be selected over another."

As in the cases involving race-conscious redistricting, Kennedy has been unreceptive to affirmative action initiatives. He was among the majority that struck down a local contracting set-aside approach for public construction projects (*Richmond v. J.A. Croson Co.,* 488 U.S. 469: 1988). He was also among the dissenters in *Metro Broadcasting, Inc. v. FCC* (497 U.S. 547: 1990), in which the Court allowed the FCC to consider minority ownership as a factor in licensing decisions. Finally, Kennedy was one of the five justices to explicitly overrule *Metro Broadcasting* in *Adarand Constructors, Inc. v. Pena* (515 U.S. 200: 1995). In *Adarand,* the Court held that even federal affirmative action initiatives must pass strict scrutiny, a level of review previously reserved only for programs of state or local origin. On a similar issue, Kennedy has been reluctant to endorse broad remedial authority for federal courts. In *Freeman v. Pitts* (503 U.S. 467: 1992), for example, the Court ruled that lower federal courts may incrementally relinquish remedial control over desegregation orders as school districts move into unitary operations. Once a particular violation has been remedied, Kennedy said, a school district should have no duty to "remedy imbalance that is caused by demographical factors." Indeed, it is beyond the "authority and . . . practical ability" of federal courts to try to "counteract . . . continuous and massive demographic shifts."

Kennedy's deference to state sovereignty is evident in the Court's rulings on state abortion regulations and federal judicial authority to review state criminal convictions on *habeas corpus* petitions. Kennedy was in the majority in both *Webster v. Reproductive Health Services* (492 U.S. 490: 1989) and *Planned Parenthood of Southeastern Pennsylvania v. Casey* (505 U.S. 833: 1992). In both of these decisions, the Court upheld various restrictions on abortions, such as informed consent provisions, modified viability criteria, and prohibitions in public-supported facilities. Yet Kennedy was among the five justices who chose to retain several underlying principles from *Roe v. Wade* (410 U.S. 113: 1973). He rejoined Justices Scalia and Thomas in *Madsen v. Women's Health Center* (512 U.S. 753: 1994), dissenting against the use of an injunction to keep abortion protesters from interfering with access to abortion clinics.

Justice Kennedy is a key vote in the Rehnquist Court's efforts to scale back federal *habeas corpus* review of state criminal cases. In *Coleman v. Thompson* (504 U.S. 188: 1992), Kennedy supported a ruling that virtually any failure to exhaust state procedures would constitute a default and preclude federal intervention. He wrote the majority opinion in *McCleskey v. Zant* (499 U.S. 467: 1991), invoking the "abuse of the writ" principle to disallow a state prisoner's second petition for review. Kennedy's position on this matter was not negotiable. Federal *habeas* review has "significant cost," he said, as it "strikes at finality" of the state trials and, as a result, "disparages the entire criminal system."

Kennedy's record on First Amendment issues is more difficult to identify. He has generally taken the position that the Court's establishment of religious standards did not sufficiently accommodate religion. He is one of the Rehnquist Court justices critical of the three-pronged test found in *Lemon v. Kurtzman* (403 U.S. 602: 1971). Yet, as Kennedy wrote in a narrow, 5-4 ruling in *Lee v. Weisman* (505 U.S. 577: 1992), it was unnecessary to reconsider *Lemon* in striking down a practice of allowing clergy to lead prayers at public school graduation ceremonies. Kennedy also provided the deciding vote in both *Texas v. Johnson* (491 U.S. 397: 1989) and *United States v. Eichman* (496 U.S. 310: 1990), which struck down, respectively, state and federal laws proscribing flag desecration. Kennedy joined the more liberal justices in dissenting in *Florida Bar v. Went For It, Inc.* (515 U.S. 618: 1995), which allowed regulation of attorney advertising. It was Kennedy's view that despite the commercial character of the advertisements it was expression protected by the First Amendment.

Thurgood Marshall (1967–1991) Thurgood Marshall was born in Baltimore, Maryland, in 1908. At the age of 18, he left Baltimore to attend Lincoln University, where he graduated cum laude in 1930. Marshall earned his law degree from Howard University in Washington, D.C., graduating first in his class. While attending law school Marshall became interested in civil rights. Following a short private practice in Baltimore, Marshall was named assistant special counsel to the National Association for the Advancement of Colored People (NAACP); he became special counsel to the organization in 1938. In 1940, the NAACP made a significant structural change. It created a new and separate entity known as the NAACP Legal Defense and Educational Fund. Marshall was named director and counsel. From this position, Marshall orchestrated comprehensive challenges to the practice of racial discrimination in a variety of areas. For example, during its first decade, the fund was successful in having outlawed the racially exclusive "white primary" used in a number of southern states (*Smith v. Allwright*, 321 U.S. 649: 1944), racial segregation on interstate buses (*Morgan v. Virginia*, 328 U.S. 373: 1946), and segregative practices in various professional and graduate educational programs. The most significant initiative was a challenge to racial segregation in public education. Marshall supervised preparation for the several cases docketed by the Supreme Court on this issue and handled presentation of arguments in one of the suits. The litigation led to the Court's landmark ruling in *Brown v. Board of Education* (347 U.S. 483: 1954). Marshall's activity with the fund continued until 1961.

In September 1961, President John Kennedy nominated Marshall for the U.S. Court of Appeals for the Second Circuit. Marshall began service under recess appointment; his confirmation was held up until late 1962 by the chair of the Senate Judiciary Committee, who opposed Marshall's nomination. The Senate eventually confirmed Marshall on a 54-16 vote. President Lyndon Johnson appointed Marshall to the position of solicitor general in 1965. He was the first African-American to hold that position. Two years later, Johnson submitted Marshall's name to fill the Supreme Court vacancy created by the retirement of Justice Tom Clark. The Senate confirmed the nomination on a 69-11 vote, and Marshall became the first African-American on the Supreme Court. Marshall retired from the Court in 1991 and was replaced by Justice Clarence Thomas. Marshall died in early 1993 at the age of 84. *See also* WILLIAM J. BRENNAN, p. 501; *NEW YORK TIMES v. UNITED STATES* (403 U.S. 713: 1971), p. 148.

Significance Thurgood Marshall came to the Supreme Court as the Warren Court period drew to a close. As the Court changed in composition over the next several years, Marshall found himself playing the role of liberal dissenter, often with Justice William J. Brennan. Marshall believed that the federal courts must play a fundamental role in safeguarding individual rights and the interests of minorities. He would have, for example, used the Equal Protection Clause to invalidate the use of property taxes to finance public schools (*San Antonio Independent School District v. Rodriguez*, 411 U.S. 1: 1973), but he was among the minority in this case. He was also in the minority on the issue of Medicaid funding for abortions. He said in *Beal v. Doe* (432 U.S. 438: 1977) that the Court had a "duty to enforce the Constitution for the benefit of the poor and powerless" when the elective branches make decisions that do not do so. In general, Marshall was dissatisfied with the Court's resistance to enlarge the scope of equal protection coverage and often urged the Court to subject various classification bases such as gender, wealth, age, and others to more stringent scrutiny. Marshall was also strongly protective of voting rights. He opposed restrictions on access conditions to voting, was unyielding in his support of the "one person–one vote" standard for legislative apportionment, and was consistently resistant to the Burger Court's relaxation of that standard (see, for example, *Mahan v. Howell,* 410 U.S. 315: 1973).

Marshall was a judicial liberal and a judicial activist. He consistently supported extensive federal judicial intervention in school desegregation situations, for example. Marshall was also an aggressive advocate of expanding the reach of the Equal Protection Clause to classifications other than race. He also supported the exercise of federal legislative authority to protect civil rights in virtually every context. He was among the minority in *Equal Employment Opportunity Commission v. Arabian American Oil Company* (499 U.S. 244: 1992), in which the Court refused to extend Title VII of the Civil Rights Act of 1964 to overseas employers. It was Marshall's view that the language and legislative history of Title VII indicated clear congressional intent to protect American workers from American employers operating abroad.

Marshall also took strongly liberal positions on First Amendment issues. He generally opposed time, place, and manner restrictions, supported demonstrations, opposed prior restraint in all forms (see, for example, his concurring opinion in *New York Times v. United States,* 403 U.S. 713: 1971), and dissented from the Court's upholding of state obscenity regulations in *Miller v. California* (413 U.S. 15: 1973). He wrote the Court's opinion in *Stanley v. Georgia* (394 U.S. 557: 1969), which held that the First Amendment and considerations of privacy do not permit a state to make it a crime to privately possess obscene materials.

Marshall typically took the position that protections afforded those accused of crimes must be steadfastly maintained. He embraced the view that protections under the Bill of Rights required compliance not only by federal agents but also enforcement agents of the states. He was a consistent dissenter in Burger and Rehnquist Court decisions modifying the *Miranda* ruling, and he supported retention of the exclusionary rule despite the majority's critical view of it. With Brennan, Marshall took the position that capital punishment is unconstitutional under any circumstance; he automatically voted to reverse death sentences in every case seeking review from the Court. With the exception of certain equality cases where Justices White, Blackmun, Powell, or Souter might be drawn to a moderate position, Justice Marshall represented the value of liberal activism from a minority position.

Sandra Day O'Connor (1981–) Sandra Day O'Connor was born in El Paso, Texas, in 1930. Her family owned and operated a sizable cattle ranch located on the Arizona–New Mexico border. Much of O'Connor's youth was spent in El Paso with her grandmother, because virtually no critical services, medical facilities, or schools were available in the remote area of the ranch. O'Connor finished high school at age 16 and entered Stanford University, where she graduated magna cum laude in 1950. Two years later, she obtained her law degree from Stanford. Failing to find employment in the private legal community, O'Connor worked a short time as deputy county attorney. When her husband completed law school, he joined the army's Judge Advocate General's Corps, and the O'Connors spent three years in Frankfort, Germany. During this time, O'Connor worked as a civilian attorney for the Quartermaster Corps. The couple returned to the United States and settled in Phoenix, Arizona. O'Connor attempted to maintain a private practice after the birth of their first child, but she gave it up to become a full-time housewife following the birth of their second child.

O'Connor returned to her legal career in 1965, when she was appointed assistant state attorney general. In 1969, she was appointed to complete an unexpired state senate term. The following year, she was elected to a full term in the state senate, and in 1972 she was elected majority leader. She was also cochair of the Arizona reelection campaign organization for President Richard Nixon. In 1974, O'Connor ended her legislative career and sought election to the Maricopa County Superior Court. She won the judgeship, and it was from this position that she was named to the Arizona Court of Appeals in 1979. When Justice Potter Stewart retired from the U.S. Supreme Court in 1981, O'Connor was nominated by President Ronald Reagan to fill the vacancy. O'Connor was the first woman nominated for service on the Court. Some questions were raised by antiabortion groups that felt that her record was not strong enough on that issue, but no real opposition developed, and O'Connor was confirmed by the Senate on a 99-0 vote. *See also FEDERAL ENERGY REGULATORY COMMISSION v. MISSISSIPPI* (456 U.S. 742: 1982), p. 362; *GARCIA v. SAN ANTONIO METROPOLITAN TRANSIT AUTHORITY* (469 U.S. 528: 1985), p. 275; WILLIAM H. REHNQUIST, p. 542.

Significance In 1981, Sandra Day O'Connor became the first woman to sit on the Supreme Court. Her appointment was in some measure undertaken to fulfill a campaign pledge, but her jurisprudence also reflected an ideological orientation sought by the new president. She is generally conservative, believes in a limited role for the federal judiciary, and prefers that the legislative branch be the source of major policy decisions. O'Connor is also highly protective of the authority of states. In this respect, she blended easily into the conservative majorities of the Burger and Rehnquist Courts. She dissented in *Federal Energy Regulatory Commission v. Mississippi* (456 U.S. 742: 1982), which held that a federal law could require state utility regulatory agencies to adopt a certain rate structure and other regulatory standards. She said that federal power is constitutionally limited to designated "channels" and cannot be used to "conscript" state utility regulatory commissions "into the federal bureaucratic army." O'Connor applied this same view in *Printz v. United States* (138 L.Ed. 2d 914: 1997), in which the Court struck down certain provisions of the Brady Act that imposed implementation obligations upon state and local law enforcement authorities. The Brady Act required local authorities to conduct the background checks on those seeking to purchase guns. The Court categorically reaffirmed the principle that the federal government could not "compel the States to enact or administer a Federal regulatory program." In a similar fashion, she dissented in *Garcia v. San Antonio Metropolitan Transit Authority* (469 U.S. 528: 1985), a decision that extended federal minimum wage and overtime regulations to employees of a public mass transit authority. She suggested the "true 'essence' of federalism is that the States as States have legitimate interests which the National Government is bound to respect even though its laws are supreme." For O'Connor, state autonomy is an "essential component of federalism." If this element is ignored in reviewing the exercise of federal power, then federalism "becomes irrelevant simply because the sets of activities" remaining outside federal reach "may well be negligible."

O'Connor has been a pivotal member of the Rehnquist Court on the issue of abortion. One year after joining the Court, she dissented in *Akron v. Akron Center for Reproductive Health, Inc.* (462 U.S. 416: 1982) and was highly critical of the trimester foundation of *Roe v. Wade* (410 U.S. 113: 1973). It was in *Akron,* however, that she introduced an "undue burden" standard for reviewing state regulations on abortion. Although state has an interest in protecting maternal and potential lives during the course of a pregnancy, there are regulations that impose an "undue burden" on the basic right to abortion. Such regulations, in her view, must be strictly scrutinized by the Court. In the two recent cases where *Roe v. Wade* was most vulnerable to reversal, *Webster v. Reproductive Health Services* (492 U.S. 490: 1989) and *Planned Parenthood of Southeastern Pennsylvania v. Casey* (505 U.S. 833: 1992), O'Connor chose not to reconsider the underlying framework from *Roe,* to the great disappointment of the four-justice minority. O'Connor will remain a critical vote in the abortion rights controversy.

O'Connor tends to join the conservatives on issues concerning rights of the accused. In *Elstad v. Oregon* (470 U.S. 298: 1985), for example, O'Connor authored the Court's opinion in a decision that allowed use of uncoerced statements made by a suspect prior to Miranda warnings if rights were subsequently waived following administration of the necessary warnings. She also dissented in *Tennessee v. Garner* (471 U.S. 1: 1985), a decision that disallowed use of deadly force to prevent the escape of any fleeing felony suspect, whatever the circumstances. O'Connor said that notwithstanding a suspect's interest in his life this interest does not encompass the "right to flee unimpeded from the scene of a burglary." O'Connor's strong commitment to state authority in the criminal justice field is clearly represented in the numerous federal *habeas corpus* cases decided by the Rehnquist Court. Generally, the Court has restricted federal *habeas* review of state criminal convictions. Among the leading cases is *Coleman v. Thompson* (504 U.S. 188: 1992), in which the Court required that *habeas* petitioners must exhaust all state remedies before seeking federal review. O'Connor said this case was "about federalism" and the respect that federal courts owe to state criminal proceedings.

O'Connor has generally taken an accommodationist position on Establishment Clause questions. She dissented in *Aguilar v. Felton* (473 U.S. 402: 1985), a decision that prohibited use of federal funds by local school districts to pay the salaries of employees providing remedial instruction and guidance services to parochial school students. And though she joined the majority in striking down Alabama's "moment of silence" policy for public schools in *Wallace v. Jaffree* (472 U.S. 38: 1985), she indicated that states could provide voluntary silent prayer time in public schools as long as there was no endorsement of prayer as the preferred activity during the period of silence. This state endorsement approach has led her to a more separationist position in such recent cases as *Lee v. Weisman* (505 U.S. 577: 1992) and probably forestalled the Court's abandonment of *Lemon v. Kurtzman* (403 U.S. 602: 1971) as the principal analytic framework for establishment issues.

O'Connor's rare departures from the conservative bloc have occurred in gender discrimination cases. In *Mississippi University for Women v. Hogan* (458 U.S. 718: 1982), she authored the Court's opinion holding that a public university could not deny admission (in this case to a male) solely on the basis of gender. In her view, gender classification could not be allowed unless the state presented "exceedingly persuasive justification." She also cast the decisive vote in *Arizona Governing Commit-*

tee for Tax Deferred Annuity and Deferred Compensation Plans v. Norris (463 U.S. 1073: 1983), which invalidated an employer-sponsored retirement plan that provided smaller benefits to women by using gender-based actuarial tables reflecting greater longevity for women. O'Connor was also instrumental in extending the reach of Title VII of the Civil Rights Act of 1964 to instances of sexual harassment in the workplace. In *Harris v. Forklift Systems, Inc.* (510 U.S. 17: 1993), O'Connor spoke for the Court and said that even without "tangible effects of workplace discrimination," conduct that is so severe as to create an abusive workplace environment "offends Title VII's broad rule of workplace equality."

O'Connor replaced Potter Stewart, a member of the Court's center or "swing" group. She has often aligned herself with members of the conservative bloc—Chief Justice William Rehnquist and Justices Scalia, Thomas, and Kennedy. Thus, the appointment of O'Connor served to generally solidify the conservative majority on the Rehnquist Court into the 1990s. Yet her opinions have a moderate tone. The recent cases involving congressional redistricting are illustrative. O'Connor spoke for the Court in *Shaw v. Reno* (509 U.S. 630: 1993) and said that states must demonstrate a "compelling interest" when using race as a factor in establishing congressional district boundaries. Although some of her more conservative colleagues felt that race could never be legally considered in making districting decisions, O'Connor did not rule out the possibility. In her view, the decision to create majority-minority congressional districts is not unconstitutional in itself. Strict scrutiny must apply, however, when "traditional districting criteria are *subordinated to race.*"

Lewis F. Powell (1971–1987) Lewis F. Powell was born in Suffolk, Virginia, in 1907. He graduated Phi Beta Kappa from Washington and Lee University in 1929. He attended law school at Washington and Lee and received his LL.B. in 1931. He pursued legal study at Harvard Law School, earning an LL.M. the following year. Upon finishing Harvard, Powell returned to Virginia and joined a prestigious Richmond firm (where he continued his private practice until his nomination to the Supreme Court much later). He became a full partner in the firm in 1937. He practiced corporate law, specializing in securities, reorganizations, mergers, and acquisitions. Among his clients were several of the largest corporations in the United States.

There was a public side to Powell as well. He had a long and extensive involvement with the American Bar Association, serving as its president in 1964 and 1965. He later led the American College of Trial Lawyers and headed the American Bar Foundation. He was widely known and highly regarded within the legal profession. Powell also became involved with public education. He was president of the Richmond Board of Education from 1952 to 1961. This was a time of turmoil in Virginia schools because of desegregation. Whereas other school systems in the state were closing to demonstrate their "resistance" to desegregation, Powell was instrumental in accomplishing orderly desegregation in the Richmond schools. Powell moved to the Virginia State Board of Education in 1961, where he served until 1969.

In 1971, Justice Hugo L. Black retired from the Court. President Richard Nixon nominated Powell to the Court despite his Democratic Party affiliations. The nomination was widely praised, and Powell was subsequently confirmed by the Senate, with only a single vote in opposition. Justice Powell retired from the Court in 1987 and was replaced by Justice Anthony M. Kennedy. *See also* JOHN M. HARLAN, p. 519; JUDICIAL SELF-RESTRAINT, p. 627.

Significance Justice Lewis F. Powell believed in a limited role for the federal judiciary. Along with former justices such as John M. Harlan II, Powell felt the Supreme Court functioned most effectively when it proceeded cautiously and with restraint. This fundamental belief manifested itself in a variety of ways. Powell consistently supported a narrowing of access to the federal courts. In *Warth v. Seldin* (422 U.S. 490: 1975), Powell wrote for the majority where a challenge to a municipal zoning decision was rejected on standing grounds. Powell believed that standing requirements ought not be met easily. This, in turn, would keep the courts from deciding "abstract questions of wide public significance" and prompt the Court to show appropriate deference to other governmental institutions that may be "more competent to address the questions."

Typical of those advocating judicial self-restraint, Powell favored legislative solutions for major policy issues. He was also highly supportive of the exercise of power at the state level. These two positions were clearly reflected in Powell's majority opinion in *San Antonio Independent School District v. Rodriguez* (411 U.S. 1: 1973). Suit had been brought challenging, on equal protection grounds, the system used in Texas for financing public education. In order for the financing scheme to be subject to the closest judicial scrutiny, education would have had to be seen by the Court as a fundamental right. Powell resisted, saying that it is "not the province of the Court to create substantive constitutional rights in the name of guaranteeing equal protection of the law." But more important for Powell was that this case constituted a "direct attack" on the way Texas chose to finance public education. The Court was asked to "condemn the state's judgment" in allowing local units to tax property to supply revenues for local schools. The challengers asked the Court to "intrude in an area in which it has traditionally deferred to state legislatures." The Court, said Powell, "has often admonished against such interferences with the states' fiscal policies under the equal protection clause." Similar deference to state legislative judgment was generally exhibited by Powell, as evidenced in the obscenity regulations, state restrictions on Medicaid funding for abortions, and state capital punishment laws.

Yet Powell was not insensitive to individual rights or inflexible in his restrained approach. On occasion (often with Justice Blackmun) he parted company with the conservative bloc to join the moderates and liberals. An example is *Weber v. Aetna Casualty and Surety Company* (406 U.S. 164: 1972), in which the Court struck down a law disadvantaging illegitimate children. Powell's majority opinion held that considerations of equal protection were sufficient in this case to invalidate a state law relating to birth status where a classification scheme "is justified by no legitimate state interest." Powell was also the decisive fifth vote in *Plyler v. Doe* (457 U.S. 202: 1982), in which the Court struck down a state law that denied free public education to school-age illegal aliens.

Powell's balancing approach was also clear in relation to rights of the accused. Though generally reluctant to require the states to meet the same standards as the federal government, Powell supported extension of the right to counsel to misdemeanor cases in which incarceration was possible (see *Argersinger v. Hamlin,* 407 U.S. 25: 1972). He sought to maintain procedural fairness in the criminal process but balanced the interests of the states in effectively enforcing criminal laws. Deference to states and to legislative judgments can be seen in his unwillingness to expand the reach of federal *habeas corpus* power, and he consistently supported state sentencing options for offenders, including capital punishment.

Most illustrative of Powell's willingness to engage in pragmatic balancing of competing interests is the highly visible affirmative action case, *Regents of the University of California v. Bakke* (438 U.S. 265: 1978), in which he was the decisive vote on three of the component issues and authored the majority opinion. He joined the conservatives in striking down the rigid quota system involved in the admission plan but aligned with the liberals to hold that race could be a factor in admitting a minority student. Powell was one of the Court's conservative justices, but throughout his tenure he demonstrated an independence and flexibility that allowed him to balance competing interests in pursuit of reasonable, middle-ground decisions. Powell served on the Court for 16 years before retiring in 1987.

William H. Rehnquist (1971–) William H. Rehnquist was born in 1924 in Milwaukee, Wisconsin, where he lived until serving in the Air

Force during World War II. He later entered Stanford University, where he graduated with "great distinction" in 1948, earning baccalaureate and masters degrees. He earned a second M.A. in political science from Harvard University in 1950. He returned to Stanford's law school and graduated first in his class in 1952. Upon graduating, Rehnquist went to Washington, D.C., as a law clerk for Justice Robert Jackson. Following his clerkship, Rehnquist established a successful private practice in Phoenix, Arizona. He became heavily involved in Republican politics in the state from the outset and aligned himself with the conservative wing of the state party.

Rehnquist was involved extensively with the 1964 presidential campaign of Arizona Senator Barry Goldwater. During the campaign he met Richard Kleindienst, who would become deputy U.S. attorney general in the Nixon administration. On Kleindienst's recommendation, Rehnquist was appointed assistant U.S. attorney general and named to head the Justice Department's Office of Legal Counsel. One of Rehnquist's responsibilities was to review all constitutional law questions involved in Nixon's executive orders and matters relating to the executive branch generally. Rehnquist was often the administration's spokesman on a range of issues. He frequently appeared before congressional committees, representing the more conservative and controversial policy positions of the Nixon administration. He defended the U.S. invasion of Cambodia as a proper exercise of executive power, for example; supported extensive presidential privilege to withhold information from Congress; and supported such crime-control policies as no-knock entries for searches, electronic surveillance, and the mass arrest of antiwar protesters.

In 1971, Justices Black and Harlan left the Court. A number of names surfaced as possible replacements, but Nixon ultimately chose Rehnquist (to replace Harlan) and Lewis Powell (to replace Black), neither of whom had been publicly discussed. The Rehnquist nomination prompted strong opposition from civil rights and civil liberties groups because of Rehnquist's outspoken conservatism on a range of issues. His nomination was eventually confirmed in the Senate on a 68-26 vote. In 1986, President Ronald Reagan nominated Rehnquist to succeed Warren Burger as chief justice, again giving rise to lengthy debate before the Senate confirmed on a 65-13 vote. *See also* ANTONIN SCALIA, p. 242 (Supp.).

Significance William Rehnquist was the Burger Court's most outspoken conservative. He consistently took the position that the Supreme Court should play a very limited role in fashioning policy. Even in matters that affected individual rights, Rehnquist emphatically rejected an interventionist function for the courts. Rather, he argued that policy decisions must emanate from the elected branches, especially the legislative branch. He typically takes a highly deferential position on initiatives coming from the states.

Rehnquist has remained committed to these positions during his more than 11 years as chief justice, but he has relinquished his role as conservative spokesman to Justices Scalia and Thomas. His narrow view of federal judicial power can be seen in his dissent in *Weber v. Aetna Casualty and Surety Company* (406 U.S. 164: 1972). The Court invalidated a state law as discriminatory against illegitimate children because the law violated a "fundamental" though unenumerated right. Rehnquist saw only those rights explicitly contained in the Bill of Rights as protected. This narrow approach is also reflected in Rehnquist's resistance to expanding the scope and coverage of the Equal Protection Clause. He examines legislative classifications using the rational basis test, a deferential and relaxed standard, rather than using strict or close judicial scrutiny. He was, for example, the only member of the Court voting to uphold different benefit requirements based on gender for military personnel in *Frontiero v. Richardson* (411 U.S. 677: 1973), saying that Congress could "reasonably have concluded" that because husbands are typically the "breadwinners" and wives the "dependent partners" different procedures for demonstrating dependency could be used.

Rehnquist's record on criminal rights reflects two strongly held views. The first is that the Court ought to lend greater support to the crime-control efforts of law enforcement authorities. The second is his deference to the exercise of state police power. Accordingly, Rehnquist has not only opposed extension of the exclusionary rule but has urged overruling *Mapp v. Ohio* (367 U.S. 643: 1961), which extended the exclusionary rule to state criminal trials. Similarly, he has given the states broad discretion in defining criminal punishments, including the death penalty. He said in *United States v. Robinson* (414 U.S. 218: 1973) that an officer's decision to search an arrestee "is necessarily a quick ad hoc judgment" and that the Fourth Amendment does not require it to be "broken down in each instance into analysis of each step in the search." Most revealing are his decisions in cases that involve federal *habeas corpus* review of state criminal convictions. Rehnquist strongly supports limiting the scope of such federal review. He wrote the Court's majority opinion in *Wainwright v. Sykes* (433 U.S. 72: 1977), which held that failure to assert a timely claim in a state criminal proceeding essentially precludes federal *habeas* review. As chief justice, Rehnquist has repeatedly maintained this position (see, for example, *Teague v. Lane,* 489 U.S. 288: 1989; *Coleman v. Thompson,* 501 U.S. 722: 1991; *Herrera v. Collins,* 506 U.S. 390: 1993).

Rehnquist's position regarding federal-state disputes is most clearly revealed in two cases involving application of the Fair Labor Standards Act (FLSA) to state and municipal employees. Rehnquist authored the majority opinion in *National League of Cities v. Usery* (426 U.S. 833: 1976), which held that state and local units are immune from the wages and hours restrictions of the FLSA. Rehnquist used the Tenth Amendment to effectively insulate certain aspects of state sovereignty from congressional reach. The *Usery* decision was reversed in *Garcia v. San Antonio Metropolitan Transit Authority* (469 U.S. 528: 1985). In dissent, Rehnquist said that he was confident that the *Usery* position "would again command the support of a majority of this Court." His inclination to protect state power from what he considers federal usurpation is reflected in three other recent decisions. In *United States v. Lopez* (514 U.S. 549: 1995) and *Printz v. United States* (138 L.Ed. 2d 914: 1997), the Court ruled that the federal commerce power did not permit Congress to criminalize possession of a firearm near elementary or secondary schools (*Lopez*) or require state and local law enforcement officers to perform administrative roles in a federal regulatory program (*Printz*). Rehnquist also wrote the Court's opinion in *Seminole Tribe of Florida v. Florida* (517 U.S. 44: 1996), which struck down, on Eleventh Amendment sovereign immunity grounds, a federal law that authorized lawsuits against states in federal courts. The Eleventh Amendment limits the power of federal courts, said Rehnquist, and Article I "cannot be used to circumvent the constitutional limitations placed on federal jurisdiction."

Rehnquist is best known for his deference to legislative judgments. In *Rostker v. Goldberg* (453 U.S. 57: 1981), he wrote for the majority upholding male-only draft registration. He said that the gender-based classification was not "unthinkingly" or "reflexively" reached by Congress nor a "byproduct of a traditional way of thinking about women." Congress was entitled to "focus on the question of military need rather than 'equity,'" and it was reasonable to conclude that males and females were not similarly situated with respect to combat duty. His deference to legislative judgment is often coupled with a strong predisposition to sustain exercise of state authority.

More than any member of the Burger Court, Rehnquist supported state governmental initiatives and usually favored states in conflicts with the federal level. Examples are numerous. He argued in *Roe v. Wade* (410 U.S. 113: 1973) that states should have the authority to impose restrictions on abortions, including prohibition of it. Subsequently, he generally supported state legislation aimed at limiting access to abortion and disallowing use of public moneys to underwrite or reimburse the costs of abortions. Rehnquist also wrote the majority opinions in *Vacco v.*

Quill (138 L.Ed. 2d 837: 1997) and *Washington v. Glucksberg* (138 L.Ed. 2d 771: 1997), in which the Court upheld state prohibitions on physician-assisted suicide. The Due Process Clause protects those fundamental rights that are objectively "deeply rooted in the nation's history and tradition" and "implicit in the concept of ordered liberty." Inquiry into the place of assisted suicide, said Rehnquist, "shows a consistent and almost universal tradition that has long rejected [such a] right." The states have, on the other hand, an "unqualified interest in the preservation of human life." As with the cases on regulation of abortion, Rehnquist deferred to state judgment.

Rehnquist has consistently upheld state capital punishment laws and dissented from the Court's holding in *Coker v. Georgia* (433 U.S. 584: 1977), where the death penalty for the crime of rape was found excessive. He felt that the states have broad discretion to act to deter crime, including use of the death penalty to that end. Rehnquist also supported a state statutory rape law that permitted prosecution of men but not women. He said in *Michael M. v. Superior Court* (450 U.S. 464: 1981) that because the most serious consequences of teenage pregnancies fall almost exclusively on the female a legislature is "well within its authority when it elects to punish the participant who, by nature, suffers few of the consequences of his conduct."

Rehnquist's responses to First Amendment challenges to governmental policies reveal the same deference to legislative judgments, particularly those at the state level. He supports most state initiatives directed at controlling production and distribution of obscene materials. This deference manifests itself in Establishment Clause cases as well. He would have upheld the Alabama "moment of silence" for meditation or voluntary prayer in public schools in *Wallace v. Jaffree* (472 U.S. 38: 1985). He would have also permitted clergy to offer prayers at public school commencement exercises (*Lee v. Weisman,* 505 U.S. 577: 1992).

Rehnquist clearly served as the Burger Court's conservative anchor and was a major ideological force on that Court. His selection as chief justice enhanced his influence as a jurist generally, but he appears to prefer that Justices Scalia and Thomas take the lead in advancing conservative positions on most issues.

Antonin Scalia (1986–) When William Rehnquist became the new chief justice following Warren Burger's departure from the Court, Rehnquist's seat was filled by Antonin Scalia. He was born in Trenton, New Jersey, in 1936. His father took a faculty position at Brooklyn College, and the family moved to Queens, New York, when Scalia was five years old. He received his B.A. from Georgetown University, where he graduated summa cum laude in history. He went on to Harvard Law School, where he graduated magna cum laude.

Scalia joined a law firm in 1961 as an associate. His practice was primarily in real estate, corporate finance, and antitrust. He left the firm in 1967 for a faculty position at the University of Virginia. Four years later, Scalia left teaching to become general counsel in the Office of Telecommunications Policy in the Nixon administration. The following year, he became chair of the Administrative Conference of the United States, an agency that advises the government on various issues of administrative law and procedure. In 1974, Scalia became assistant U.S. attorney general for the Office of Legal Counsel in the Justice Department. In that position, he functioned as legal adviser to the executive branch.

Scalia returned to teaching in 1977, first going to Georgetown and then to the University of Chicago, where he remained until 1982. It was during that period that Scalia served as chair of the American Bar Association's section on administrative law. In 1982, President Ronald Reagan appointed Scalia to the U.S. Court of Appeals for the District of Columbia Circuit; he served on the circuit bench for four years, being nominated to the Supreme Court by Reagan in June 1986. Scalia was confirmed by the Senate unanimously three months later, becoming the first person of Italian ancestry to join the Supreme Court. *See also MORRISON v. OLSON* (487 U.S. 654: 1988), p. 126 (Supp.); WILLIAM H. REHNQUIST, pp. 542; CLARENCE THOMAS, p. 252 (Supp.); *UNITED STATES v. MISTRETTA* (488 U.S. 361: 1989), p. 63 (Supp.).

Significance Antonin Scalia is an advocate of a "textualist" approach to judicial interpretation, that is, he views the actual text of the law (whether the Constitution or a statute) as the only appropriate basis for judicial decisionmaking. The language adopted by legislatures provides objective and reliable grounds for judicial decisions. Conversely, legislative history and representations of legislative intent are unreliable and distort judicial interpretation. Scalia also holds something other than a traditional view of stare decisis: He is more willing than many of his colleagues to reconsider principles seemingly resolved by prior decisions. Scalia clearly prefers to revisit questions if he feels they were improperly decided in the past. Although this approach occasionally puts him on the same side of cases with the Court's moderates, Scalia is generally regarded as the anchor of the conservative bloc on the Rehnquist Court. In recent terms, Scalia has been most closely aligned with Chief Justice Rehnquist and Justice Thomas. During his tenure on the circuit court, he was regarded as prepared and suited for the give-and-take of oral argument. It was during this period that he exhibited his strong belief that courts must play a limited role in the U.S. governmental system, a view that is evident in his Supreme Court writings.

Scalia's conservatism is most easily seen on several civil liberties issues. Yet he has significantly influenced the current definition of separation of powers. Scalia is not uncomfortable with the exercise of federal judicial power as such, but his views on the standing question would clearly preclude courts from entertaining suits where "concrete injury" is not present. Even Congress cannot confer standing in cases lacking this "core requirement" of standing. His textualist approach was apparent in his dissent in *Morrison v. Olson* (487 U.S. 654: 1988), which upheld the independent counsel provisions of the Ethics in Government Act. It was Scalia's conclusion that the prosecutorial function was an exclusively executive function and could not be performed by the legislature. Similarly, Scalia dissented in *United States v. Mistretta* (488 U.S. 361: 1989), which upheld congressional authorization for the creation of a commission to formulate federal sentencing guidelines. In Scalia's view, Congress can only delegate its lawmaking power in "conjunction with the lawful exercise of executive or judicial power." In this case, the sentencing commission neither exercised executive power nor was it subject to the control of the president.

Scalia prefers to paint bright lines—to establish clear legal rules through the Court's decisions. Recent rulings involving First Amendment, equal protection, and privacy issues are representative. It is his view that the First Amendment prohibits viewpoint discrimination. As a result, he voted to strike down a city's attempt to regulate hate speech in *R.A.V. v. St. Paul* (505 U.S. 377: 1992). He also joined the Court in *Rosenberger v. University of Virginia* (515 U.S. 819: 1995), allowing a public university to subsidize religious activities by a student organization. To allow the university to withhold such support would give it the power to select favored and disfavored expression for financial support, including religious expression. Similarly, Scalia has been at the forefront of the Rehnquist Court's accommodationist approach to interpreting the religion clauses. Long critical of the three-pronged establishment test from *Lemon v. Kurtzman* (403 U.S. 602: 1971), Scalia would permit church-state interaction as long as the state does not influence a person's religious beliefs or practices through coercion. Scalia also wrote the majority opinion in *Employment Division, Department of Human Resources of Oregon v. Smith* (494 U.S. 872: 1990), in which the Court returned to a less protective general secular purpose standard in free exercise of religion cases. In *Smith,* the Court upheld a state criminal prohibition against using peyote even though the drug was part of the ceremonial rituals of the Native American Church. Scalia said for the majority that the Court had never ruled that an "individual's beliefs excuse him from compliance with an otherwise valid law prohibiting conduct that the State is free to regulate." The government's ability to enact and enforce generally applicable regulations directed toward "socially harmful conduct," Scalia continued, "cannot depend on measuring the effects of a governmental action on a religious objector's spiritual development." To make an individual's obligation to comply with a law "contingent on the law's coincidence with his religious beliefs, except where the State's interest is 'compelling,' . . . contradicts both constitutional tradition and common sense."

Scalia takes an essentially absolutist equal protection position in affirmative action cases. He said in *Adarand Constructors, Inc. v. Pena* (515 U.S. 200: 1995) that government can never demonstrate a "compelling interest in discriminating on the basis of race in order to 'make up' for past racial discrimination." Scalia has carried this same view into recent cases involving race-conscious congressional districting plans. He joined Justice Thomas's opinion in *Holder v. Hall* (512 U.S. 874: 1994), for example, which criticized lower federal courts for segregating voters into "racially designated districts to ensure minority electoral success." Such a course was termed a "disastrous misadventure in judicial policymaking." This view is substantially influenced by his concerns about the exercise of federal legislative and judicial power. Scalia vigorously protested the Court's decision in *Chisom v. Roemer* (501 U.S. 380: 1991), extending provisions of the Voting Rights Act to judicial elections. Scalia said the act was not an "all-purpose weapon for . . . judges to wield as they please in the battle against discrimination." Similarly, Scalia wrote for a five-justice majority in *Printz v. United States* (138 L.Ed. 2d 914: 1997), striking down the provisions of the Brady Act that passed on some enforcement responsibilities to state and local law enforcement officials. Scalia said the basic principle of state sovereignty cannot be balanced away by federal statute.

Finally, Scalia has been the most outspoken opponent of abortion on the Rehnquist Court. The basis of his position is that there is no constitutional right to privacy since it is not expressly contained in the Constitution. Accordingly, there can be no rights, such as the right to abortion, that stem from the privacy right. In upholding the Missouri abortion regulations in *Webster v. Reproductive Health Services* (492 U.S. 490: 1989), the Court came within one vote of overruling *Roe v. Wade* (410 U.S. 113: 1973). It was Scalia's view that *Roe* had been effectively overruled in *Webster*, and he was critical of Chief Justice Rehnquist for not explicitly acknowledging that result. He said the Court "needlessly" prolonged its "self-awarded sovereignty over a field where it has little proper business" since its responses to most critical questions are "political and not juridical." Scalia stated his position even more strongly in his dissent in *Planned Parenthood of Southeastern Pennsylvania v. Casey* (505 U.S. 833: 1992). The question in *Casey* was not whether the "power of a woman to abort her unborn child is a 'liberty' in the absolute sense; or even whether it is a liberty of great importance to many women." Scalia acknowledged both to be true. Rather, he maintained, the issue is "whether it is a liberty protected by the Constitution." His answer was, "I'm sure it is not," a conclusion based on the fact that the "Constitution says absolutely nothing about it." On a related matter, Scalia concluded that states can impose criminal penalties on physicians for assisting a patient to commit suicide (see *Washington v. Glucksberg,* 138 L.Ed. 2d 772: 1997; *Vacco v. Quill,* 138 L.Ed. 2d 834: 1997).

David H. Souter (1990–) David Hackett Souter was the first of the two appointments by President George Bush. Souter was born in Melrose, Massachusetts, in 1939. His family eventually took up residence in his grandparents' farmhouse in rural New Hampshire. His undergraduate education was at Harvard, where Souter was elected to Phi Beta Kappa and graduated magna cum laude. He attended Oxford University for two years on a Rhodes Scholarship before beginning Harvard Law School. Upon his graduation from law school in 1966, he joined a prominent Concord, New Hampshire, law firm as an associate. His practice was in general corporate law and litigation.

Souter left private practice after a short time to join the staff of the New Hampshire attorney general. In 1971, he became deputy attorney general to Warren Rudman, under whom he served for five years. He was appointed attorney general in 1976 when Rudman left the office. Two years later, Souter was appointed associate justice of the Superior Court, New Hampshire's general-jurisdiction trial court. In 1983, Governor John Sununu appointed Souter to the New Hampshire Supreme Court. During his tenure on that court, he developed a reputation as a "scholarly, tough-minded intellectual with a deep respect for precedent and history." After a seven-year tenure on the New Hampshire Supreme Court, he was appointed to the U.S. Court of Appeals for the First Circuit by President George Bush. Bush nominated him to replace U.S. Supreme Court Justice William J. Brennan upon his retirement in 1990. His performance during the Senate Judiciary Committee hearings left those trying to label him unable to do so. Indeed, the media referred to him as the "stealth nominee," for virtually nothing definitive came out of the hearings. Nonetheless, Souter was eventually confirmed by the Senate on a 90-9 vote. *See also* RUTH BADER GINSBURG, p. 224 (Supp.).

Significance David Souter's voting record on the Supreme Court is generally conservative, but increasingly he takes more moderate positions, particularly on First Amendment, equal protection, and abortion issues. He has even distanced himself from the conservatives on certain questions of criminal rights. Since Justices Ginsburg and Breyer joined the Court, Souter has become the critical fifth vote in a number of cases in which he, along with Ginsburg and Breyer, joins Justices O'Connor and Stevens to create moderate majority coalitions.

Early in Souter's tenure, he could be found among the conservative majorities in most criminal-rights cases. More recently, Souter has moved away from the conservative majority. In *United States v. Foster* (509 U.S. 688: 1993), Souter dissented from the Court's ruling, which abandoned the more protective "same-conduct" test for double jeopardy. Justice Souter was also among the dissenters in *Vernonia School District 47J v. Acton* (515 U.S. 646: 1995), in which the Court upheld the random drug testing of junior and senior high school student athletes as a condition of participating in varsity athletics. Along with the other dissenters, Souter was troubled by the privacy interests violated by the blanket searches performed without individualized suspicion. Souter also joined the Court in disallowing exclusion of jurors on the basis of race or gender, and he frequently disagrees with the Rehnquist Court's attempts to diminish the scope of federal *habeas corpus* review of state criminal convictions.

Souter voted to uphold flag desecration laws against symbolic speech claims. He was part of a five-justice majority in *Rust v. Sullivan* (500 U.S. 173: 1991), upholding a federal regulation that prohibited physicians in clinics receiving federal grant funds to offer counsel about abortion or from referring patients to agencies where such counsel could be obtained. Souter was also the decisive vote in *Barnes v. Glen Theatre* (501 U.S. 560: 1991), which upheld a state decency law prohibiting nude dancing. His response to First Amendment issues in later cases changed substantially. He wrote the Court's opinion in *Hurley v. Irish-American Gay, Lesbian, and Bisexual Group* (515 U.S. 557: 1995), which protected the expression interests of an organization that sought to keep a homosexual group from participating in a parade it sponsored. A "fundamental rule" of the First Amendment provides a speaker with the "autonomy to choose the content of his own message." All speech, said Souter, "inherently involves choices of what to say and what to leave unsaid"; one important manifestation of free speech is that "one who chooses to speak may also decide what not to say." Souter has also been less accommodationist in establishment cases. For example, he dissented in *Rosenberger v. University of Virginia* (515 U.S. 819: 1995), in which the Court ruled that a public university must subsidize the religious expression of a student organization if it subsidizes nonreligious expressive activities of other campus groups. In Souter's view, this was "direct religious aid beyond anything justifiable for the sake of access to speaking forums."

Finally, Souter broke with the conservative bloc on two other significant issues in the 1990s. The first is abortion. Souter joined the Court after the ruling in *Webster v. Reproductive Health Services* (492 U.S. 490: 1989). It was in *Webster* that the Court may have had the votes to reverse *Roe v. Wade* (410 U.S. 113: 1973). Chief Justice Rehnquist opted not to do so. Rehnquist would later vote to overrule *Roe v. Wade* in *Planned Parenthood of Southeastern Pennsylvania v. Casey* (505 U.S. 833: 1992), but Justice Kennedy changed his position as well. Justice Souter then became part of the tenuous five-justice majority in *Casey*. The two Clinton appointments to the Court have strengthened the bloc that would retain the *Roe* framework. The second issue is equal protection. One example of Souter's views is reflected in the congressional redistricting cases. He was on the dissenting side in *Miller v. Johnson* (515 U.S. 900: 1995), in which the Court set aside a plan designed to enhance the chances of electing African-American candidates to Congress in Georgia. The following year, Souter again dissented as the Court set aside congressional redistricting plans in Texas and North Carolina on the grounds they were excessively race-conscious (see *Shaw v. Reno*, 135 L.Ed. 2d 207: 1996; *Bush v. Vera*, 135 L.Ed. 2d 248: 1996).

Souter is the most likely of the Reagan-Bush appointees to support the exercise of federal legislative and judicial powers. Souter joined Justices Stevens, Ginsburg, and Breyer in dissent in *United States v. Lopez* (514 U.S. 549: 1995) in support of the federal law that would have made it a crime to possess a firearm within 1,000 feet of public or private elementary and secondary schools. The other justices appointed by Reagan and Bush took the narrower and more predictable position (that the federal commerce power cannot be used to reach local schools, even on matters clearly pertaining to the safety of schoolchildren). Souter felt the federal commerce power also allowed Congress to require state and local law enforcement officials to conduct background checks on prospective gun purchasers. The Court struck down this provision of the Handgun Violence Prevention Act (known popularly as the Brady Act), concluding that Congress could not compel states to enact or enforce a federal regulatory program. Souter, on the other hand, embraced the Hamiltonian view that state governmental machinery can be "incorporated" into the nation's operation because state officials are obliged to support federal law, even if they do not agree with the law. Similarly, Souter expressed the view in *Seminole Tribe of Florida v. Florida* (517 U.S. 44: 1996) that the commerce power permitted congressional authorization of suits by private parties against unconsenting states notwithstanding the Eleventh Amendment. Finally, Souter was among the majority in *Wyoming v. Oklahoma* (502 U.S. 437: 1992), which ruled that a state law requiring coal-fired electric utilities to burn a mixture of coal containing at least 10 percent coal mined within the state violated the Commerce Clause.

John Paul Stevens (1975–) John Paul Stevens was appointed to the Supreme Court in 1975 by President Gerald Ford to replace Justice William O. Douglas. Stevens was born in Chicago, Illinois, in 1920, a member of a prominent family. He pursued his undergraduate education at the University of Chicago, graduating in 1941. After a tour of duty in the navy, Stevens entered Northwestern University Law School. His career at Northwestern was distinguished; he served as coeditor of the law review and graduated at the top of his class. Stevens then spent almost two years as law clerk to Supreme Court Justice Wiley Rutledge. He returned to Chicago in 1948 and joined a leading law firm. There he developed an expertise in antitrust law. Twice during his early private practice Stevens put this expertise to work in the public arena. In 1950, he served as Republican counsel to the House Judicial Subcommittee on Antitrust and Monopoly. Several years later, Stevens served as a member of the National Committee to Study Antitrust Laws, a panel assembled by the U.S. attorney general under Eisenhower. Stevens maintained his Chicago practice throughout and added teaching to his activities; he became a part-time member of the law faculties at both Northwestern and Chicago, regularly teaching antitrust law.

Stevens was first appointed to the federal bench in 1970, when Richard Nixon nominated him for a seat on the U.S. Court of Appeals for the Seventh Circuit. During his tenure as a federal appellate judge, Stevens was regarded as a moderate and seemingly free of ideological orientation. He also established a reputation for clear and sound judicial opinions. When Justice Douglas retired from the Court in 1975, Ford nominated Stevens; the nomination was confirmed by a unanimous Senate soon thereafter.

Significance Justice Stevens was the Burger Court's most difficult member to predict. He based his decisions on fine-line distinctions and, as a result, he positioned with either the liberal or conservative blocs, depending upon the particulars of each case. He currently seems to be the least ideologically driven member of the Court and is often referred to as the "swing" or pivotal vote on the Court. Certainly no liberal or even moderate outcome can occur without his vote. On balance, Stevens seldom aligns himself with the Rehnquist Court's conservative bloc. Indeed, Stevens ranked just behind Justices Brennan and Marshall as the most receptive member of the Burger Court to claims of individual rights violations. He is in the minority, with Justices Ginsburg and Breyer, on the Rehnquist Court on civil liberties issues. Stevens's fine-line drawing manifests itself in two significant ways. First, he issued more individual opinions than any other member of the Burger Court. He often feels the need to offer a concurring opinion or a separate dissent to develop a distinction. Secondly, Stevens can be found supporting challenges on certain issues—but not categorically, as Justices Brennan and Marshall were wont to do. For example, Stevens deferred to state statutes that structured or guided the judgment of sentencers in death penalty cases. Yet he offered the Court's rationale in *Woodson v. North Carolina* (428 U.S. 280: 1976), in which mandatory death sentences were invalidated. Stevens also joined the majority in *Coker v. Georgia* (433 U.S. 584: 1977), which found the death penalty to be excessive punishment for the crime of rape. He has also been willing to expand the reach of particular protections afforded the accused. He wrote the Court's opinion in *Department of Revenue v. Kurth Ranch* (511 U.S. 767: 1994), which held that levying a drug tax on persons already subjected to criminal penalties for the same conduct was a multiple punishment prohibited by the Double Jeopardy Clause. Similarly, Stevens dissented in *United States v. Foster* (509 U.S. 688: 1993), in which the Court abandoned the more protective "same-conduct" approach to double jeopardy.

Stevens's line-drawing is also evident on the abortion issue. Generally, he has opposed regulation of abortion and has stood with the minority in those cases where limitations on public funding of abortions have been upheld. Yet he has supported state restrictions on abortions for minors, restrictions he views as impermissible if applied to adults (see, for example, *Planned Parenthood of Central Missouri v. Danforth,* 428 U.S. 52: 1976; *H.L. v. Matheson,* 450 U.S. 398: 1981). In the most recent and significant abortion rulings, *Webster v. Reproductive Health Services* (492 U.S. 490: 1989) and *Planned Parenthood of Southeastern Pennsylvania v. Casey* (505 U.S. 833: 1992), Stevens voted with the moderates and maintained his support of the basic components of *Roe v. Wade* (410 U.S. 113: 1973).

Similarly, Stevens has generally opposed regulation of expression, yet he did not see it as "wholly immune." He supported, for example, the use of municipal zoning power to regulate the location of adult bookstores and theaters in *Young v. American Mini Theatres* (427 U.S. 50: 1976). More frequently, however, Stevens is receptive to claims of First Amendment violations. He joined the Court, for example, in striking down a municipal hate-speech ordinance (see *R.A.V. v. St. Paul,* 505 U.S. 377: 1992) and Ohio's ban on the distribution of anonymous campaign literature (*McIntyre v. Ohio Elections Commission,* 514 U.S. 334: 1995). Stevens tends to take a firm separationist position in establishment cases. He has consistently opposed aid to nonpublic schools (see, for example, the "shared-time" case, *Grand Rapids School District v. Ball,* 473 U.S. 373: 1985). He dissented in *Zobrest v. Catalina Foothills School District* (509 U.S. 1: 1993), in which the Court allowed a public school district to place a sign-language interpreter for a deaf child in a parochial school. Stevens wrote the Court's opinion in *Wallace v. Jaffree* (472 U.S. 38: 1985), the decision that struck down Alabama's "moment of silence" statute. He is more likely than most of his colleagues to see an indication of state preference or endorsement in establishment situations. He said in dissent in *Capital Square Review and Advisory Board v. Pinette* (515 U.S. 753: 1995) that a private party ought not be allowed to display a religious symbol on public property because it "implies official recognition."

Stevens's performance on equal protection issues is generally moderate to liberal. Although criticized at the time of his nomination as being insensitive to various forms of discrimination, Stevens can usually be found supporting claims of constitutional violations. Indeed, Stevens is usually positioned with Justices Brennan and Marshall on these issues, except in cases where racial minorities are given preference (where he began by withholding support). In such cases (see, for example, *Regents of the University of California v. Bakke,* 438 U.S. 265: 1978; *Fullilove v. Klutznick,* 448 U.S. 448: 1980), Stevens rejected race as a basis for compensatory or remedial preference. More recently, however, Stevens has supported affirmative action initiatives. He disagreed with the Court in *Adarand Constructors, Inc. v. Pena* (515 U.S. 200: 1995) as it subjected federal programs to the same strict scrutiny previously reserved for state and local governments. In addition, Stevens sees congressional districting plans that take race into account as sustainable against claims of unlawful racial gerrymandering. In *Miller v. Johnson* (515 U.S. 900: 1995), he supported a plan that created a second minority-majority congressional district in Georgia. He said that the Constitution does not mandate a form of proportional representation but that it "certainly permits a State to adopt a policy that promotes fair representation of different groups." More recently, he dissented in *Bush v. Vera* (135 L.Ed. 2d 248: 1996). Stevens concluded that in determining whether to apply strict scrutiny to the Texas redistricting plan the Court improperly ignored the "complex interplay" of political and geographical factors that led to the plan containing the three challenged minority-majority districts. It was Stevens's view that *Shaw v. Reno* (509 U.S. 630: 1993) fundamentally misperceived the relationship between race and districting principles. Stevens has steadfastly supported federal efforts to legislatively protect voting rights typically supporting the most expansive application of such federal laws as the Voting Rights Act and its amendments.

Stevens is one of the Court's least visible members because of his moderate and fact-focused decisions. As the Court has become more conservative, Stevens views frequently appear quite liberal by comparison. He is certainly more comfortable than many of his colleagues ruling against claims of state sovereignty. He wrote the opinion of the Court in *U.S. Terms Limits, Inc. v. Thornton* (514 U.S. 779: 1995), in which the Court held that the Qualifications Clause of Article I, Section 2 precludes states from limiting the number of terms that can be served by members of the House and Senate. In the absence of explicit delegation of power in Article I, states are without the power to add or change qualifications of members of Congress. Permitting states to fashion diverse qualifications for representatives, Stevens said, would result in a "patchwork of state qualifications, undermining the uniformity and the national character the Framers envisioned and sought to ensure. . . ." Stevens disagreed with the Court in *United States v. Lopez* (514 U.S. 549: 1995) and would have permitted Congress to use its interstate commerce power to criminalize possession of a firearm near local schools. Similarly, he was among the minority in *Printz v. United States* (138 L.Ed. 2d 914: 1997), in which the Court struck down the background-check provisions of the Brady Act. Stevens was of the view that Congress had the power to direct state and local law enforcement officers to participate in the administration of federal handgun regulation. Stevens has also supported extensive exercise of federal *habeas corpus* review authority over state criminal cases.

Clarence Thomas (1991–) President Bush's second appointee was Clarence Thomas. He was born in Pin Point, Georgia, in 1948. Early in his life, Thomas and his brother went to live with their grandfather in Savannah. The grandfather wanted Thomas to become a priest and enrolled him in a Catholic boarding school. Although Thomas excelled academically, he encountered significant racial prejudice. He experienced similar prejudice after beginning at a seminary in Missouri and abandoned his pursuit of the priesthood. Following a brief break from school, Thomas enrolled at Holy Cross, a Jesuit college in Massachusetts. Thomas graduated from Holy Cross with honors in English in 1971. He graduated from Yale Law School in 1974. He spent two years with the staff of John Danforth, the attorney general of Missouri. When Danforth was elected to the U.S. Senate in 1976, Thomas went to work for Monsanto, a large chemical company headquartered in St. Louis. Thomas joined Senator Danforth's staff as a legislative assistant in 1979.

He sought to avoid involvement with race-focused issues, preferring instead to work on environmental and energy policies. When Ronald Reagan became president, Thomas was appointed assistant secretary for civil rights in the Department of Education. He nearly declined the appointment because he did not define his professional objectives in the area of civil rights. Less than a year after this appointment, Thomas was made director of the Equal Employment Opportunity Commission (EEOC), the agency responsible for enforcement of federal laws prohibiting employment discrimination. During his eight-year tenure with the EEOC, Thomas generally reflected the conservative themes of the Reagan administration. He declined, for example, to use affirmative action quotas and timetables as the basis of legal actions against employers whose workforces underrepresented minorities.

In 1990, President George Bush appointed Thomas to the U.S. Court of Appeals for the District of Columbia Circuit. A year later, Bush selected Thomas to replace Justice Thurgood Marshall on the U.S. Supreme Court. The confirmation process was extremely contentious. The African-American community was split over the nomination. A number of civil rights groups, most notably the NAACP, did not endorse the Thomas nomination, noting his failure to embrace the traditional civil rights agenda. Prior to the Senate confirmation vote, allegations were made by Anita Hill, a University of Oklahoma law professor and former EEOC employee who claimed that Thomas had sexually harassed her. Thomas emphatically denied the charges. The Thomas nomination was returned to the Senate Judiciary Committee for additional hearings. These hearings were highly visible, with live national television coverage. The Thomas nomination eventually came to a vote in the Senate, where he was confirmed by a slim 52-48 vote. *See also ADARAND CONSTRUCTORS, INC. v. PENA* (515 U.S. 200: 1995), p. 95 (Supp.); WILLIAM H. REHNQUIST, p. 238 (Supp.); ANTONIN SCALIA, p. 242 (Supp.).

Significance Justice Clarence Thomas has clearly established a position on the Rehnquist Court's conservative wing. He subscribes to much the same judicial philosophy as Justice Antonin Scalia, joining him nearly 90 percent of the time. Like Scalia, Thomas is willing to break with precedent in pursuit of closely held conservative principles. His approach to constitutional interpretation is a variant of original intent. Rather than attempting to discern the Framers' intent as such, Thomas prefers historical practice as the basis for his decisionmaking. For example, the Court was asked to consider in *McIntyre v. Ohio Elections Commission* (514 U.S. 334: 1995) whether a state could prohibit anonymous distribution of materials designed to influence election outcomes. Thomas was part of a six-justice majority that struck down the law on First Amendment grounds. Unlike the others in the majority, however, Thomas focused on whether free speech protection as "originally understood"—as it existed at the time the Constitution was written—protected distribution of anonymous political material. He concluded that it did.

Notwithstanding his previous service at the top of a federal agency, Thomas generally does not support an expansive view of federal governmental authority. To the contrary, he typically can be found supporting state power over that of the federal government. This view is manifested in a number of ways. Thomas consistently votes to limit the authority of federal courts to review state criminal cases through *habeas corpus* petitions. He was also among the majority in *United States v. Lopez* (514 U.S. 549: 1995), striking down the federal Gun-Free School Zones Act of 1990. It was Thomas's view that federal commerce power had "drifted far from the original understanding of the Commerce Clause" and could not be made to reach local school zones. Thomas also issued a lengthy dissent in *U.S. Term Limits, Inc. v. Thornton* (514 U.S. 779: 1995). The Court ruled in *Thornton* that states could not limit the terms of members of Congress. Thomas strongly disagreed, saying that the people of the states "need not point to any affirmative grant of power in the Constitution in order to prescribe qualifications for their representations." He rejected the contention that the Qualifications Clauses of Article I prevented states from enacting terms limits. As long as the candidate sent to Congress meets the age, citizenship, and inhabitancy requirements of Article I, a state has not violated the Qualifications Clauses.

Thomas's most outspoken opinions have come in cases where federal power and equal protection converge. Thomas has opposed the practice of racial gerrymandering, that is, creating congressional districts from which minority candidates are likely to be elected. Thomas has steadfastly resisted the creation of minority-majority districts, even when states assert that their motive is to comply with provisions of the Voting Rights Act of 1965. Thomas said in a concurring opinion in *Holder v. Hall* (512 U.S. 874: 1994) that such a rationale allows federal courts to "segregate voters into racially designated districts." If the Supreme Court permits such districting, it "collaborate[s] on what might be called the racial 'balcanization' of the Nation." In *Missouri v. Jenkins* (515 U.S. 70: 1995), Thomas supported limiting the authority of federal courts to remediate the effects of segregation in public schools. He took the occasion to comment more broadly. Case law stemming from *Brown v. Board of Education* (347 U.S. 483: 1954) has been read to support the notion, said Thomas, that black students "suffer an unspecified psychological harm from segregation that retards their mental and educational development." Such an approach rests not only on questionable social science but also on the "assumption of black inferiority." He also objected to the extent to which federal courts had been allowed to fashion remedies to constitutional violations. The exercise of such broad authority has "trampled upon principles of federalism and separation of powers" and has allowed federal courts to "pursue other agendas unrelated to the narrow purpose of precisely remedying a constitutional harm." The "mere fact that a school is black," he concluded, does not mean that it is the "product of a constitutional violation." Finally, Thomas has strongly opposed affirmative action initiatives. In *Adarand Constructors, Inc. v. Pena* (515 U.S. 200: 1995), the Court ruled that all federal affirmative action initiatives based on race are to be subject to strict judicial scrutiny. Thomas suggested that such initiatives were based on an underlying premise that there is a "racial paternalism exception to the principle of equal protection." He saw a "constitutional equivalence" between laws intended to "subjugate a race" and those that attempt to allocate benefits on the basis of race "in order to foster some current notions of equality." Such so-called benign discrimination is destructive because it conveys the message that because of "chronic and apparently immutable handicaps, minorities cannot compete with them without their patronizing indulgence." Affirmative action programs "stamp minorities with a badge of inferiority" and may cause minorities to "develop dependencies or to adopt an attitude that they are 'entitled' to preferences."

Byron R. White (1962–1993) Byron R. White was born in Fort Collins, Colorado, in 1917. White went to the University of Colorado on scholarship and graduated Phi Beta Kappa and first in his class in 1938. He also distinguished himself in athletics, winning ten varsity letters during his undergraduate career. He was named All-America in football and was known as "Whizzer" White, a nickname he detested. Combined achievements as a scholar-athlete earned White a Rhodes Scholarship, and he attended Oxford University in 1939 and 1940 (while in England White met John F. Kennedy). White began law school at Yale upon returning stateside. He also pursued a professional football career with great success. His educational and athletic pursuits were interrupted by the war and his tour as a naval officer. White completed his law degree in 1946 and then clerked for Supreme Court Chief Justice Fred Vinson. During this time he renewed his acquaintance with Kennedy, who was serving his first term in the U.S. House. White returned to Colorado in 1947 and joined a prominent Denver firm, specializing in corporate law.

Thirteen years later, Senator John Kennedy sought the presidency. White joined the campaign, first working in securing the Democratic nomination for Kennedy, then playing a major role in the general election campaign organization. Following Kennedy's election, White was named deputy U.S. attorney general. For the next 15 months, he recruited Justice Department staff and had extensive responsibility for supervising the operations of the department. Specifically, he monitored antitrust and civil rights suits and evaluated judicial nominees for the Kennedy administration. In March 1962, Justice Charles Whitaker resigned from the Court; White was nominated to replace him. The Senate confirmed his nomination two weeks later. He served until 1993, when he was replaced by Justice Ruth Bader Ginsburg. *See also* POTTER STEWART, p. 549.

Significance Justice Byron R. White was President John Kennedy's first appointment to the Supreme Court (Kennedy also appointed Arthur Goldberg). It was expected that White would take a solidly liberal course, but that did not occur. From the outset, White approached constitutional issues in a fashion independent of ideology. Indeed, White's tenure of 30-plus years defies easy ideological characterization. During the Warren era, White typically aligned with centrist and conservative justices—Stewart, Clark, and Harlan. Especially revealing is White's record on rights of the accused. During the 1960s, White resisted extending certain provisions of the Bill of Rights to the states. His dissents in *Robinson v. California* (370 U.S. 660: 1962) and *Malloy v. Hogan* (378 U.S. 1: 1964), opposing incorporation of the cruel and unusual punishment and self-incrimination clauses, respectively, are representative. He also disagreed with the Warren Court majorities in two landmark decisions involving custodial interrogation of suspects: *Escobedo v. Illinois* (378 U.S. 478: 1964) and *Miranda v. Arizona* (384 U.S. 436: 1966).

White was among the Burger Court majority that limited the scope of *Miranda*'s protection (see, for example, *Harris v. New York,* 401 U.S. 222: 1971). Similarly, White tended to support law enforcement on Fourth Amendment questions. White was in the majority in upholding the stop and frisk practice in *Terry v. Ohio* (392 U.S. 1: 1968) and dissented in *Chimel v. California* (395 U.S. 752: 1969), in which the Court limited the scope of warrantless searches incidental to lawful arrests. White also supported use of the death penalty by states. In *Furman v. Georgia* (408 U.S. 238: 1972), White was among the majority that struck down the wholly discretionary use of capital punishment. With Justice Stewart, he found that the changes in procedures following *Furman* met the demands of the Eighth Amendment.

White was not a leading libertarian on First Amendment issues. He was among the Burger Court majority in *Miller v. California* (413 U.S. 15: 1973) in which the Warren Court's standards for obscenity regulation were redefined to permit greater governmental control. White also wrote for the Court in *Zurcher v. Stanford Daily* (436 U.S. 547: 1978), allowing the search of a newspaper office for evidence pertaining to a criminal investigation. He also voted with the majority in *Branzburg v. Hayes* (408 U.S. 665: 1972), which required journalists to disclose sources to grand juries. White's establishment clause record was essentially accommodationist, especially in school aid cases. He was with the majority in *Lynch v. Donnelly* (465 U.S. 668: 1984), where the Court ruled that a municipality could include a nativity scene in its annual holiday display; he also supported the holiday displays in *Allegheny County v. ACLU* (492 U.S. 573: 1989). White was also part of the majority that allowed a religious group to access public school facilities in *Lamb's Chapel v. Center Moriches Union Free School District* (508 U.S. 384: 1993). White also would have permitted participation of clergy in public school commencement exercises (*Lee v. Weisman,* 505 U.S. 577: 1992) and would have upheld Alabama's "moment of silence" for mediation or voluntary prayer in *Wallace v. Jaffree* (472 U.S. 38: 1985). Similarly, White was willing to allow some state regulation that affected free exercise of religion protections. He disagreed with the Court in *Sherbert v. Verner* (374 U.S. 398: 1963), which required that a state demonstrate a compelling interest when any action affected free exercise of religion. Almost three decades later, White was part of the majority that returned to the less protective "general secular purpose" approach in *Employment Division v. Smith* (494 U.S. 872: 1990).

Yet White was something of a liberal activist on questions involving equal protection. Generally aligned with Justices Brennan and Marshall, he regularly supported those claiming racial discrimination. He also supported affirmative action as a means of remediating previous racial discrimination. He supported a congressional initiative to set aside a portion of federal construction grants for minority contractors in *Fullilove v. Klutznick* (448 U.S. 448: 1980) and supported the FCC policy of considering minority ownership as a factor in licensing decisions in *Metro Broadcasting, Inc. v. FCC* (497 U.S. 547: 1989). White was also receptive to extending the Equal Protection Clause to other classes. In *Frontiero v. Richardson* (411 U.S. 667: 1973), White supported the designation of gender classification as "suspect," thus invoking strict judicial scrutiny. More recently he opposed the male-only draft registration policy upheld in *Rostker v. Goldberg* (453 U.S. 57: 1981). Similarly, he took a strong position on economic discrimination in *San Antonio Independent School District v. Rodriguez* (411 U.S. 1: 1973).

White generally supported state initiatives to regulate abortion. In fact, White dissented with Justice Rehnquist in *Roe v. Wade* (410 U.S. 113: 1973), arguing that an inferred right of privacy was not sufficient to preclude state prohibition of abortion. He preferred to leave policies about reproductive rights to the legislative process. White voted in favor of most state regulations of abortions and in many of his opinions called for the overturning of *Roe v. Wade.* (see especially his last abortion case, *Planned Parenthood of Southeastern Pennsylvania v. Casey,* 505 U.S. 833: 1992).

White was basically a New Deal liberal. He generally supported the exercise of federal legislative power, particularly the commerce power. In *Chemical Waste Management, Inc. v. Hunt* (504 U.S. 334: 1992), for example, White voted to strike down a state law that imposed a higher disposal fee for hazardous wastes brought from other states on the grounds that the law discriminated against interstate commerce. Similarly, White was among the majority in *Wyoming v. Oklahoma* (502 U.S. 437: 1992), in which the Commerce Clause was used to strike down a state law that imposed a requirement that coal mined within a state be used in preference to coal brought in from other states. White, along with Stewart, was a "swing" vote on the Burger Court and often cast the decisive vote on important cases. The retirement of Stewart in 1981 and the subsequent appointment of Sandra Day O'Connor solidified the conservative bloc and made White less of a swing vote. From that point on, White seemed comfortable as part of the conservative majority on most issues until the time he left the Court in 1993.

APPENDIX B: JUSTICES OF THE SUPREME COURT

Justices of the Supreme Court

	TENURE	APPOINTED BY	REPLACED
JOHN JAY*	1789–1795	Washington	
John Rutledge	1789–1791	Washington	
William Cushing	1789–1810	Washington	
James Wilson	1789–1798	Washington	
John Blair	1789–1796	Washington	
James Iredell	1790–1799	Washington	
Thomas Johnson	1791–1793	Washington	Rutledge
William Paterson	1793–1806	Washington	Johnson
JOHN RUTLEDGE	1795	Washington	Jay
Samuel Chase	1796–1811	Washington	Blair
OLIVER ELLSWORTH	1796–1800	Washington	Rutledge
Bushrod Washington	1798–1829	John Adams	Wilson
Alfred Moore	1799–1804	John Adams	Iredell
JOHN MARSHALL	1801–1835	John Adams	Ellsworth
William Johnson	1804–1834	Jefferson	Moore
Brockholst Livingston	1806–1823	Jefferson	Paterson
Thomas Todd	1807–1826	Jefferson	(new judgeship)
Gabriel Duval	1811–1835	Madison	Chase
Joseph Story	1811–1845	Madison	Cushing
Smith Thompson	1823–1843	Monroe	Livingston
Robert Trimble	1826–1828	John Q. Adams	Todd
John McLean	1829–1861	Jackson	Trimble
Henry Baldwin	1830–1844	Jackson	Washington
James Wayne	1835–1867	Jackson	Johnson
ROGER B. TANEY	1836–1864	Jackson	Marshall
Phillip P. Barbour	1836–1841	Jackson	Duval
John Catron	1837–1865	Jackson	(new judgeship)
John McKinley	1837–1852	Van Buren	(new judgeship)
Peter V. Daniel	1841–1860	Van Buren	Barbour
Samuel Nelson	1845–1872	Tyler	Thompson
Levi Woodbury	1846–1851	Polk	Story
Robert C. Grier	1846–1870	Polk	Baldwin
Benjamin R. Curtis	1851–1857	Fillmore	Woodbury
John A. Campbell	1853–1861	Pierce	McKinley
Nathan Clifford	1858–1881	Buchanan	Curtis
Noah H. Swayne	1862–1881	Lincoln	McLean
Samuel F. Miller	1862–1890	Lincoln	Daniel
David Davis	1862–1877	Lincoln	Campbell
Stephen J. Field	1863–1897	Lincoln	(new judgeship)
SALMON CHASE	1864–1873	Lincoln	Taney
William Strong	1870–1880	Grant	Grier
Joseph P. Bradley	1870–1892	Grant	Wayne
Ward Hunt	1872–1882	Grant	Nelson
MORRISON R. WAITE	1874–1888	Grant	Chase

**Chief justices capitalized*

continued

	TENURE	APPOINTED BY	REPLACED
John Marshall Harlan	1877–1911	Hayes	Davis
William B. Woods	1880–1887	Hayes	Strong
Stanley Matthews	1881–1889	Garfield	Swayne
Horace Gray	1881–1902	Arthur	Clifford
Samuel Blatchford	1882–1893	Arthur	Hunt
Lucius Q. C. Lamar	1888–1893	Cleveland	Woods
MELVILLE W. FULLER	1888–1910	Cleveland	Waite
David J. Brewer	1889–1910	Harrison	Matthews
Henry B. Brown	1890–1906	Harrison	Miller
George Shiras Jr.	1892–1903	Harrison	Bradley
Howell E. Jackson	1893–1895	Harrison	Lamar
Edward D. White	1894–1910	Cleveland	Blatchford
Rufus W. Peckham	1895–1909	Cleveland	Jackson
Joseph McKenna	1898–1925	McKinley	Field
Oliver Wendell Holmes	1902–1932	T. Roosevelt	Gray
William R. Day	1903–1922	T. Roosevelt	Shiras
William H. Moody	1906–1910	T. Roosevelt	Brown
Horace H. Lurton	1909–1914	Taft	Peckham
Charles Evans Hughes	1910–1916	Taft	Brewer
EDWARD D. WHITE	1910–1921	Taft	Fuller
Willis VanDevanter	1910–1937	Taft	White
Joseph R. Lamar	1910–1916	Taft	Moody
Mahlon Pitney	1912–1922	Taft	Harlan
James McReynolds	1914–1941	Wilson	Lurton
Louis D. Brandeis	1916–1939	Wilson	Lamar
John H. Clark	1916–1922	Wilson	Hughes
WILLIAM H. TAFT	1921–1930	Harding	White
George Sutherland	1922–1938	Harding	Clarke
Pierce Butler	1922–1939	Harding	Day
Edward T. Sanford	1923–1930	Harding	Pitney
Harlan F. Stone	1925–1941	Coolidge	McKenna
CHARLES EVANS HUGHES	1930–1941	Hoover	Taft
Owen J. Roberts	1932–1945	Hoover	Sanford
Benjamin N. Cardozo	1932–1938	Hoover	Holmes
Hugo L. Black	1937–1971	F. Roosevelt	Van Devanter
Stanley F. Reed	1938–1957	F. Roosevelt	Sutherland
Felix Frankfurter	1939–1962	F. Roosevelt	Cardozo
William O. Douglas	1939–1975	F. Roosevelt	Brandeis
Frank Murphy	1940–1949	F. Roosevelt	Butler
James F. Byrnes	1941–1942	F. Roosevelt	McReynolds
HARLAN F. STONE	1941–1946	F. Roosevelt	Hughes
Robert H. Jackson	1941–1954	F. Roosevelt	Stone
Wiley B. Rutledge	1943–1949	F. Roosevelt	Byrnes
Harold H. Burton	1945–1958	Truman	Roberts

continued

	TENURE	APPOINTED BY	REPLACED
FRED M. VINSON	1946–1953	Truman	Stone
Tom C. Clark	1949–1967	Truman	Murphy
Sherman Minton	1949–1956	Truman	Rutledge
EARL WARREN	1954–1969	Eisenhower	Vinson
John M. Harlan	1955–1971	Eisenhower	Jackson
William J. Brennan	1957–1990	Eisenhower	Minton
Charles E. Whittaker	1957–1962	Eisenhower	Reed
Potter Stewart	1959–1981	Eisenhower	Burton
Byron R. White	1962–1993	Kennedy	Whittaker
Arthur J. Goldberg	1962–1965	Kennedy	Frankfurter
Abe Fortas	1965–1969	Johnson	Goldberg
Thurgood Marshall	1967–1991	Johnson	Clark
WARREN E. BURGER	1969–1986	Nixon	Warren
Harry A. Blackmun	1970–1994	Nixon	Fortas
Lewis F. Powell	1971–1988	Nixon	Black
William H. Rehnquist	1971–	Nixon	Harlan
John P. Stevens	1975–	Ford	Douglas
Sandra Day O'Connor	1981–	Reagan	Stewart
WILLIAM H. REHNQUIST	1986–	Reagan	Burger
Antonin Scalia	1986–	Reagan	Rehnquist
Anthony M. Kennedy	1988–	Reagan	Powell
David H. Souter	1990–	Bush	Brennan
Clarence Thomas	1991–	Bush	Marshall
Ruth Bader Ginsburg	1993–	Clinton	White
Stephen G. Breyer	1994–	Clinton	Blackmun

APPENDIX C: COURT COMPOSITION SINCE 1900

Court Composition Since 1900

The table below represents the members of the U.S. Supreme Court since 1900. By locating the term in which a particular case was decided, the reader may readily determine the names of the justices on the Court at the time of the decision.

THE FULLER COURT (1900–1909 Terms)									
1900–01	Fuller	White	Gray	Peckham	Brown	Shiras	Brewer	Harlan	McKenna
1902	Fuller	White	Holmes	Peckham	Brown	Shiras	Brewer	Harlan	McKenna
1903–05	Fuller	White	Holmes	Peckham	Brown	Day	Brewer	Harlan	McKenna
1906–08	Fuller	White	Holmes	Peckham	Moody	Day	Brewer	Harlan	McKenna
1909	Fuller	White	Holmes	Lurton	Moody	Day	Brewer	Harlan	McKenna
THE WHITE COURT (1910–1920)									
1910–11	White	VanDevanter	Holmes	Lurton	Lamar	Day	Hughes	Harlan	McKenna
1912–13	White	VanDevanter	Holmes	Lurton	Lamar	Day	Hughes	Pitney	McKenna
1914–15	White	VanDevanter	Holmes	McReynolds	Lamar	Day	Hughes	Pitney	McKenna
1916–20	White	VanDevanter	Holmes	McReynolds	Brandeis	Day	Clarke	Pitney	McKenna
THE TAFT COURT (1921–1929)									
1921	Taft	VanDevanter	Holmes	McReynolds	Brandeis	Day	Clarke	Pitney	McKenna
1922	Taft	VanDevanter	Holmes	McReynolds	Brandeis	Butler	Sutherland	Pitney	McKenna
1923–24	Taft	VanDevanter	Holmes	McReynolds	Brandeis	Butler	Sutherland	Sanford	McKenna
1925–29	Taft	VanDevanter	Holmes	McReynolds	Brandeis	Butler	Sutherland	Sanford	Stone
THE HUGHES COURT (1930–1940)									
1930–31	Hughes	VanDevanter	Holmes	McReynolds	Brandeis	Butler	Sutherland	Roberts	Stone
1932–36	Hughes	VanDevanter	Cardozo	McReynolds	Brandeis	Butler	Sutherland	Roberts	Stone
1937	Hughes	Black	Cardozo	McReynolds	Brandeis	Butler	Sutherland	Roberts	Stone

continued

Court Composition Since 1900

1938	Hughes	Black	Cardozo	McReynolds	Brandeis	Butler	Reed	Roberts	Stone
1939	Hughes	Black	Frankfurter	McReynolds	Douglas	Butler	Reed	Roberts	Stone
1940	Hughes	Black	Frankfurter	McReynolds	Douglas	Murphy	Reed	Roberts	Stone
THE STONE COURT (1941–1945)									
1941–42	Stone	Black	Frankfurter	Byrnes	Douglas	Murphy	Reed	Roberts	Jackson
1943–44	Stone	Black	Frankfurter	Rutledge	Douglas	Murphy	Reed	Roberts	Jackson
1945	Stone	Black	Frankfurter	Rutledge	Douglas	Murphy	Reed	Burton	Jackson
THE VINSON COURT (1946–1952)									
1946–48	Vinson	Black	Frankfurter	Rutledge	Douglas	Murphy	Reed	Burton	Jackson
1949–52	Vinson	Black	Frankfurter	Minton	Douglas	Clark	Reed	Burton	Jackson
THE WARREN COURT (1953–1968)									
1953–54	Warren	Black	Frankfurter	Minton	Douglas	Clark	Reed	Burton	Jackson
1955	Warren	Black	Frankfurter	Minton	Douglas	Clark	Reed	Burton	Harlan
1956	Warren	Black	Frankfurter	Brennan	Douglas	Clark	Reed	Burton	Harlan
1957	Warren	Black	Frankfurter	Brennan	Douglas	Clark	Whittaker	Burton	Harlan
1958–61	Warren	Black	Frankfurter	Brennan	Douglas	Clark	Whittaker	Stewart	Harlan
1962–65	Warren	Black	Goldberg	Brennan	Douglas	Clark	White	Stewart	Harlan
1965–67	Warren	Black	Fortas	Brennan	Douglas	Clark	White	Stewart	Harlan
1967–69	Warren	Black	Fortas	Brennan	Douglas	Marshall	White	Stewart	Harlan
THE BURGER COURT (1969–1985)									
1969	Burger	Black	Fortas	Brennan	Douglas	Marshall	White	Stewart	Harlan
1969–70	Burger	Black		Brennan	Douglas	Marshall	White	Stewart	Harlan
1970	Burger	Black	Blackmun	Brennan	Douglas	Marshall	White	Stewart	Harlan
1971	Burger	Powell	Blackmun	Brennan	Douglas	Marshall	White	Stewart	Rehnquist

1975	Burger	Powell	Blackmun	Brennan	Stevens	Marshall	White	Stewart	Rehnquist
1981	Burger	Powell	Blackmun	Brennan	Stevens	Marshall	White	O'Connor	Rehnquist
THE REHNQUIST COURT (1986–)									
1986	Rehnquist	Powell	Blackmun	Brennan	Stevens	Marshall	White	O'Connor	Scalia
1987	Rehnquist	Kennedy	Blackmun	Brennan	Stevens	Marshall	White	O'Connor	Scalia
1990	Rehnquist	Kennedy	Blackmun	Souter	Stevens	Marshall	White	O'Connor	Scalia
1991	Rehnquist	Kennedy	Blackmun	Souter	Stevens	Thomas	White	O'Connor	Scalia
1993	Rehnquist	Kennedy	Blackmun	Souter	Stevens	Thomas	Ginsburg	O'Connor	Scalia
1994	Rehnquist	Kennedy	Breyer	Souter	Stevens	Thomas	Ginsburg	O'Connor	Scalia

INDEX